THE ART OF INVESTMENT

THE ART OF
INVESTMENT

A. G. Ellinger

BOWES & BOWES

LONDON

This edition © *A. G. Ellinger, 1971*
ISBN 0 370 00150 8
Printed and bound in Great Britain for
Bowes & Bowes Publishers Ltd
9 Bow Street, London, WC2 7AL
by C. Tinling & Co. Ltd, Prescot
First published 1955
Third revised edition 1971

CONTENTS

GRAPHS

INTRODUCTION TO
THE FIRST EDITION

The object of this book is to explain in comprehensible terms a theoretical basis for practical investment. No claim is made that the methods discussed are the only methods by which the investor can achieve success. Methods of this sort are said to be used extensively in America; very little is known about the extent of their use in this country.

While the Americans make great use of charts, presumably because they believe that the things which they see being done in their charts are data of a more reliable kind than the things that they hear being said in Wall Street, there is no necessity that the theoretical bases of investment in U.S.A. need be the same as the theoretical bases of investment in Britain. The practical differences between the New York and London markets are so great that the two need not work on one common theory.

Nevertheless, the main reason for the Americans' use of charts is valid also for their use in London. The things which we can see being done in charts that cover the London market are often data of a more reliable kind than the things that one hears being said in Throgmorton Street.

Quite apart from their prophetic uses, which a reader at this stage has every right to question, charts are of the greatest value in illustrating what has happened in the past and what is happening in the present. So no excuse is needed for illustrating this book with charts. So many people find it so much easier to understand what they can see in a picture than what is described to them in words, and for the writer it is often much easier to explain by a picture something that would defy his powers of explanation in words.

The first need for a book of this sort is that it should be written from the beginning in terms that the ordinary reader can easily understand. As the work advances, technical terms can be introduced, explained and used. But the basic assumption is that the reader, at the start, knows nothing about the subject; the reader who does know must grant his forgiveness and skip.

Much that has been written about security charts has been expressed—perhaps through inadvertence, perhaps by a deliberate policy—in a language private to the chart-reading fraternity. The terminology is not

9

always difficult but to the beginner it is absolutely baffling. As a result the chartists have rather driven people away from their tenets instead of converting investors to them.

It is the intention that this book should be written with the object of explaining things to the reader, not concealing things from him; this is the purpose with which our terms will be chosen.

People may believe that practical investment does not need a theoretical basis. You can argue that of the 9,706 securities which were quoted on the Stock Exchange on 2nd April 1951 one was just as good as another, but this argument does not stand the test of time. Since 2nd April 1951, some of those securities have gone up in price and some have gone down. You can argue that these rises and falls occur by pure chance and that securities can be picked for investment with a pin as well as by any other method. Nevertheless, the number of questions asked every day argues strongly a widespread belief that some people, namely those to whom the questions are put, have some means of knowing what is going to go up and what is going to go down.

The general public expects that the experts will be able to make prudent decisions about investment, decisions which are presumably rational and based on some principles. If those principles are coherent, that is they stick together, as a jig-saw puzzle can be stuck together, they form a theory; if that theory fits into the facts outside, it is almost certainly right. If the principles are not coherent but are self-contradictory, some of them must be wrong (and all of them may be wrong).

If the theory is to be of any use, it must be not only internally coherent but must stand up also to the external test of practice. It must lead to success in investment, that is to the preservation or increasing of capital and the securing of a useful income from it.

A theory of this sort requires two major virtues; it must be comprehensible and practicable. You, the investor who read this book, must be able to understand its tenets and, having understood them, to put them into practice.

We must consider next the area of discussion, what is going to be brought in and what is going to be left out. Broadly, our subject is investment in securities that can be bought and sold on the Stock Exchange, London. As the Council of the Stock Exchange permits its members (the Stock Exchange is in theory a private club, in practice a public institution) to deal in securities that are quoted on any other stock exchanges, these will, to a lesser extent, fall within the area of discussion. We shall have to consider the other stock exchanges of the British Isles and perhaps some of those in Europe as well as the Johannesburg Stock Exchange in South Africa and the New York Stock Exchange.

So much for the stock exchanges, the places where they deal in securities. What are the securities in which they deal? These are the loans raised by governments and municipalities and public boards, the loans raised by companies, usually called debentures in Britain and bonds in America, and the shares of companies. Shares are of two broad classes, preference shares which are entitled to a fixed rate of dividend out of the profits, and ordinary shares which are entitled to what is left after the rights of the preference shareholders, if there are any, have been satisfied. We have to consider individual shares, and also the behaviour of groups, like oil shares or shipping shares; and we find it convenient to make averages, taking the prices of, say, ten shares and working out the average price from week to week.

We can pass, in this way, not only from the share to the group; we can also proceed further to the market as a whole. When one asks 'What is the market like?' one wants to know the general behaviour of very large sections of the Stock Exchange, and the question assumes that there is one sort of behaviour that is, at any time, common to the market as a whole. In general we find that there is, at any time, one sort of behaviour for all securities which pay a fixed rate of interest, one for the great bulk of variable dividend securities (the ordinary shares), one which is often different for gold mining shares, and frequent exceptions among other mining shares and plantation shares.

Among fixed interest securities the loans of one's own government reflect most faithfully the changes of one's own country's rate of interest (if War Loan $3\frac{1}{2}\%$ falls from 100 to $87\frac{1}{2}$, the rate of interest has risen from $3\frac{1}{2}\%$ to 4%). Foreign government loans may reflect the changes of the rate of interest, if expectations that the foreign government in question will go on paying its debts are high; if those expectations are not so high or are non-existent, influences quite different from the rate of interest cause large changes in the prices of the bonds. Similarly, the debentures and preference shares of companies are influenced mainly by the changes of the rate of interest as long as the credit of the company is high, but if there is doubt whether the company will pay the dividend on the preference share or the interest on the debenture, then the questions 'Whether?' and 'How much?' are of far greater importance than changes in the general rate of interest.

There are available averages composed of the prices of British Government stocks only and of British Government stocks and industrial fixed interest securities of the highest grade; through these we can study the changes in the long-term rate of interest. These averages represent conveniently the market in fixed interest securities. There are also averages of ordinary share prices, where the shares have been selected with the intention of the average's representing the ordinary share market.

For individual shares (and also for the whole market and for group averages, whose movements depend on individual shares) we must study first the prices. Income may be the main object of investment, but capital is the key to income and therefore the price at which any security stands is always the matter of first importance. Next we must consider the interest or dividend that the security is paying. If we divide that interest or dividend by the price and multiply the answer by 100, we work out the 'yield per cent'. This is always called 'the yield' and it shows what income is obtained, as long as the current rate of interest or dividend persists, from an investment of £100 in that particular security at that particular price. Finally, we have to study 'earnings', the total sum available for distribution among shareholders divided by the total capital of the security in question. There are three things we can find from earnings, a notion how secure the present dividend is, a notion how much more the directors could divide, if they felt so inclined, a notion how much the concern is increasing its earning power by investing its undistributed profits in the business instead of paying them out to shareholders.

It is necessary also, for our understanding of the forces that influence prices and the means by which they do it, to make some study of the machinery of the market. Much of this machinery is irrelevant to our purpose. A book of this sort is no place for a description of the routine of a stock exchange settlement nor of the workings of a broker's office. What the investor needs to know is what the market is and how the market works and who are the people and the institutions that influence it. He must understand that the Stock Exchange is one market formed from the meeting there of more than 9,700 smaller markets, for each security has a market of its own with different characteristics and different patrons.

At this point I may be permitted to strike a personal note. People sometimes ask me what qualifications I have to write about investment. I am not an economist, nor an actuary nor a statistician. Although I live at Cambridge (because I like living at Cambridge), my university was Oxford and my subject there Classics. The reader need, therefore, have no fear that he will be baffled by abstruse mathematics; the mathematical equipment required is that which used to be suitable, between the wars, for obtaining a pass in Elementary Mathematics in the School Certificate. After Oxford I spent three years in the Lancashire trade (partly in Manchester and partly in the Far East) till the Japanese and the slump put an end to that. Then came ten years in a broker's office in London. Five and a half years were spent in the army; after demobilization I set myself up as an investment consultant.

The period from the end of the war to 1950 might well be described as one of practical seclusion, seclusion because a distance of fifty-five miles

separated me from the bustle and distraction of Throgmorton Street and
allowed me ample time to think, practical because the theoretical conclusions at which my thinking arrived could always be tested in the
practical laboratory of the Stock Exchange. When my theories led me to
believe that a certain security was likely to rise, I could reach for the
telephone and, within my small means, buy some. When my theories led
me to believe that a certain security was likely to go down, I could ring a
broker and, perhaps beyond my means, sell some. This period of practical
conclusion has been spent in assembling data, forming conclusions, and,
sometimes, putting those conclusions to the test of practice. These methods
seem the only ones by which one can make discoveries about investment.

My greatest debt is owed to the investors who had the hardihood to consult me in 1946; it is on the results of my work for them that my conclusions
have been built. I am grateful to the editors of the *Investors' Review*, the
Stock Exchange Gazette and *Investors' Chronicle* who have allowed me space
(and paid me) for ventilating my views and especially to the readers of the
Investors' Review who put up with my writings for so long. I owe an
immeasurable debt to my predecessors in authorship and to my contem-
poraries in journalism, and I must mention two books, *Investment* by Mr.
L. L. B. Angas, and *Ordinary Shares* by the late Hargreaves Parkinson,
which no student of investment should leave unread.

My thanks are also due to the *Financial Times*, the London & Cambridge
Economic Service and Moody's Service for their permission to use and
reproduce in graphical form various of their index numbers.

PREFACE TO
THE THIRD EDITION

The First Edition of this book was written mainly in the second half of 1952 and in 1953 and completed early in 1954. A Second Edition with some additions and alterations was prepared in 1960 and this Third Edition has been written between January and July 1970. Very substantial changes and additions have been made, but much of the original edition remains as valid as when it was originally written and has no need of change.

Changes have been required for two main reasons. One is that the market and its whole background has changed vastly since the late forties and the early fifties. The second is that the author has learnt much that he did not know fifteen to twenty years ago.

Investment analysis in this country existed on quite a small scale up to the beginning of the fifties. The way to extensive fundamental analysis was opened by the Companies Act of 1948, and it was not till the middle fifties that the Society of Investment Analysts was founded. (We have had to wait till 1969 for the Association of Chart and Technical Analysts.) There has been an enormous expansion of research activity; brokers who had research departments have expanded and improved them and harnessed computers to the work, while brokers who employed a man whom they called their statistician or perhaps nobody at all are now covering at least a small field with careful research.

Not only the brokers have changed; the market has changed too. The unit trusts were kept on a tight chain till the late fifties and these have expanded through the sixties, especially in the last few years through a multiplication of the number of trusts and the growth of equity linked life assurance. The growth of the unit trusts and of contractual saving seems to have reduced the market activity of the private investor and the institutional business has become more and more important. Turnover figures for the Stock Exchange do not go back many years and turnover may have reached its highest level so far in the recent boom, but for the highest number of bargains marked in the Industrial sections we have to go back to the General Election of 1959.

The sixties have been the decade of the cult of equity, which shows how blind investors are; they had only to look across the sea to Europe to see a

14

number of markets where the high prices of 1960, 1961 and 1962 have not so far been regained. In 1970 we have seen the *Financial Times* industrial ordinary index below the top of 1959, although the F.T. Actuaries 500, starting at a not very high level in April 1962, has done moderately better.

Over this period there has been a great growth of the interest in and use of charts. Before 1948, when we had only rudimentary figures from the companies, it might well have been argued that charts were indispensable (I certainly thought that they were), but since then there has been such an improvement in the quality of the data at the disposal of the fundamental analyst that one could argue that the need for charts has been much reduced. The argument possibly does not give enough weight to the un-availability of charts before Investment Research started a chart library and sold photoprints, or to the likelihood that charts were so grossly under-used in 1947 that a reasonable usage in 1970 would multiply their study a thousandfold (probably an under-estimate, in my opinion).

There has also been a considerable widening of the view. One must not imagine that investment overseas began with Poseidon; the Australian mining boom is only one of a long series of overseas flows by British investment capital. The appeal of the distant prospect has often been strong; look back to the South Seas Bubble. There has been a continuing interest in the American market for well over a century; in the 1850s Robert Benson, now merged into Kleinwort Benson, was taking an active part in the financing of American railroads, as were Heseltine, Powell, still a highly respected firm of London stockbrokers. The Kaffir boom that broke out after the discovery of the Main Reef on the Rand comes nearer to human memory. The number of important oil companies registered in the middle of the first decade of this century suggests that there was then something of an oil boom, and a year or two later the great rubber boom, when the companies were generally floated with florin shares, spread interest in the stock exchanges widely through Britain. There were Kaffir booms in the forties and fifties, probably not as big as that of the thirties, and a Canadian oil boom in 1956 and 1957. Interest in European stocks began to grow in the late fifties, and investors' experience there has so far been rather unhappy. But if Britain is to go into the Common Market, European shares are likely to become a more important medium for British investment, and how better to make their acquaintance quickly than through looking at their charts?

We have to cope too with new currencies and new media for investment. The American balance of payments deficit, combined with the financial ingenuity of the City of London, has created the Euro-dollar, and this has brought us some American investment practices, the convertible bond (which in Britain is generally not a bond at all but an unsecured loan stock) and the warrant. Warburg's have invented the bond with the floating interest rate. No doubt we shall have more strange innovations.

Perhaps it is more important for my readers to decide how much I have learnt since I wrote the First Edition with my eye on the late forties and early fifties. I have been using charts and, I hope, learning from doing it, for an additional eighteen years. The market has changed and presented new experiences; I doubt if the 'Head & Shoulders' pattern was really important in the period between the end of the war and the 1952 bottom, but it has become very important since. I owe an immense debt to *Technical Analysis of Stock Trends* by Edwards & Magee which stresses the importance of the 'Head & Shoulders' and clarifies ideas about support and resistance. I have learned a lot from the *Odd Lot Studies* which Garfield Drew publishes weekly in Boston and from the *Indicator Digest*, founded by Sam Coslow. I have had much more time in which to test my own ideas, and some of them have, alas! been found wanting. Confidence, which looked on its pre-war and immediate post-war record to be a splendid leading indicator for ordinary shares, has turned out to be nothing of the sort but, if Mr Heath gives us in the seventies an economy in which dividends fluctuate more and gilt edged less, its old importance may return. It must not be ignored; it still seems far the best measure of the market's dearness or cheapness, much better than the P/E Ratio which has become so popular in the last five years.

Another American invention which seems useful is the Advance/Decline Line which Investment Research did not start to use till the sixties. This is a very useful tool for keeping a check on the share index; when the two do not keep in step, one is wise to be as alert as the old-fashioned Dow Theorist who noted a divergence between Rails and Industrials.

I must acknowledge my indebtedness to all the various analysts whom I have met and with whom I have conversed, to all the investors who have corresponded with me and improved me by asking awkward questions, and most especially to my partner, Harvey Stewart, whose wide experience in security and commodity charts is always at my disposal, to my secretary, Miss Judith Gowler, who has typed all the more tedious parts of the script, and to my draughtswoman, Mrs Margaret Norris, who has prepared for publication more than seven dozen charts.

Cambridge   *September 1970*

CHAPTER ONE

The Market

The Stock Exchange is a market place, primarily for the purchase and sale of the securities that are quoted in the Daily Official List. Once a year the number of securities is counted and their total market values calculated at the lower of the two prices that are quoted for each security (the reason for the quoting of two prices for one security will appear when we reach the rôle played by the jobber).

The count for 1969 was made on 31st March; it showed that 9,356 securities appeared in the List. These were divided into forty different categories. The total value at market price of the securities quoted was £131,678,611,255.

It is not easy to appreciate the relative importance of the various categories unless one has a clear picture of their respective values. For this reason we are reproducing here from the booklet issued by the Council of the Stock Exchange the columns which show the details that are important for our purpose; the extreme right hand column which shows the percentages is our calculation and is not published by the Stock Exchange Council.

A glance at this list will show how wide are the differences between the values of the categories and of the issues of securities of which they are composed. British Government stocks work out at an arithmetic mean round £350mn. for the average loan; Rubber near the other extreme has 130 different securities for a total value of £114mn. or about £875,000 to a security. There are at least 20 British companies in the List which each showed, on 31st March 1969, a market value exceeding £250mn. This comparison helps to put the Rubber market in proper proportion.

Approximately 14% of the total represents the borrowing of governments, national or local; the remainder covers the borrowings and share capital of companies. Far the largest group of company securities is the Commercial & Industrial section. The next largest market is Oil—but both the Royal Dutch and the Shell companies, each of which have

B   17

Section		Number of Securities	Market Valuation	% of Total
I	British Funds: British Government	38	£13,395,364,385	10·1
2	Gtd. & Nationalisation	20	1,343,295,877	1·0
3	Northern Ireland Loans	6	58,940,000	0·1
4	Trade Facilities and other Acts			
5	Corp. & County Stocks—Gt. Britain & N.I.	567	1,309,821,583	1·0
6	Public Boards, etc.—Gt. Britain & N.I.	93	247,927,906	0·2
7	Commonwealth Govt. & Provincial	136	612,391,504	0·5
8	Commonwealth Corporation	20	50,866,760	0·1
9	Foreign stocks, bonds, etc.	300	1,416,129,467	1·1
10	Corporation Stocks—Foreign	48	24,023,595	
11 12 13	U.K. & other Commonwealth Rlys.	25	763,937,029	0·6
14	Railways: American	16	66,933,936	0·1
15	Foreign	31	35,741,460	
16	Banks & Discount Companies	116	6,641,650,720	5·1
17	Breweries & Distilleries	323	2,475,750,515	1·9
18	Canals & Docks	26	21,961,810	
19	Commercial, Industrial, etc.	4,630	57,485,570,491	43·5
20	Electric Lighting & Power	39	306,194,023	0·3
21	Financial Trusts, Land, etc.	192	1,090,689,306	0·8
22	Gas	15	71,833,688	
23	Insurance	80	2,338,533,552	1·8
24	Investment and Unit Trusts	1,021	5,148,652,225	4·0
25	Iron, Coal & Steel	100	1,562,874,279	1·2
26	Mines: Australian	22	1,055,789,081	0·8
27	Miscellaneous	65	2,027,224,886	1·5
28	Rhodesian & East African	36	500,899,383	0·4
29	South African	127	3,013,062,445	2·3
30	West African	13	3,003,515	
31	Diamond	13	2,663,547,803	2·0
32	Nitrate			
33	Oil	59	21,272,244,764	16·1
34	Property	394	1,515,565,048	1·1
35	Rubber	130	114,077,163	0·1
36	Shipping	79	402,502,488	0·3
37	Tea & Coffee	178	30,880,779	
38	Telegraphs and Telephones	12	2,480,417,656	1·9
39	Teamways and Omnibus	31	18,905,625	
40	Water Works	355	111,406,508	0·1
	TOTAL	9,356	£131,678,611,255	100·0

securities, quoted in London, with a market value over £2,300mn. have quotations on stock exchanges abroad including Wall Street; a small part of the business in Shell and the largest part of the business in Royal Dutch is always being transacted on foreign stock exchanges.

The next most important is Mines, which is subdivided in the List into Australian, Miscellaneous, Rhodesian & East African, South African, West African and Diamonds. The order was originally alphabetical, but, when reform came to the List and Diamonds were extracted from the South Africans, they were put at the end. A little later the shares of the Barrier companies, which work the lead-zinc lodes of Broken Hill in Australia, were logically transferred from Miscellaneous to Australian. It would probably benefit the investor if the mines were grouped not by a geographical classification but by the minerals that they extract. Australian mines are mainly working lead-zinc, and to a lesser extent gold and copper, while nickel, still mainly in the exploration or development stage, has recently assumed great importance. In West Africa the main metal as far as investors are concerned is tin; the gold mines have been either nationalised or taken over. In Rhodesia and East Africa copper, and to a lesser extent gold, are the main metals (here also nickel may become important). Most of the South African mines work gold, some of these uranium as well; there are also collieries and mines working copper, platinum and antimony. A company that mines manganese in South Africa has its shares quoted in the Commercial & Industrial section. This digression will serve to show that these matters are not wholly controlled by logical considerations.

After Mines the next biggest category is Banks, followed by Investment Trusts; after this there is a big gap and then Telegraphs & Telephones, Breweries & Distilleries and Insurance come close together. (This greatly exaggerates the importance of the Telephone & Telegraph section in London. It accounts for 1·9% of the value and 0·007% of the bargains marked. The value is inflated by the two lines of the List which cover two very large American issues whose companies applied for and obtained London quotations.) Thus, by the time we get down to the eighth most substantial category, we are discussing groups which account for less than 2% of the total value of the List.

This, then, is the material in which the Stock Exchange deals, securities to the number of 9,356 different issues, with a market value on 31st March 1969 of £131,678,611,255. (It should be noted that members are also entitled to deal in any security which has been granted a quotation on any stock exchange in the world.)

We must now turn from the things dealt in to the people who deal. These fall into three classes, the client, the broker and the jobber. The client is any John Doe or Richard Roe, or perhaps the Prudential Assurance; to be a client he must have the means and the will to buy or sell a stated amount of a certain security. The broker is the client's agent; his part is to buy or sell the securities in question, buying from or selling to another member of the Stock Exchange. This other member is usually a jobber. The broker is an agent who transacts business in any of the 9,356 different securities in which any of his clients happens to want business done. The jobber is not an agent but a principal; he trades for his own account in a limited number of those securities. The securities in which he trades are called his market; he may deal in all the rubber shares quoted, or those only which are of £1 nominal value; he may deal in oil shares only or in some group or groups within the Commercial & Industrial list. A firm of jobbers consists of a small or large number of members in partnership who are helped by 'authorised clerks' and by full members who are 'associates'. Thus, while a small firm of jobbers will be dealing in only one or two markets, a large firm is able to deal in a very large number of markets. In recent years the number of jobbing firms has been enormously reduced while a few firms have become very large.

The jobber stands at his post in the Stock Exchange ready to 'make a price' in any security in which he deals. Let us suppose that he deals in textile shares. A broker comes to him and says 'What are Courtaulds?' By convention it is the ordinary shares that are meant when a company is named without qualification. The jobber, who does not know if the broker is a buyer or a seller or merely wants to find out the price, will quote two prices, say 1·44 to 1·47, meaning that he is prepared to buy a normal marketable amount at 1·44 per share or to sell a normal marketable amount at 1·47 per share. If the broker has business to do, he will probably test the quotations of various jobbers, and on a reasonably active day he finds that the best bid was 1·45 and the cheapest offer 1·46. If his client were a buyer of 100 shares, the broker could then secure them at 1·46; if the client were a seller, he could dispose of the lot at 1·45.

This, of course, is the ideal picture. All shares are not as easily marketable as Courtaulds; all days are not reasonably active. Some days are unreasonably active and the price may be changing quickly while the broker is testing the market. Some stocks are unreasonably unmarketable; the price quoted may be 'wide' like 2·25–2·5 or worse still it may be 'one way' 2·25–2·5 sellers only. That means the jobber is prepared to sell stock at 2·5 and that he thinks that, if he were prepared to buy, he would be prepared to buy at 2·25. But, as he is not prepared to buy, the information is not very helpful to an intending seller.

The jobber earns a living by taking risks. He makes a price without knowing whether the broker wishes to buy or to sell, and he must be prepared to buy shares that he does not want and to sell shares that he has not got. The broker charges his client a commission of $1\frac{1}{4}\%$ on shares that he buys or sells for his client (there are a number of different rates for other kinds of stock). Many clients think that commission is easily earned. But the good broker must know his job thoroughly, must know at any particular moment which jobbers are likely to buy at high prices and which are likely to sell at low, must know the state of the market and whether it is more prudent to take 1·45 that is bid or to spend time, in which the price may move down, looking for a higher bid. The broker has also important functions outside the market; he sees that his client's shares are collected from their sellers and delivered to their buyers, he arranges for the transfer and registration of securities that his clients buy, he claims his dividends due from sellers and in addition is expected to know about, or find out about, every one of the 9,356 securities that are officially quoted. For these purposes he must rent an expensive office near the Stock Exchange and maintain a large staff of skilled clerks. In addition it has grown more necessary in recent years that he must have the use of a research department, which must be staffed by able, well qualified and very expensive people. A number of brokers now possess their own computers, and many others have access to computer time.

Our description of the market should have given some idea of its mechanism. The geography of the market is equally important. Where does the client live and how does he get access to the market? During 1948 an attempt was made on behalf of the *Financial Times* to count the number of company investors. The work was done by the author, because he wanted to know the answer, and by Professor C. F. Carter, who was then a Fellow of Emmanuel College and was persuaded into or fascinated by the task. The answer reached was about 1,250,000; this figure excluded all investors who held Government securities only. Subsequent investigations, which show figures which are larger (much larger if investors who hold only Unit Trusts are included), have suggested that this figure was reasonably accurate for 1948. As a by-product of the investigation there emerged a very rough picture of the geographical distribution of clients; the figures are shown in the table on page 22.

The investors in the London postal district will do their business either by instructing a broker to whom they are known or by asking their bankers to handle it. Every branch of the clearing banks and every office of most other banking houses is prepared to pass the investment business of its customers to its brokers. The broker gives the banker a rebate of commission; it does not normally cost the investor any more to do his business through a bank instead of working directly with a broker. These same facilities, direct contact with a stockbroker in London or indirect contact through a bank, are open to investors in any part of the world.

Area		Population %	Investors %
1	London Postal District	9·7	23·8*
2	Home Counties (including Sussex)	15·4	20·4
3	Southern England	3·5	5·3
4	South-western England	3·1	5·1
5	Monmouth and Glamorgan	3·0	0·7
6	Rest of Wales	1·8	1·3
7	Western England	3·5	2·3
8	Eastern England	3·7	3·7*
9	Midlands (including Oxon. and Beds.)	12·7	9·3*
10	Lancashire and Cheshire	12·0	6·2
11	Yorkshire	8·6	3·9
12	Northern England	4·9	3·3*
13	Scotland	9·9	10·0*
14	Northern Ireland	2·6	1·5
15	Eire	5·6	1·8
16	Rest of World	—	1·4

*The sample on which the investigation was based was not selected for the purpose for which it was used here; the methods employed were bound to inflate the figures marked with an asterisk at the expense of the others. The figures should be accepted as 'a very rough picture'.

There are also stockbrokers in the provinces. Here the scene is changing very rapidly as the stockbroking world moves in the direction of federation. Formerly there were two main organisations, the Associated Stock Exchanges, whose member exchanges were situated mainly in a few large towns, especially Glasgow, Edinburgh, Manchester, Liverpool and Birmingham, and the Provincial Brokers' Stock Exchange, whose members operated in smaller towns like Northampton, Scottish burghs like Selkirk and even villages like Quorn. But in recent years there has been some federation in the provinces and there is now one stock exchange for the Midlands and West, based mainly on Birmingham and Bristol but extending from Nottingham into Wales, one for the North to cover the former exchanges of Lancashire, the West Riding and Newcastle, and one for Scotland. The Provincial Brokers' Stock Exchange remains independent. Brokers in the provinces were formerly allowed 'dual capacity' which means that the same firm could do business as a broker and a jobber. This will shortly come to an end; the dual capacity firms will hive off their jobbing activities into separate businesses. These exchanges in the provinces provide two valuable facilities. They are a market for local securities, shares of companies that are well known in the district and are satisfied with a quotation on the local stock exchange. The brokers are also in touch, by telephone, with the Stock Exchange, London, and with the other stock exchanges in the provinces. So the local investor can obtain through his local broker expert advice from a man whom he knows and also swift negotiation of any business that he wishes to transact. One of the tasks of a broker in the provinces is to decide where it is best to transact his client's business. It may be best to do it within his own exchange; it may be better to go to London. But an order given in Manchester may be best transacted neither on the Northern Exchange nor in London, but possibly on the Midland or the Scottish. The London broker is very much limited to his own exchange; there may be some virtue in dealing in the provinces where the brokers are more free to choose the best market. It is also worth noting, apart from the matter of dealings, that the broker in a provincial city has an outlook that is different from his London counterpart. The London broker is a City man who moves in a world of finance. The provincial centres are interested far more in matters of commerce and industry. A London broker may lunch with accountants, solicitors, ship-brokers, Lloyds underwriters; his counterpart in Manchester is far more likely to meet manufacturers and merchants.

Let us now imagine a company with a thousand shareholders on its register. If the geographical distribution of these shareholders is normal, there will be 238 in the London postal district, 204 in the Home Counties, and so on down the list in our table. The share is quoted in London; three firms of jobbers keep a book in it. Let us assume that the company is called Consolidated Fence Posting Ltd and that it makes fence posts.

A retired Lancashire cotton spinner, who lives in Prestatyn, decides to fence the end of his garden. He makes enquiries about posts; he finds that the best fence posts are made by Consolidated Fence Posting and that they can promise him delivery in two years and eight months. The next day he receives £800 from the executors of a relative. He remembers the name of the company and its full order book; so he writes to his broker in Manchester for particulars of the company. The broker asks his agent in London; the news comes back that Consolidated Fence Posting £1 shares earned 40% and paid 20% last year and the price is 2·37 to 2·62. The client in Prestatyn thinks this is satisfactory and uses his legacy to buy 300 shares.

The jobber who sold the shares did not hold any; he now wants to make his book even by buying 300. He knows the company's chief factory is in Doncaster, and he knows which broker deals for the provincial brokers in Doncaster. So the jobber goes to these brokers with a tentative bid of 2·44 for 300 shares in the hope that he will thus tempt a sale from Doncaster. If that fails he can try a firm of brokers which deals for the issuing house that bought the shares of Consolidated Fence Posting from the original owners and arranged the underwriting and sold the shares to the investing public (an issuing house usually arranges the underwriting of any issue that it makes, that is to say it finds guarantors who are prepared, for a small commission, to guarantee to take up a stated proportion of any shares for which buyers cannot be found among the investing public). The jobber, through his knowledge of the brokers who have in the past been interested in Consolidated Fence Posting, will probably be able to secure the 300 shares that he has already sold to the broker in London who acts for the broker in Manchester who is acting for the client in Prestatyn.

This example should give some idea of the network that is spread all over the country. At the centre you have the London jobbers; they are in contact with the London brokers. The London brokers are in contact with clients directly, big clients like insurance companies, investment trusts and unit trusts, merchant bankers, industrial companies, and smaller clients, mainly private investors. The London brokers are also in contact with all the branches of the joint-stock banks, with the members of the Associated Stock Exchanges in the big provincial towns and with the scattered members of the Provincial Brokers' Stock Exchange.

It is these clients with whom the jobbers are so indirectly in touch who are the real market. Although they are scattered all over the British Isles and farther, yet almost all the business that they initiate is transacted with the small number of jobbers in London. The whole two million of them make up 'the market' but 'the market' consists of over 9,000 smaller markets, roughly one for each security quoted. The constituents of each market are the investors, actual or potential, who do hold and might sell, do hold and might buy, do not hold and might buy the security in question. To them must be added the brokers through whom they deal and the jobbers with whom those brokers deal.

This conception of the market is of great importance in the study of the art of investment. The whole market consists of all the investors and all other persons with the money and the inclination to become investors. It is an organism with about two million members. Those members are scattered, unevenly of course, over the whole country. They move in many different walks of life. They work in many different trades and professions. Some of them are unimportant individuals; others are great corporations with access to the best information and advice that is available.

There are certain investors of great weight and importance who by their nature are active. Life assurance, whether it is industrial and collects pennies on the doorstep every week or ordinary and receives a premium cheque once or twice a year, brings in a constant inflow of funds which exceed the payments out (and will go on exceeding them till the death-rate and birth-rate are in the right balance and possibly even after that if inflation goes on at a significant rate). The pension funds of big industrial companies are still generally young; they are receiving more in contributions than they are paying out in pensions. Insurance and pension funds of these types are building up their investment portfolios; an unwinding stage may come later but it does not concern us now. Every week they have new money to invest; there are times when they may delay the investment for a week or two but the concern of their managers is always to earn interest in long term investments that are good for their purposes. In the last ten years the unit trust movement has enjoyed a great expansion, and the successful unit trusts are generally trying to secure a constant inflow of funds.

Investors who do not enjoy a constant inflow of investible funds are naturally less active. The professionals—a vague term to cover those who are in constant touch with markets and are frequently shifting their funds from one security to another—may be the next most active class. They are a group which cannot, by its very nature, be subjected to close study. A man may be a professional investor one week and away on a sea voyage the next. You cannot pin him down. He may spend his whole active life in Throgmorton Street; less frequently he reads the *Financial Times* in bed before breakfast and makes all his decisions for the day. More influence is exerted by the large corporations, especially the insurance companies with large reserves behind their accident, fire and other funds, the investment trusts and, to a smaller extent, the companies engaged in various sorts of business which own large invested funds.

The personal investors are numerically the largest class, and they must still account for the bulk of the sum invested. But they hold investments in much smaller packets; their individual resources are generally small. Soon after the end of the war more than 40% of them were women, and the percentage may now be greater. The less than 50% who are men are partly retired, to a small extent they are rentiers who live solely on their investment incomes, to a much greater extent they are professional or business men who trade for their own accounts or they are employed in a managerial or technical capacity by some company. (In addition to male and female investors there are some joint and some nominee accounts.)

Many of these independent and employed investors are well placed to have special knowledge about one or more companies that have shares quoted on the Stock Exchange. They may be employed by such a company or be one of its customers or suppliers. The purchasing manager, for example, of a motor manufacturer is in a position to have special knowledge not only of the company that employs him but also of many of those from which it buys through him.

Thus in each little market, whether the individual investors are bound

25

together by their ownership of shares in a Midland motor company, a Manchester textile warehouse, a Tyneside shipping line, a Falkirk iron-founder, there is almost always a useful fund of special knowledge. Further, when a company is developing well, new investors with special knowledge are induced by their knowledge to buy the shares.

Your new investor in the Falkirk iron foundry may be the proprietor of a firm of builders' merchants in Ipswich. The special knowledge about the Manchester textile warehouse may be found in the textile buyer of a department store in Edinburgh. These markets have no geographical contiguity. They are linked by telephone, telegram and post, through the banking and broking links that have been described, to the jobbers on the floor of the Stock Exchange in London.

To understand how prices change it is necessary to have grasped the rôles of client, broker and jobber and the nature of the market that their relationships form. Let us suppose that a company, which has paid 10% for some years on its £1 shares, declares a dividend of 12½%. Before the announcement the shares stood at 2·4. As the dividend appears on the board in the Stock Exchange, it is transmitted over private telephone wires by brokers in London to their counterparts in the provinces (in some cases it may be published simultaneously in stock exchanges outside London). The news goes out on the 'tape' to all subscribers to the 'ticker'. (The Exchange Telegraph Company leases a machine to City customers for recording the stock prices being quoted. The machine ticks as it prints on a paper tape). The dealers on the floor of the Stock Exchange telephone the information to their principals in the brokers' offices. The brokers ascertain from their records if any clients are interested and pass the news on to them. Thus you have brokers, jobbers, clients all thinking about the new dividend, forming their opinion about it and so on. Some clients will think the dividend (or the figures which now accompany its publication) good in relation to the price; they may want to buy some shares. Others will find it disappointing because they knew the company had been doing well and they had been hoping for 15%; they may want to sell shares. The jobbers have to estimate quickly what the reaction of the market will be, whether it is likely to provoke more selling or more buying. If they expect that there will, on balance, be buyers, they will mark the price up, say, to 2·45–2·48. If they expect that there will, on balance, be sellers, they will mark the price down, say, to 2·35–2·38. Their object is 'to keep their book even', that is to buy as many shares as they sell and to sell as many shares as they buy. If they 'make' a price that is too low (quoting a double price, implying their willingness to buy at the lower or sell at the higher, is called 'making a price'), they will find that they have sold shares which they cannot repurchase without raising their bid and incurring a loss. Similarly, if they make a price that is too high, they will find that they have bought shares which they cannot sell except by lowering their offer and incurring a loss.

Let us suppose that the jobbers feel the dividend is disappointing and they make 2·35–2·38. Some of the clients may be disappointed too and they sell at 2·35. The jobber lowers the price to 2·33–2·37. More clients, disappointed and frightened of a further fall, sell their shares. The jobber makes 2·31–2·35. Other disappointed clients are unwilling to sell as low as 2·31; for a moment business comes to a stop. But a broker who is disappointed but believes that the company's profits are still growing and that better results will be reported next time tells some of his clients that the stock is now on offer at 2·35 and looks to him a good investment. His clients agree and he goes to the jobber and buys at 2·35. Thus the price moves up and down, responding to the changes in supply and demand. If supply and demand are in balance, the price does not move; competition between jobbers may close the price in to 2·34–2·36. What happens when supply and demand become unbalanced? If supply exceeds demand, the jobber must lower his price to avoid becoming a 'bull' of stock which he can sell only at a loss; if demand exceeds supply, he must raise his price to avoid becoming a 'bear' of stock that he can buy back only at a loss. (When he puts stock on his book and becomes a bull, he is said to be 'long' and when he sells stock which he does not hold and becomes a bear, he is said to be 'short'.) He may, however, be helped by the system of 'limits'. Clients give brokers orders to buy or to sell at prices which they state and these orders are called limits. The broker leaves the limits with appropriate jobbers. Thus, a jobber in the case we are describing may have a limit from a broker whose client wants to sell at 2·38. He then knows that if he is short and raises his bid (the lower of the two prices which he quotes) to 2·38, he will get back some, or all or more than all of the stock of which he is short.

As the price moves, its changes are reported over brokers' private telephones to all the provincial stock exchanges. Other brokers advise their private clients who are likely to be interested, also their broker clients on the other stock exchanges. These brokers in the 'country' pass on the news to any clients of theirs who are likely to be interested. (Investors who deal through banks are not likely to hear about it till they read it in the newspaper).

Perhaps there are several brokers who take the view that the prospects are still good. Then orders to buy will continue to flow into the market. The jobbers will raise their prices and more holders are then likely to sell. This helps to bring supply and demand back into balance, and, when the price has reached a level at which the market thinks that it fully discounts the improvement which they expect, buying orders will fall away till demand and supply are once again in balance.

The changes in one market help to cause changes in others. One investor who has sold shares on the $12\frac{1}{2}$% dividend at 2·35 will buy in their place shares in another company, also paying a $12\frac{1}{2}$% dividend but with shares standing at 2·1. He thus secures a higher return on his money—for the moment at any rate. He also tends to raise the price of the share bought at 2·1; after his purchase the quotation may move up to 2·2–2·5. So a piece of news about Company A, which results in the sale of shares of Company A and the purchase of shares in Company B, may bring about a change in the price of a share in a company whose connection with the news is remote. The nine thousand markets of the Stock Exchange are all one market, and the one market is nine thousand separate markets.

There is one important characteristic of markets of this sort which is obvious but is nevertheless often overlooked. There is no mysterious pool from which would-be buyers can draw shares and into which would-be sellers can discharge them. There is a certain small give and take in the system due to the willingness of jobbers and professionals to sell short, that is to make a sale of securities that they do not hold in the expectation that at a later date they will be able to repurchase those securities at a lower price and so close their commitment. But these short sales must all, sooner or later, be closed by purchases. The general rule is firm that nobody can get into the market unless somebody else is willing to get out, nobody can get out of the market unless somebody else is willing to get in.

The sort of image which one should keep in mind is something like the Inner Circle railway with over a million passengers travelling round the circuit. But no traveller can get into this Inner Circle simply by buying a ticket; he cannot pass through the entry turnstile unless some other traveller simultaneously passes through an exit turnstile. When there are a large number of would-be travellers pressing on the entry turnstiles, waiting for admission to be permitted by the exit of another traveller, then there is loose talk of 'pressure of money' and share prices most certainly have a tendency to rise. When the situation is reversed and there is a crowd of travellers pressing on the exit turnstiles waiting for some would-be traveller from outside to pass through the entry turnstile, then there are more sellers than buyers and share prices most certainly have a tendency to fall.

One must doubt how much 'pressure of money' is reduced when money passes at rising prices from would-be investors to holders of shares. One suspects that in most cases what happens is that the would-be investors become holders of shares and the holders of shares become would-be investors. This is not the process by which demand for shares is usually reduced. Demand is reduced when an investor sells his securities in order to spend the proceeds on consumer goods (if he sells shares to buy a house he may well be matched at the other end of the chain of transactions by someone who sells a house to buy shares). Supply is increased when companies offer new shares to their stockholders at favourable prices in order to augment their own capital resources.

This is a matter in which there are important differences between shares and commodities. When prices go up, sellers are more willing, but the seller of securities, once he is possessed of cash instead of securities, is likely to be in his turn a buyer of securities or to buy in their stead some asset which is held by somebody who will be glad to hold securities in its place. So the rise in the price of securities, while it does increase supply, tends also to increase demand. It is only in so far as it encourages new issues of securities that it really increases the supply without a corresponding increase in the demand.

In a commodity market a rise in the price does tend to increase the supply. If the price rises more than the cost of production, then the acres that can be profitably tilled or the veins that can be profitably mined are more in number than they were before. The total quantity of a commodity that enters into a market is capable of variation over a shorter or longer period; the quantity of securities is capable of a much smaller variation. Securities can be increased in number by new issues or decreased by repayments of borrowing or capital. The volume of securities is also sometimes decreased by the liquidation of companies, but when a company comes to an unfortunate end the value of the securities dies with the securities and in this case the going out of existence of the security does not leave its former owner in the possession of any cash equivalent.

If a single security rises in value, the yield or return on the money invested shows a corresponding decline. This tends to reduce the demand for the particular security. But when securities in general rise in value, the relationship between their yields is little altered. Many holders are tempted to sell by the higher prices; but, as they still want their money to be invested, they soon buy other securities. Thus markets tend to be more active when prices are high; though it is true that the higher prices are caused by the increase of demand, it is also true that the higher prices themselves cause an increase of demand.

CHAPTER TWO

History of Prices

Price is obviously important to the speculator whose interest in stocks and shares lies in his hope of making profitable deals; but it used to be argued that the investor for income makes the best bargain for income that he can at the time of his investment and has no further concern with the price of the security that he has bought. Even before investors became concerned with inflation and the declining value of money, this argument was not valid. The investor may at some time after his investment wish to exchange for something else the income which he has bought, for example a new car, a larger house, more education for a child, a long sea voyage. The quality of the car, the size and location of the house, the excellence of the education, the luxury and duration of the voyage will depend entirely on the prices realised for the securities. Buying securities is turning capital into income by a reversible process, and the investor, in making his purchase of a security, must consider not only the reliability of the security's income but also the price at which he will be able to realize, if need or the desire arises.

The object of investment is to preserve capital and at the same time, or in the future, to secure income from it, and the investor of today is aiming not at the preservation of the monetary value of his investments but wants to maintain their real value, that is to be able to buy with the proceeds of sale years after the purchase as much as he could have bought with the money he invested at the time when he made the purchase. In former times this idea of 'growth' did not play so prominent a part in investment, and people thought more of success achieved by buying securities at prices which turned out to be low. Some measure of success could also be achieved by selling securities at prices which turned out to be high. Accordingly we must treat the movements of security prices among the most important aspects of investment.

There are two ways of approaching prices. We can start with individual securities, study their price behaviour and then go on to see whether smaller or larger groups have a common price behaviour that can conveniently be studied by means of averages. Alternatively we can assume at once that there is a common price behaviour for large sections of the securities market and proceed without further ado to the study of averages. Let us make this assumption now and justify it later.

When this book was originally written, there was very little recent history for the stock market. Although the market was functioning through the war, there was a feeling that history began again when the war ended, and we selected for study two periods of twenty-eight years, one of which began in 1920 and covered a time well within recent memory, one of which ended in 1913 (of this period memories were fewer, more dim and less reliable, and none went back to the earlier part of it). This study still appears valuable, but we can now add to it a large chunk of recent history, the progress of the market from 1946 to 1969. The first part of this chapter deals with the ancient history.

The curves we require are plotted on a chart which is divided into a lower and an upper section. The upper section contains the bold dramatic movements of the years 1920–47, the lower section the more sedate patterns of the Victorian and Edwardian eras. In this chart, as in most of the others that will appear later in this book, the time intervals go from side to side across the chart and are all the same distance apart. In this case each vertical line shows the end of a year and each year takes up the same space on the chart. But the horizontal lines which show the changes of the price level are not the same distance apart. Theirs is a logarithmic scale, arranged so that the distances 40:80::50:100::60:120::70:140::80:160 ::90:180 are all the same. Again the distance from 40 to 120 is the same distance as from 60 to 180. This is far the best kind of scale when you want to use a chart to compare the movements of two different securities or averages. If you use ordinary squared paper for charts, then the distance from 60 to 70, which Consols covered in a few months of 1932, is only half the distance from 120 to 140, which Moodys share index covered between November 1935 and November 1936. But the percentage gain if one buys at 60 and sells at 70 or buys at 120 and sells at 140 is $16\frac{2}{3}$, the same in both cases.

There are two curves plotted in each section of the chart, one for each of the two main divisions of securities, fixed interest and variable dividend. A simple example of the fixed interest security is the Liverpool Corporation $3\frac{1}{2}\%$ Stock which is redeemable only by purchase or by agreement with stockholders. It is, in effect, a contract to pay a certain income in perpetuity, and the Liverpool Corporation will be able to fulfil its bargain as far into the future as any investor dares to look. Preference shares used to be considered as perpetual incomes of the same sort, with the proviso that no company could be thought as safe and sound as a city like Liverpool, but in recent years decisions of the courts have shown that reductions of capital can be enforced by ordinary shareholders so that preference shareholders are paid off at the nominal value of their shares. Consols 2½% and Treasury 2½% are British Government obligations of almost the same type, but there are clauses in their deeds which allow the Treasury to redeem the stocks at par after 1923 in the first case and after 1975 in the second. It was naturally assumed in 1921 that Consols could never be repaid; the same assumption did not look quite so sound in 1946 when the stock rose within a fraction of its par value. At the other end of the fixed interest scale there are stocks that are issued for repayment in a very short time, like the Serial Funding 1¾% 1952 which was issued in the autumn of 1951 and repayable in the autumn of 1952. These securities that are issued with a promise of repayment, whether in one year or one hundred years, have in them an element of money and are not pure stock like the Liverpool 3½%. These dated securities, as they are called because they have a fixed final date by which they must be redeemed, are the titles to a loan of money which must be repaid and which in the meantime bears interest. Pure stock is simply a title to an income; the value lies in the income and not in the promise of ultimate repayment.

The types of securities that we are studying at this moment are all 'pure stock'. Ordinary shares are a title to an income, which may be stable in some cases, variable in others, and in a third merely a memory of the past or the hope of a future. The holder of an ordinary share is entitled to as much of the profits available as the directors elect to divide. His dividend may, if he is unlucky in his choice of a share, fall to nothing; it may, if he is lucky, rise to 100% or more.

On our upper chart we can trace the course of Consols 2½% from 1920 to 1947. In 1920 we see the price declining (this was, in fact, the last stage of the decline which, as we shall see later, began in 1896). But with the turn of the year the price began to rise and at the end of 1921 it passed out of the 40–50 range into the 50–60. In that range it stayed till the early months of 1932; by then a steep rise was in progress which took the stock by the end of the year to 75. The rise then continued at a slower pace; by the beginning of 1935 it was over 90. Then began a decline, the first serious downward movement since the rise began in 1921. Most of 1935 and all of 1936 saw the stock in the 80–90 range; in 1937 it fell to the 70–80 range and in the second half of 1938 it was falling again. The outbreak of war in 1939 saw it in the low sixties, but the five-year decline was by this time finished. For 1940 the range was 70–80, for 1942 over 80. Prices were slightly lower, round 80, for 1943 and 1944 but improved in the first half of 1945. In the second half of 1945 the Labour Government was in power and the rise was fairly steep; it went on till the price came within a hairsbreadth of par in the last months of 1946.

Consols is not a suitable stock for our study in the period before 1914.

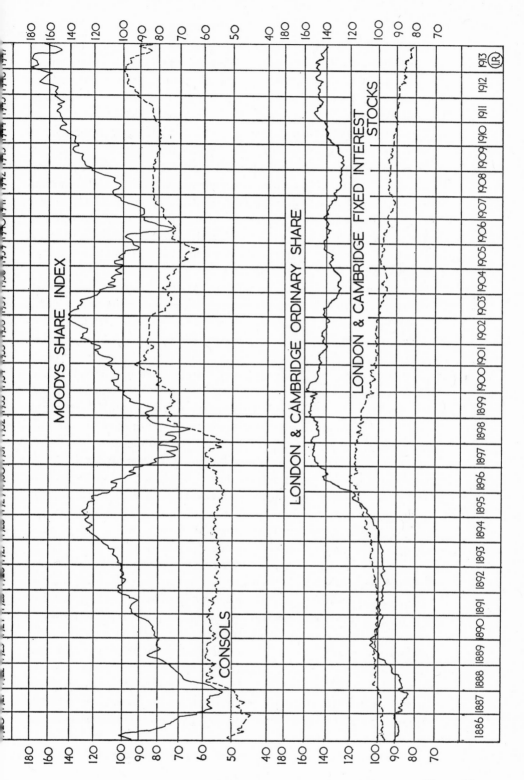

MOODYS SHARE INDEX

CONSOLS

LONDON & CAMBRIDGE ORDINARY SHARE

LONDON & CAMBRIDGE FIXED INTEREST STOCKS

1886 1887 1888 1889 1890 1891 1892 1893 1894 1895 1896 1897 1898 1899 1900 1901 1902 1903 1904 1905 1906 1907 1908 1909 1910 1911 1912 1913 ⓘⓡ

Chart No. 1

It had always been a 3% stock, but the Goschen conversion brought it down to $2\frac{3}{4}$% in 1888 and $2\frac{1}{2}$% in 1902 and these changes would vitiate comparisons over our period. We have therefore substituted the London & Cambridge Economic Service's fixed interest stock index (an index is an average which is adjusted to a given base, normally '100 in such-and-such a year'. The figures then express the changing values as percentages of the base). This is an average of the prices of very high grade fixed interest securities. The index is rising when the chart begins in 1886; it reaches a temporary peak in 1888 and the rise is not resumed until 1892. It continues to the middle of 1896; then values turn downwards and decline with little dramatic change to 1913. (The mean price of the high and low points of Consols for that year were 73·3; for 1920 they were 47·8. This gives some idea of the extent to which the 1914 war and its aftermath accelerated this long decline of fixed interest stocks.)

We can now form some idea of the characteristic movement of fixed interest stocks. In the pre-war period the movement was gentle and it had, for very long periods, one main direction. The decline which ran for twenty-four years from 1896 to 1920 was the counterpart of an even longer, if less violent, upward movement that culminated in 1896. It is possible to treat the twenty-six-year rise from 1921 to 1946 as one single upward movement; but it is clearly divided into chapters bounded by the financial crisis of 1920, its successor in 1930 and the outbreak of war in 1939. The fall from 1896 to 1913 is a much steadier movement. If you draw a line from the point where the index stood in December 1896 to the point to which it had fallen in December 1913, you will see that it never diverged far from this straight path. The divergences have been larger but still regular in the decline of Consols since 1946. In this case the angle of the fall has been much steeper than for the decline from 1896. In both cases there is a marked contrast with the wide and irregular divergences if you draw a line joining a 1921 level of Consols with one in 1946.

When we turn to Moodys share index for the years 1920–47, we see that it moved in a succession of huge waves. The rise from 1915 was spent in 1920 and our chart begins with an abrupt decline in which shares lost nearly half their value in less than two years. By 1925 the ground lost had been regained and the rise went on and up into new high levels till the beginning of 1929. Then came two and a half years of steep decline and a final downthrust a year later; values were little above the low level of 1921 and were about half the high level of 1929. From this point we see a rise of four and a half years which more than doubled prices. Next comes a three-and-a-half-year fall which nearly halves them. The next rise runs for six and a half years.

Before we turn to the lower section of the chart where we have used the

London & Cambridge ordinary share index, it is worth noting that in the period between the wars it stood at 266 for 1926 when Moodys was 100 and 375 for 1936 when Moodys was round 130. This suggests that there is no startling difference of volatility between the two but that the more volatile of the two is the London & Cambridge. We did not use it for the period after 1920 because its figures run only from 1925; its compilers omitted the period 1915–24 which had been studied by the late Mr J. Kitchen.

The character of the share market before 1914 appears to have been utterly different. Late in 1887, the second year that our chart shows, it reached the low point of a decline that began in 1880 (some might say in 1873). There are no examples since of declines that persisted through so many years, but it may, at some date in the future, be important to remember that shares, which have often shown long rises, have also, on some few past occasions, shown long declines.

The market rose briskly to the winter of 1889–90, by which time it was under the influence of the events which preceded the Baring Crisis. The rise was arrested, but the decline which succeeded took the character more of a movement sideways rather than downward. It was not till 1893 that the rise began once more to take control. The pace quickened through 1894, 1895 and 1896 but slackened in 1897. 1898 was a year of reaction but new high levels were reached in 1899 and a final spurt at the end of the year took prices to a peak in the first months of 1900.

This long rise had lifted the index from its level round 100 in 1890 to round 150. But by 1900 the rise was exhausted and a decline set in which carried the index down below 130. This decline lasted four and a half years (longer than any decline has lasted since). It was succeeded by a brief rise to the winter of 1905–6. 1906 was a year of hesitation and at the beginning of 1907 the peak of the previous winter was attained once again. These twin peaks were a little above 140 and well below the peak of 1900. Next we have a broad trough, associated with the American crisis of 1907–8. Once again the index dropped below 130; but the decline was checked at a level similar to that of 1904. In 1909 the rise began again and reached a peak in a little less than two years. This 1911 peak was above those of the period 1905–7 but below 1900. Thereafter prices moved sideways above the 140 level till near the end of 1913.

While the movements before and after the 1914 war differed greatly in violence and amplitude, there are certain characteristics which persist through the barrier of the war. The rate of interest on long-term stocks appears to have an oscillation with a very long period. Fixed interest stocks were high in 1896 and low in 1920–21 and high again in 1946–47; the period seems close to a quarter of a century. The equality of the swing up and the swing down may be purely fortuitous; the Chamberlain peak of 1935 may be a more natural eminence than the Dalton peak of 1946.

On the other hand, the decline of Consols from 1935 to 1939 is the only substantial countermovement in the whole fifty-six years that our charts cover. It is certainly the habit of changes of the long-term rate of interest to persist for long periods, and this is a habit that a second war has not changed.

The character of the share market is quite different. A turning point was reached in 1887 and the next may be placed as far off as 1900. The next was in 1904, a decline of four and a half years. Next comes a rise of, at the most, two and a half years. Then comes a two-and-a-half-year decline followed by a two-year rise. The record was broken in 1914 when the Stock Exchange was closed; the level was lower when the market reopened in 1915. From there it rose to the peak we see on our chart in 1920, declined for twenty-two months, and then set off on the series of great rolling swings that persisted to 1947.

The period before our chart begins was a period of declining prices for ordinary shares, but throughout the years since 1887 the general tendency has been either upwards or sideways. The rises of 1887–1900 and 1915–20 were great lifts of values to new high levels; the subsequent rises were of a different character, great in amplitude but little in progress because each started unlike the two predecessors, at levels so deep below the preceding peaks.

The ordinary share market has two characteristics which differ, over this period, from the fixed interest market. The ordinary share index has a series of low points separated one from the other by a small number of years and a series of high points separated one from the other by a small number of years. The fixed interest stocks run up to a peak in 1896, down to a trough in 1920, up to a peak in 1946. The cycle here is long and unprogressive; the rate of interest at the second peak does not seem to have been very different from that at the first. But the ordinary cycle is progressive; there is a tendency for the later peaks to be higher than the earlier. Sometimes a long period elapses before a new peak is reached. It was not till 1896 that the index rose above the level of 1873, nor till the middle of the first war that the 1900 level was excelled. The peak of 1920 was excelled in 1925, 1929 in 1936, 1936 in 1944. By all these precedents the peak of 1947 was, in due course, to be exceeded, and the new high was in fact achieved in April 1954, some months before this book was first published.

It is now time to leave the old historic chart and to consider the performance in the post-war period. The charts used for this purpose are not historical exhibits like that on page 33 but are actual working charts in current use by Investment Research. They are constructed on a different principle; most of them are 'bar charts', not 'line charts'. A bar chart shows the range of price covered in a certain period while a line chart shows the price at the end of a period, or the average for a period. In the post-war period the divergence between fixed interest stocks has been developed more strongly even if you allow for the great decline of fixed interest stocks that occurred in the period omitted in the first chart, the years of the first war. Further, the divergence between Consols $2\frac{1}{2}\%$, the fixed interest stock we have chosen, and the *Financial Times* industrial ordinary share index, developed so strongly that it is not possible to present the two curves clearly on a single chart. So instead of one chart with four curves, we have to use two charts with one curve each.

Let us take first Consols $2\frac{1}{2}\%$ in Chart No. 2. This is a very good stock to chart; the dividend is paid four times a year so that the breaks in the curve caused by adjustment of the price for the stock's going 'ex-dividend' are comparatively small, even when the running yield rose over $9\frac{3}{4}\%$ in 1969. You will note that two lines, in addition to the price bars, have been drawn on the chart. The upper line joins the peaks of 1946, 1954, 1963 and 1967, while the lower line joins the low points of 1952, 1957, 1961 and 1969. These two lines are parallel. They are called 'trendlines'. You will find that trendlines can often be drawn whether single stocks or averages are being plotted, sometimes on one side of the price curve, sometimes on the other, rather less frequently on both, and in some of the cases where two trendlines can be drawn they are parallel. But it is not usual for a single, parallel trend channel to extend over a period of twenty-three years (perhaps longer as the trend has still to be broken). The long swings that appeared in the fixed interest market between the nineties and the end of the war had a duration of about twenty-five years. If anybody mocks at a study of the history of the stock market, remind him how useful it should have been to holders of War Loan in 1946 to know that fixed interest stocks which had risen 120% in the latest quarter of a century had in the previous quarter of a century declined about 60%, a performance which could be repeated. It is comforting for holders of War Loan at its present low price to know that there is a precedent for a rise, over twenty-five years, of 120%!

The chart of Consols is a commentary on Britain's financial history since the war. We start with the stock being inflated to an entirely artificial value from which the price declined with very poor rallies till it found the lower trendline in 1952. You can see the 'Convertibility Crisis' in the summer of 1947, the run-down to the devaluation in 1949, the slide through the 'Korean Crisis' of 1951 followed by the Conservatives' change in fiscal policy and the first raising of the Bank Rate. Then you have the rise of the Butler period in 1952/54 and a new decline, interrupted

37

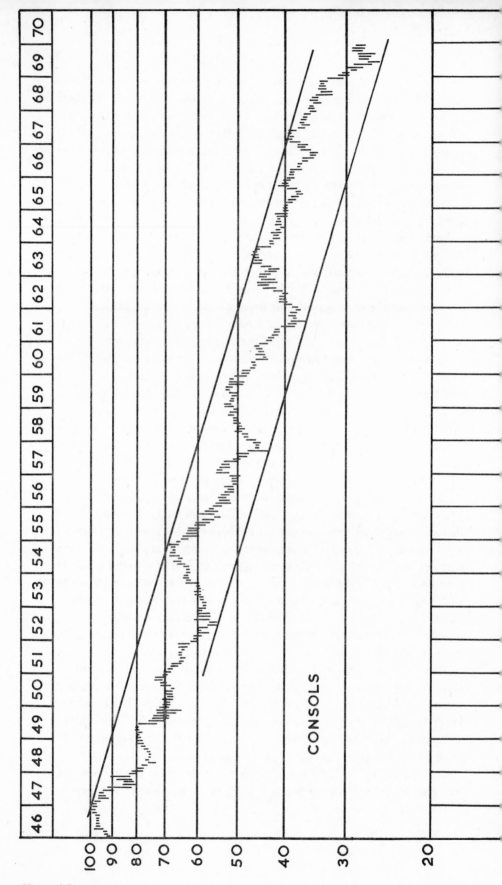

Chart No. 2

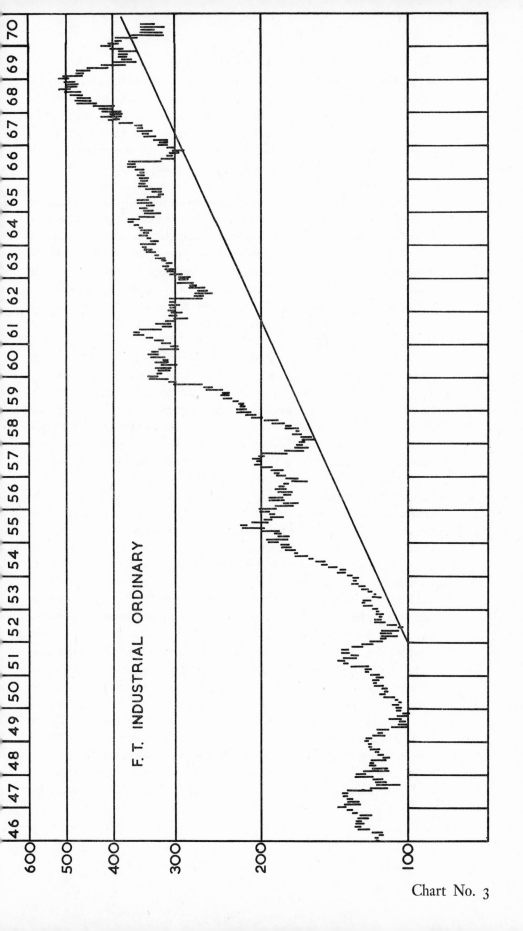

F.T. INDUSTRIAL ORDINARY

Chart No. 3

by a weak rally after Suez, with a swift resumption of the decline to the Thorneycroft Bank Rate of 7% in 1957. The subsequent rally petered out without reaching the trendline and a new decline came down to the lower trendline in 1961, when Selwyn Lloyd put the Bank Rate to 7% again. A tighter squeeze helped the price up to the upper trendline by 1963; but by this time a new General Election was in sight and the price turned down again. From then there was little but decline with a feeble rally for the recovery of 1965, and slightly less feeble rally for the measures of July 1966, then a graceless slide from the middle of 1967, accelerated in its later stages by American financial policy which induced a worldwide rise of interest rates to unexampled levels. Then a brave budget in 1969 restored a proper balance between Britain's savings and investment, with a substantial margin for the repayment of foreign debt and our overseas payments swung suddenly and vigorously into a large surplus. Consols rallied from the lower trendline, and that is as far as the story goes in the early months of 1970.

The chart of the *Financial Times* industrial ordinary share index for the same twenty-four years (Chart No. 3) presents a very different picture. When the *Financial News* was merged in the *Financial Times* after the war, the index which was continued under the name of the *Financial Times* was the old *Financial News* index with only one or two changes of constituents. The *Financial News* index had flattened out in August 1944 and moved in a narrow horizontal range up to April 1946; it then ran up through the top of that range to a level just over 140 at the beginning of 1947. Then it subsided and within a very few months collapsed to the bottom of the range. Then it rallied but made no great progress and settled down for the rest of 1948 in a range from just below 110 to just above 120. In 1949 the downward movement started in 1947 was completed with a decline to 100 in June and, after the September devaluation, to a slightly lower level in November. The next upward movement ran to the summer of 1951 and carried the index to the top level of 1947 but no higher. And by June 1952 it had fallen most of the way back to the low point of November 1949. But the next move upwards was really substantial and more than doubled the index number in the space of three years. The pattern here consists of an initial rise from the bottom lasting eight months, a reaction of three months, and then an upward sweep without significant interruption from May 1953 to February 1955. In March the rise was renewed but this was its last phase; it reached a peak in July 1955 and this was followed by a period of decline to February 1958, a decline interrupted by a strong rally in the spring of 1957. The new big rise of 1958 lasted into January 1960, and again the index was more than doubled. In 1960 the market declined, rallied and declined again; from its low point in December it rose strongly for five months to a level $7\frac{1}{2}\%$ above the peak of January 1960. Then it fell in two stages, first through the low levels of 1960 where it steadied for seven months, then down about the same distance again to a bottom in the summer of 1962. The next period was much less exciting; there was first a recovery of just over two years to a level little over the best of 1961, then a decline after the 1964 General Election, a rally in the first quarter of 1965 and a decline in the second, then a rather longer rally to the summer of 1966 which was ended by a sudden collapse. You will note that a lower trendline has been drawn under the curve through the low points of 1952 and 1958; the 1962 bottom did not approach this line but the 1966 trough sat on it. This contact with the lower trendline was followed by a new rise of nearly 80% which culminated in tops in September 1968 and January 1969. The subsequent decline of that year brought the index down to the lower trendline again, and it is not clear at the time of writing whether the trendline once again marks an inviolable frontier which the index cannot penetrate or whether a new decline is still in store which will break the trendline, which might mean the ending of this phase of market history and the beginning of a new one.[1] The market of 1920/40 was quite different from the markets known before 1914; its rises were much larger and so were its declines. The market after 1952 produced rises as big as those of 1920/40, but the succeeding declines were very much smaller. This was the market of inflation and the gold-exchange standard. The gold-exchange standard seems to have come very near its end, but it is generally assumed—'part of the conventional wisdom' Professor Galbraith might say—that inflation must go on. A decline of the index through the trendline might mark a decision by the market that inflation as a market sustaining factor might be able to persist no longer. In that case the market would need a new philosophy which it would probably seek in uncertain movements, just as it did between 1944 and 1952.

[1] The chart shows how the trendline was broken in the second quarter of 1970; the new low point lay on a trendline drawn through the bottoms of 1962 and 1966.

CHAPTER THREE

How Prices Move

In the preceding chapter we have given some account of the history of security prices in modern times and have described the characteristics of the long-term movements of ordinary shares in general and of fixed interest stocks. We showed first two combined charts, each of which showed the movements of both ordinary shares and fixed interest stocks by separate curves and each of which covered periods of twenty-eight years. These charts were composed by plotting monthly average figures, twelve to a year. The earlier chart covered a period that ended in 1913, the later one that ended in 1947. We then turned to more recent events in two charts, each plotted by monthly ranges, one for the *Financial Times* industrial ordinary share index and the other for Consols 2½% for the period from 1946 to 1969.

But the movement of prices goes on not merely from month to month through the years but from week to week through the months and from day to day through the weeks. Investment consist in buying and selling securities (some people might add that holding them is even more important), and the decision whether one should buy or sell today or alternatively put off the decision till tomorrow may be very important. It is therefore necessary to study the manner in which prices move not only from month to month but from week to week and from day to day. It is easy to see from the chart of Moodys share index from 1920 to 1947 that the big movements up and down did not consist of one single rise or one single fall. The rise and fall has generally a saw-toothed appearance which suggests that falls were frequently interrupted by rises and rises by falls. But in the long rises the falls failed to persist; in the long falls the rises failed to persist.

We must think of the market (or of an individual security) as always looking for the 'right' price; at the same time we must bear firmly in mind that the notion of a 'right' price is illusory. The investor's greatest mistake is to fall into the error of Mr William Saroyan's Armenian musician. This gentleman played the 'cello; he played it at home; he played only one note the whole time, and this troubled his wife. After several years she remonstrated with him and pointed out that other 'cellists moved their fingers up and down the strings and thus made the instrument sound different notes. To this he replied magnificently, 'Oh! woman of little sense! Other men are looking for the right note; I have found it.'

There is no right price for the market to find; for the price which seems right today seems wrong tomorrow and the market must move on in its search. Sometimes it moves too slowly and must pursue tomorrow the same direction as today. Sometimes it moves too fast and must pursue the reverse direction. Sometimes it seems to have found the right price and it then stands still for two days or three; then the right price dodges away from it and it must proceed on its eternal chase.

If you look at the chart on page 33 you will see that for the whole of the fifty-six years there portrayed there are only two periods in which you could not say firmly either 'Shares are going up' or 'Shares are going down'. (There would have been a third if we had been using the *Financial News* ordinary for the period 1944/46.) Exclude the year 1906 and the two year period from the spring of 1911 to the spring of 1913; at almost any other point on the record, except the actual turning points, you can decide by inspection whether shares were in course of a rise or a fall. These long movements, which last for a year or sometimes for years, are called primary. The primary movements are composed of shorter secondary movements; the secondary movements, whose direction is the same as that of the primary, are usually long and the secondary movements, whose direction are counter to the primary, are generally short. These secondary movements last a few weeks or many months. They in their turn are composed of shorter movements, lasting days or weeks, which are called tertiary. The secondary movements are visible, in curtailed form, in the chart on page 33; the tertiaries are not.

In order to examine the tertiary movement we have drawn up Chart No. 4—the *Financial Times* industrial ordinary share index for the first forty-four weeks of 1946. For this large scale chart an ordinary arithmetic scale has been used; the range from 113 to 129 does not require a logarithmic scale, especially when no comparison is being made on the chart. The months show at the bottom of the chart and at the top the numbers of the weeks appear.

The *Financial Times* industrial ordinary share index is computed four times a day from the prices of 30 leading industrial shares. They are shares which are popular and are widely distributed among investors. They are 'marketable', that is to say, there are always sellers of them and always buyers. The index is based on a 'geometric mean' that is to say it is calculated not by adding up the prices and dividing the sum by thirty but by multiplying the prices together and extracting the thirtieth root. The

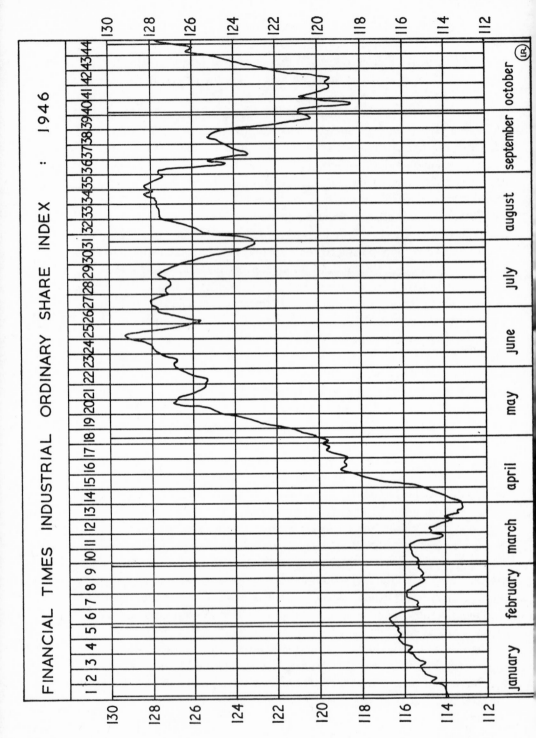

FINANCIAL TIMES INDUSTRIAL ORDINARY SHARE INDEX : 1946

Chart No. 4

arithmetic mean of 95 and 105 is 100 but the geometric mean is something less. This sort of average went right out of fashion in the fifties and early sixties, but it has now come back and at least one American advisory service, Indicator Digest of Palisades Park, N.J., computes an unweighted geometric mean of all the common stocks listed on the New York Stock Exchange. An index like the *Financial Times* industrial ordinary need not reflect accurately the behaviour of the whole corpus of industrial ordinary shares and it is not weighted to show accurately the changes in the market valuation of British industry. These, perhaps, were not the purposes for which it was composed; it is an index of representative ordinary shares and it serves well to show how the feeling of the market changes from day to day.

The fashion recently has been for indices like Standard & Poor in America, *The Times* and the F.T. Actuaries in Britain (and similar indices in most other countries), which are based on a refined arithmetic mean (the calculation takes account of relative changes of price, not absolute changes which would make a 1% move in a share at £100 much more important than a 1% change in a share at £1) and are weighted. This means that a movement in Imperial Tobacco or Imperial Chemicals counts more than a movement in Carreras or Albright & Wilson because Imperial Tobacco is more important than Carreras and Imperial Chemicals more important than Albright & Wilson. This is a much better method of using averages to estimate how much the value of the market as a whole has changed, and these weighted arithmetic means are probably the best instrument we have for measuring changes in the value of the market, as long as nobody will take the trouble to feed the whole market into a computer every day. But it is very doubtful whether these weighted indices are good for studying the behaviour of the market as opposed to its value. They are influenced far too much by the shares which are not bought and sold, like the Government's holding of British Petroleum or the American parent's controlling interest in F. W. Woolworth & Co. Ltd, or the millions of shares in Imperial Chemicals which are held by family trusts and insurance and pension funds and which never change hands. The case for the unweighted mean is that it is the shares which people buy and sell which matter and that the holdings that never change hands should not enter into the calculations of students of movements of price. That is what investors should be studying.

After that digression we must return to the tertiary movement. A glance at Chart No. 4 will show that it divides easily into five separate phases, weeks 1–13, 14–25, 25–34, 34–40 and 40–44. The first phase which covers the first quarter of the year is a period of stable equilibrium. The index had been confined within the range 105–119 since August 1944. It had looked for the right price near the top of that range just before the declaration of the poll in 1945 and near the bottom just after. For the first five weeks of 1946 the index was moving quietly upwards. At the beginning of most weeks it seems to have advanced a bit too sharply; there is often a tiny tertiary counter-movement from Monday to Tuesday. But the main movements up to the middle of the sixth week were upwards. This was not unnatural; Mr Dalton, the Chancellor of the Exchequer, was working hard at his cheap money policy, augmenting the resources of the banks so that they increased their holdings of Government securities. What the banks were buying, other investors were selling, and these other investors were likely to be reinvesting in other securities.

Although the banks added £11mn. to their investment portfolios between the middle of January and the middle of February, by the sixth week of the year the rise was losing momentum. The first full-scale Socialist budget was only a few weeks ahead. Investors felt cautious. The rise stopped; the market began to look for the right price at lower levels. During the previous rise would-be sellers had often abstained from selling in the hope that prices would rise a little higher. Now they came in to sell, and the would-be buyers held off for a little in the hope that prices would fall a little lower. At the end of the seventh week there was a little recovery. The price steadied for a few days, but the buyers were still timid and the sellers still wanted their money. So the sellers pressed the price down in Week 8. Then they became less eager to sell and the buyers a trifle more eager to buy. The market was looking for the right price at a slightly higher level and the movement through Weeks 9 and 10 was gently upward. Then in Week 11 the sellers pressed urgently for their money. They pushed prices down too far; sellers were too few and buyers were more than sufficient, so the price rose to the middle of Week 12. Then again the urgency of the sellers prevailed over the timidity of the buyers; there was one insignificant rally at the end of Week 12 and in Week 13 the index reached the lowest point on this chart. This first phase was one of stable equilibrium. The market never looked for the right price above 117 nor below 113. It worked quietly upwards for five and a half weeks and quietly down again for seven and a half. This phase covers the last three months of a prolonged movement sideways, a movement which had started a few weeks after the Normandy landings. It was a period of stable equilibrium.

Then at the beginning of April the whole character of the market changed. All of a sudden a large number of investors came to the conclusion that a Socialist Budget need not end the world for investors, especially as it was going to abolish Excess Profits Tax. Throughout April and for two weeks in May the market was dominated by buyers.

46

Except for a pause before the Easter holiday there was no sign of equilibrium; the balance was weighted firmly down by buyers. In Week 20
there came a check; perhaps some of the buyers of early April took their
profits and some of the would-be sellers who had been holding off came
in to sell. This tertiary reaction lasted a fortnight; then the profit-takers
were sated and the sellers pressed less urgently. The buyers regained control
of the market and looked for the right price at higher levels till Week 25.
This second phase was one of disequilibrium, of dominance of buyers
over sellers. From Week 14 to Week 20 it might be described as stable
disequilibrium.

From Week 25 to Week 34 we are again in a period of equilibrium. But
this is not like the first three months of the year. The movements are
sharp and the fluctuations wide. The movement of a few days in Weeks
25–26 covers almost as wide a range as the whole fluctuation of the first
thirteen weeks; the decline from Week 29 to Week 31 covers a wider.
The recovery from Week 31 to Week 34 covered more ground than any
movement since Week 20.

At Week 35 we move into disequilibrium again. This time it is the
sellers who are looking for the right price at lower levels; and the buyers
withdrew before their urgency. The sellers were prudent, over prudent
it turned out, but they had good reasons for their alarm. Prices on Wall
Street were crumbling at the end of August and collapsing at the beginning
of September. Collapses of Wall Street in 1929 and 1937 had been followed
by dire falls of security prices in London; sellers in London were afraid
that the same might happen again. There was a short period in Weeks
37–38 in which buyers were able to assert a superiority over sellers; then
fear prevailed once more and the sellers drove the index down towards
118 in Week 40.

In the event the buyers were right and the sellers were wrong. A crash
on Wall Street was no match for a Socialist Government in those brave
days. Mr Dalton, the Chancellor of the Exchequer, was bent on converting
Local Loans 3% (Treasury 2½% 1975 or after was offered in exchange
later in the autumn when he called Local Loans for redemption); Mr
Barnes, the Minister of Transport, had to announce the terms on which the
railways were to be nationalised. The news that more than a thousand
million of Home Rails, much of it giving a high percentage return on its
quoted prices, was going to be converted into a guaranteed stock that
would probably yield 3%, impressed on many inexperienced investors
that they must, if they were to preserve a fraction of their standard of
living, sell their Home Rails and buy something that would give more
than 3%. Their brokers told them to buy first-class ordinary shares.
First-class ordinary shares rose—you can see how steeply they rose

through Weeks 42–44. Not only were holders of Home Rails buying; but other investors had been selling their holdings of gilt edged to the banks to whose resources the cheap money policy was constantly adding, and those other investors were tempted into the rising market for ordinary shares. Thus there was once again a stable disequilibrium with buyers in unshakable control of the market.

The tertiary movement is changeable and unpredictable. It may last as little as one day; it may last two or three weeks. Its various zigs and zags build up the secondary movements which last for weeks and months. The decline from Week 25 to Week 40 is an example of a secondary reaction, or countermove downwards against the direction of a primary rise. The complete secondary decline from Week 25 to Week 40 appears to consist of 19 different tertiary movements. Some lasted as little as one day; one persisted for nearly three weeks. But in order to study the secondary movement we need a chart of quite a different scale. The Investment Research Gold Producers share index for the years 1946–49 (Chart No. 5) provides an example that is useful because it conforms fairly closely to the classical pattern.

Chart No. 5

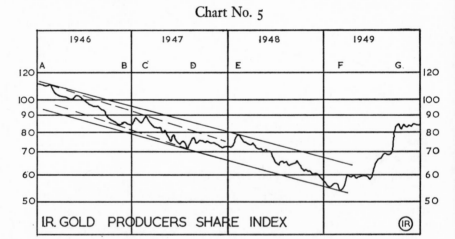

The war had been a bad time for gold mining. Once Lend-Lease was arranged gold production did not aid the war effort. Labour was wanted for other purposes, and the mines had no priority for equipment. Operations were curtailed and development was neglected. When the war ended the mining community was full of hope of better times, and the prices of shares rose. But by the beginning of 1946 a new danger was appearing—inflation. It would raise the cost of mining; it would make other occupations attractive for labour which had formerly come to the mines. The prices of everything else would rise but not the price of gold.

Investors who grasped what was happening began to sell their gold producers shares, and the mining finance houses may have been sellers too, as they needed funds to finance their development of the new field in the Orange Free State.

The main secondary movements on this chart are marked by the capital letters above the 120 line. The movements are of two classes, the phases which follow the direction of the primary movement, in this case downwards, and the rallies which run counter to the primary movement upwards. (When the primary movement is upwards, the countermovements are known as reactions.) The movement consists of three phases, AB, CD, and EF. It was interrupted by two rallies, BC and DE. During the downward phase AB there were a few rallies, but these were only of tertiary duration and extent; they each lasted a few days but no more. But in the autumn of 1946 the climate became a little more propitious. The shares of the developing mines had reached a peak in June, had crumbled quietly through July and August and collapsed on the break of Wall Street in September. By November that collapse had overrun itself, and a strong secondary rally in the developers, combined with a hope that the decline of Wall Street was the forerunner of an end to inflation, checked the fall of the producers and caused the small secondary rally that ran from B to C. The fuel crisis of February 1947 may have helped the rally; a shortage of coal in Britain had forced the Government to curtail the supply of electricity and close every factory that depended on electric power, a misery which South African gold mines were spared. As normality returned after the fuel crisis, it was plain that inflation was still a dominant force; the decline of gold producers was resumed.

This decline was arrested at D by the impact of the Convertibility Crisis. This might lead to deflation and reduce the cost of mining, or it might lead to a depreciation of sterling and a rise in the price of gold. These hopes seemed ill-founded; they were raised again by some juggling with the franc early in 1948. But this point E marked the limit of the secondary rally. The decline was continued to F when a well-founded conviction that the pound would be devalued brought the primary decline to an end.

This Gold Producers chart that we have been considering presents an excellent opportunity for introducing the notion of trend and the terminology that goes with it. You will remember how we described on page 34 the manner in which the London & Cambridge fixed interest stocks index came down steadily from 1896 to 1913 without ever diverging from its path and the even longer decline within narrow bounds of Consols 2½% from 1946 on page 37. What we called, in the case of the London & Cambridge fixed interest stocks index, a path is the same thing as a trend;

D

the trend of a security price or of a price index, and of other prices and indices too, is the way that it is going. If you look at Moodys share index (Chart No. 1 page 33) there is little difficulty in deciding for most years what the trend was. The turning points that separate downtrends from uptrends are clearly visible. An uptrend ended early in 1920; then a downtrend ran to the end of 1921. The next turning point was in 1929.

The Gold Producers chart shows the classical pattern and this time we have a much larger scale. From this chart we can learn how trendlines are drawn. You will remember that the top of the post-war rise in Gold Producers came at A. Some weeks later there was a sharp tertiary rise, and it is the top of this tertiary rise that turns out to be one of the key-points for this downtrend. (A tertiary rise of this sort need not be the key-point; in this case it is a matter of sheer necessity as it would have been impossible to draw a satisfactory trendline from the absolute top.) The index declined as far as B before there was a substantial rally, and then from B came a sharp rally which lasted several weeks and carried the index up to C. Then prices turned down again. At this point it is possible to draw (in pencil as a continuous line) the broken line which joins the tertiary peak A of February 1946 with the secondary peak C of February 1947. For the moment that will stand as one of the trendlines. At the same time one can hopefully draw in a broken line, parallel to the line AC through the point B where the index made its low before the secondary rally. The upper line is a trendline, joining two or more extreme points on the trend. The lower line is a parallel, drawn parallel to the trendline on the opposite side of the trend channel. These two lines mark out tentatively the limits in which the index is likely to move while the trend persists. Unfortunately, as you will see in a moment, this index did not long remain in the trend channel that was thus marked out. But before we discuss that behaviour we must note that the second secondary phase of decline terminated at D, on the lower parallel already drawn in. At this point the chartist would redraw his parallel as a continuous line because the second contact argues strongly that it too is a trendline.

From D, which had confirmed the trend, the index rallied through the upper trendline to E. This might have signalled the completion of the downtrend, but the subsequent fall into new low ground put that possibility out of court. A new tentative trendline must be drawn and AE would probably be chosen in preference to CE which is also a possibility. And the chartist's faithful friend, the india-rubber, would be used to erase the extinct trendline AC. At the same time we can draw a tentative new lower parallel through D without erasing the existing lower trendline which has not yet been invalidated. We now have a new trend channel bounded by the upper trendline AE and the lower parallel drawn through

D, and you will observe that this is the final trend channel which does contain the whole of this decline of the Gold Producers index. Further you will note that when the broken lines were drawn as parallels the decline to D carried the index down to the lower parallel and no further, and the subsequent decline to F carried the index down to the lower parallel and no further. You must note that you cannot rely in every case on the trendlines being parallel one to the other nor that every parallel which you draw will ultimately be confirmed as a trendline.

If a line is drawn halfway between the upper and lower trendlines (or between trendline and parallel), it is called the axis of the trend. There is no necessity, either in logic or fact, for the trendlines to be parallel and in such cases the axis may be useful to denote the assumed direction of the trend. Reference may be made sometimes to 'the trendline'. If there is only a trendline and a parallel, the meaning is obvious, but if there are two, an upper and a lower, 'the trendline' is the right hand trendline, the upper boundary of a declining trend channel and the lower boundary of a rising trend channel. As an uptrend cannot change to down nor a downtrend to up without cutting through the right hand trendline, you will see why this is chosen for the title and not the other.

In a case like the Gold Producers we find that there is a certain distance above the axis of the trend at which the optimists always lose heart and the pessimists assert themselves; in the same way there is a certain distance below the axis of the trend where the pessimists always lose heart and the optimists assert themselves. (If you are using logarithmic paper, you could write percentage instead of distance; if you are using arithmetic paper, that is squared, you could write difference.) The upper trendline in such a case is a declining trend of waxing pessimism and the lower trendline a declining trend of waning optimism. When you have an uptrend in place of a downtrend, the upper trendline is a rising trend of waning pessimism and the lower trendline a rising trend of waxing optimism.

Inside our primary trend channel we can also draw in secondary trends up and down; these secondary trends would zig-zag across the channel of the primary trend.

This pattern of the Gold Producers, which we have just been examining, is almost classical. It has one imperfection; the rally from B to C is too short. The normal secondary rally or reaction retraces one-third to two-thirds of the ground lost or gained in the previous secondary phase; if the rally from B to C had reached normal dimensions it would have gone on to the final upper trendline and given us a truly classical pattern.

We must now turn to a pattern that appears regrettably unclassical, that of the *Financial Times* industrial ordinary share index in the years

1946/49 (Chart No. 6). In the first year the behaviour of the index was orthodox; most of this we have examined in greater detail when we were considering the tertiary movement. In the chart below, the secondary highs and lows are indicated by capital letters. A shows the summer peak of 1946, B the bottom of the secondary reaction that succeeded it, and C the top of the primary rise in January 1947. In the case of the Gold Producers, the six letters from A to F were sufficient to carry us through a primary decline that lasted over three years; on this industrial chart we have a decline that lasts less than three years and requires the letters C to P. It is a much more complex decline. Its start is orthodox enough with the decline to D and rally to E. Then we get the collapse to F, which turns out to be only a little above the actual bottom of the decline at P more than two years later. Next comes the big rally to G. After that comes more than a year of movement that is almost horizontal; it includes a rally from J to K that retraces more than the whole of the movement which preceded it. Then in 1949 the pattern returns suddenly to orthodoxy. The decline from K to L is corrected by a rally of normal dimensions to M; the decline from M to N is corrected by a rally of normal dimensions to O. The decline from O to P makes no significant extension into new low ground.

Chart No. 6

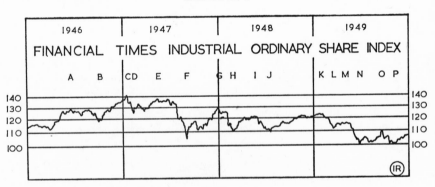

Although no parallel trendlines can be drawn for this decline, nevertheless the upper trendline runs through C, E and K and a contact was missed by a hairsbreadth at G. This turned out early in 1950 to be a useful trendline; it was cut by the rising index just as investors were beginning to realise that the downward trend of 1947/49 was a thing of the past and that what was important was the upward trend from 1949.

We can now bring the three trends into proper focus. The primary trend is the main direction in which the market is carrying out its search for the right price. These primary trends endure usually for more than one year and sometimes for much longer periods. The secondary trends zig-zag up and down across the axis of the primary trend; these are the directions in which the market seeks the right price for periods of at least several weeks and perhaps many months. The tertiary trends zig and zag across the axis of the secondary trends; they endure for a day or two and at the most for a few weeks.

The old nomenclature of bull and bear market or primary upward or primary downward trend has not been entirely suitable. The bull markets, or primary upward trends have been well developed but the bear markets or primary downward trends have not. What has happened has been a sequence of the following sort. Starting at a bottom the market rises irregularly while it is arguing whether it is still in a primary decline or a primary rise has begun. Then the buyers take control and the index moves up in a very stable disequilibrium, all primary uptrend, no significant secondary correction. Then instability appears and there is a well marked secondary reaction and this is followed by a strong rally, perhaps into new high ground. The next stage is a period of substantial irregularity in which over two to three years the market has a tendency to drive down to successively lower levels, but this tendency does not preclude it from also reaching higher levels, as in the case of 1961 and, to a much less marked extent, in 1966.

CHAPTER FOUR

Do the Indices Forecast?

In former times when the direction of ordinary share prices changed, many business men expected to see fairly soon a corresponding change in the activity of business. This expectation gained belief partly from experience, partly from its plausibility. It is true that business activity, as recorded by *The Economist*'s index, turned down in 1929 some months later than Moodys share index or the London & Cambridge, turned up late in 1932 and turned down late in 1937. There was the record of experience.

Was this a logical necessity? Or was it sheer chance? The normal answer is that there are all over the country—all over the world, if you like—investors who are in positions of special knowledge. When the activity of business is going to decline, a shadow is cast in front of the deterioration. Sales managers note that their order books are emptying; buyers note that their suppliers are more eager to make sales. Everywhere shrewd investors are putting two and two together, and their sums are adding up to mean lower profits for this company or for that corporation. Holders of the shares come to hear that the prospects are not so good; so the ranks of the sellers are reinforced and the ranks of the buyers are attenuated. That was a fair enough statement of the position just after the war and up to the early fifties when the first edition of this book was written. But since 1945 there has been a great change in the composition of the body of shrewd investors. Investment analysis has become a profession whereas before the war it was very largely a matter of inside information and hunch. The influence of institutional investors on the market has increased and that of personal investors has diminished. Your shrewd investor now is likely to be an investment trust or an insurance company or a pension fund or a merchant bank, drawing on a number of teams containing economists and investment analysts who are busy not only in considering the likely achievements of individual companies or industries but also considering what is going to happen to the economy as a whole.

If the deductions of the shrewd investors of the past were sound, it was reasonable to treat the stock market as a 'leading indicator' for the economy as a whole, and again now if the deductions of the shrewd investors of the present are right, it would still seem reasonable to expect ordinary share prices to change direction in front of a change of direction of the economy as a whole. On the other hand the shrewd investors may not be infallible or may not be as closely concerned as is assumed with the behaviour of the economy. So we have here a plausible answer; it seems to explain how the Stock Exchange has been a good forecaster and can still be a good forecaster without excluding the possibility that its forecasts could be wrong. For if something were to happen that made enough shrewd investors put two and two together so that the answer was five instead of four, if in fact shrewd investors were quite wrong in their reasoning, then there could be a substantial turn in the direction of ordinary share prices which did not forecast a change in business activity.

If we turn back to the long-term chart of ordinary share prices on page 33, we shall see that in the period 1920–47 there were four major turning points at the top, in 1920, 1929, 1936–37 and in 1947 and three major turning points at the bottom in 1921, 1932 and in 1940. Let us take the first top and bottom. The Trade Unions' returns of the percentage of the members unemployed were:

Year	%
1919	2·4
1920	2·4
1921	14·8
1922	15·2
1923	11·3

Here you have the orthodox pattern. Share prices dip down, and unemployment begins to increase only several months after the decline of shares began. Share prices rise, but the worst year for unemployment is the year after that in which the rise of share prices began. In this case shares turned up at the end of 1921, the worst year for unemployment was 1922 and the upturn came in 1923.

You get the same thing in 1928–33 with the Ministry of Labour's percentage of unemployment (these figures were not available for the year 1919 and immediately thereafter):

Year	%
1928	10·8
1929	10·4
1930	16·0
1931	21·3
1932	22·1
1933	19·9

55

The downturn of prices came at the beginning of 1929, but that was a better year for unemployment than 1928. The rise of prices came in 1932, the worst year for unemployment. The pattern is very much the same for 1936–38:

Year	%
1936	13·1
1937	10·8
1938	12·7

Share prices turned down right at the beginning of 1937, but the unemployment figure for the year was much better than for 1936. The bottom of 1940 must be omitted; there can be no answer to the objection that the curve of share prices at that point was influenced mainly by the development not of business activity but of the war. But when we come to the top of 1947 we are beyond the influence of war. This was peace, and in time of peace ordinary shares turned downwards and declined with a speed and ferocity unknown since 1920. The fall of prices in 1947 between January 17th and September 3rd showed a larger decline than that of the first seven months of the 1929–32 slump and the 1937–40 bear market. In fact, the bulk of this decline was crammed into a few weeks between July and September. Later an even fiercer decline developed in the first seven months of 1969.

Now that we have seen the end of it, it may be fashionable to argue that the bear market of 1947–49 was small, shallow and insignificant. That is the view which would be put forward by those who demand that a real bear market should enjoy the dimensions of 1929–32. Such a disaster may overtake us once in thirty years; so those who want to reserve the term 'bear market' for so great a convulsion are unlikely to have much opportunity for using it. On the other hand, the slacker kind of journalist will apply the term to any sharp decline of share prices and will presumably see two bear markets in the 1947–49 period. It is difficult to fit the second use into a satisfactory terminology.

The 1947–49 bear market appears to have been quite normal for extent and duration. If you compare it with the fall from January 1937 to January 1939 you will find the dimensions similar. If we ignore the extension of the 1937 bear market into 1940 on the ground that it was due to the war, it seems reasonable to compare the development of unemployment after 1937 with that after 1947. We have seen that there was a $17\frac{1}{2}\%$ increase of unemployment in the average figure for 1938 over that for 1937. It would be reasonable to expect that a decline of similar dimensions for share prices after the war would have been the forerunner of a similar increase of unemployment (or larger, if one takes account of the numbers of men being released from the forces). Unemployment did fall between 1946 and 1947, just as we should have expected. It did increase, as we should have expected, between 1947 and 1948. But in the whole period (except, of course, for the weeks of the fuel crisis in 1947) the percentage of unemployment was less than 2; and the increase for 1948 over 1947 was roughly of the order of 1·5 over 1·4.

This 1947–49 bear market was much shallower than the catastrophic declines of 1920–21, 1929–32, 1937–40; but it was almost as large as the decline from January 1937 to Munich, which corresponds roughly to the period of declining business activity in those years. It was half as large again as the decline that ran from 1900 to 1904 and it was twice as deep as the decline associated with the American Crisis, the bear market of 1907–9.

The Central Statistical Office produces an interim index of industrial production, covering at that time twenty-one different industrial groups. Out of all these only one, manufactures of wood and cork, showed a lower figure for 1947 than for 1946; only one, leather, leather goods and fur, showed a lower figure for 1948 than for 1947. The former had a weight of 25:1000, the latter of 6:1000. The total for all industries rose from 100 in 1946 to 108 in 1947, 121 in 1948, 129 in 1949 and 140 in 1950. If the decline of ordinary share prices in 1947 was forecasting a depression of trade, it was wrong, utterly wrong. (But the upward turn from November 1949 seems to have been a very shrewd appraisal of the increased activity of business that was coming in 1950.)

The association between declining share prices, declining business activity, and rising unemployment can be traced back to 1873, if not further. The association was close from 1900 to 1912 and from 1920 to 1938. But the post-war share slump of 1947 did not bring in its train any general decline of business activity. After this example it is no longer possible to argue that there is an inevitable association in peace time between a primary decline of share prices and a falling off of business activity. We are forced back to the position either that the Stock Exchange is not an accurate forecaster of business declines or that it is an accurate forecaster but what it forecasts need not be a decline of business. In that event we must define what it is that a Stock Exchange decline forecasts, and to this the short answer must be trouble.

Formerly the expectations of a business man after a Stock Exchange slump were fairly clear. There was going to be a decline of public demand, a growth of competition, a falling off of profits, an increase of unemployment. These things would continue for a time to get worse; then, after a time, they would get better. This was what his father had told him, when he first came into business. His own observation in the twenties and thirties confirmed his father's experience of the eighties, nineties and nineteen hundreds.

Then in 1947 it just did not happen.

The stock exchanges are concerned with investors who are engaged in buying and selling securities, and these investors are interested not in the activity of business but in what they are going to get out of their shares. We used to think that it was the dividend which was the shareholder's primary concern; but as you can now clearly persuade him to buy shares which do not and never will pay a dividend it is plain that the dividend by itself is not of prime importance. The investor now is interested in the whole return from his investment, the sum of all the dividends that he will receive from it plus the difference, which may of course be negative, between the price that he pays for it and the price at which he ultimately sells it.

His valuation of shares in terms of their dividend is by no means stable. Chart No. 7 on page 59 shows the *Financial Times* industrial ordinary share index plotted against a dividend curve deduced from the yield figures which the paper regularly prints. (As a yield is dividend divided by price, it follows that dividend is yield multiplied by price.) In the years 1946–52 the investor tended to value dividend on a declining basis, i.e. the yield on shares was going up. In the next period up to the beginning of the sixties the shareholder was willing to pay more and more for his dividends but in the early sixties he relapsed towards the attitude of the late forties and prized dividends less. This attitude suffered a startling reversal after 1966 up to the end of 1968, but for this period a statistical defect inherent in our method seems to have invalidated the series, and the chart is therefore not to be trusted beyond 1965.

The obvious difference between the two curves is that price fluctuates in the first few years and then surges upwards, fluctuates, surges upwards, fluctuates. The periods of fluctuation are the bear markets; even if a new high level is reached after the fluctuation begins, the lowest level of the period of fluctuation always immediately precedes the next upsurge. The dividend curve moves in a different way. There is little fluctuation; the curve is either rising or not rising and periods of significant decline are difficult to find and always extremely short. This is quite different from what happened between the wars; there was a very substantial decline of dividend from 1929 to 1933 and a lesser decline running from 1938 to 1942. The larger of these two declines fell little short of 40%!

In the years just after 1945 dividend was vulnerable to a very small extent. Dividends were generally very well covered by earnings. But since the early fifties cover has diminished, largely because the threat of a take-over urges directors on to distribute as much as they dare. It is thus

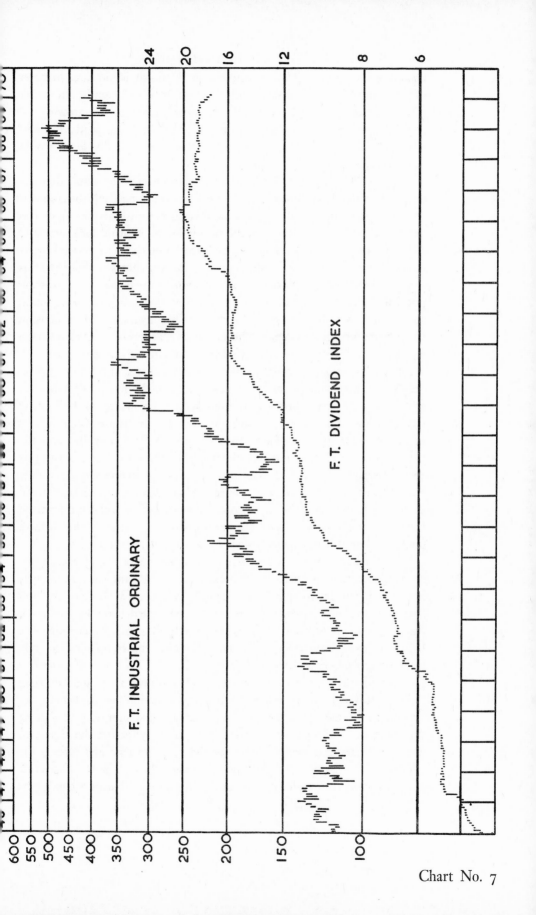

F. T. INDUSTRIAL ORDINARY

F. T. DIVIDEND INDEX

Chart No. 7

becoming more difficult for directors to maintain dividend rates in times of declining business activity, and competition is sufficiently strong for profits to decline at times when the economy is growing but growing too slowly. If our economy runs into trouble and production actually declines, as it used to do between the wars, the resultant cuts in dividends would now be severe.

So far we have assumed that all the decisions except the actual declarations of dividends are made by the investors. But it need not be true that share prices go up and down because investors want shares more or less keenly. There can be changes in the supply of and demand for shares and some of these changes may be imposed from outside. The general treatment of this question is simple. The demand for shares is thought of as that proportion of their investible surplus which the managers of growing portfolios want to invest in shares; and these growing portfolios are found almost entirely among institutional investors like insurance offices, pension funds and unit trust managers. The supply of shares is thought of as (a) the surplus of sales over purchases effected by private investors who, on account of taxation, are always selling off more shares in retirement or at death than their successors are buying, plus (b) the new shares that are offered by companies through the stock exchanges, mainly in the form of rights issues. The simple assumption that the institutions are always buying and the private sector always selling is far too crude; and the private investor is still a potent influence in the making of prices. But this short description makes it clear that supply can fluctuate quite widely from month to month and year to year. There can also be fluctuations in demand. On the whole the supply of money is growing, and if it is growing fast there is more of it available for investment, that is on the side of demand, than if it is growing slowly or actually being reduced.

These changes in supply and demand can operate on the market in two ways, either through their direct impact or through the earlier anticipation by some of the investors. The changes are cyclical as they are imposed largely by the Government. At times it increases the demand by increasing the supply of money and reduces the supply of shares by enabling the banks to lend more freely, with the result that the companies can rely more on borrowing and less on issues of shares. This tendency, which is pleasant for the electorate, is democratically allowed to go too far; then the Government has to try to rectify the situation by slackening the growth of the money supply, or even reducing the supply, thus cutting down demand for shares and at the same time increasing the supply of shares by making it more difficult for the banks to lend and forcing the companies to raise some of the funds they need through issues of shares.

So the modern investor has to guess not only what business conditions will be like, because they will affect the dividends which the companies can pay, but also what the Government may do to try to change those business conditions because, even if the Government is unsuccessful in achieving the particular change that it wants, it may in the process of trying affect the supply of and demand for shares.

CHAPTER FIVE

The Controlling Factors

In the preceding chapter we discovered that ordinary share prices, if they had any prophetic qualities, were not forecasting accurately the conditions of business or the fluctuations of dividends. In any case, the investor is interested in the forecasting powers of ordinary shares so far as they will help him to accurate forecasts about the courses of ordinary shares. He does not want to use the present movement of ordinary shares as a means to foretelling the future behaviour of something else; he wants some present movement or movements that will enable him to foretell the future movement of ordinary shares.

Unfortunately, the number of present movements available is not very large. Most of them can be found in the Stock Exchange Official List; for that document contains in addition to the daily prices the daily numbers of bargains marked (not for each individual line of securities but for the List as a whole and for each of its separate sections). Changes of dividends are also readily available, as they are reported to the stock exchanges which have granted a quotation for the shares as soon as the directors reach their decision. Dividend changes, however, are not a frequent statistic like changes of price. Bargains are marked every business day in active securities but dividends for a security are declared usually only twice a year. With these dividends, interim or final, a report of earnings is now usually given. Even then, the new dividend refers to times gone by, as it is based on the profits earned in a period that ended a month or several months before the declaration (although current conditions may influence the directors' decision about the dividend).

Other economic data are not presently available. They are published at various intervals after the event to which they refer. The Overseas Trade Returns give details of January's imports and exports towards the end of February. But the orders that initiated those imports and exports were placed months earlier; so January's figures, published in detail quite promptly three or four weeks later in February, refer to business decisions that were taken three, six or nine months earlier. The gold mines of the Rand publish their figures of values, profits and tonnages milled, a day or two after the end of the month to which the figures refer. Other companies publish information about their activities, if at all, at much longer intervals. The figures for beer production appear about six weeks after the end of the month to which they refer.

The fully known factors which influence share prices from day to day are few. Is dividend one of them? The object of investment is to preserve or increase capital and at the same time to earn a useful return on it. This is assumed, even by the investor who admits that he is in search only of capital appreciation. His capital appreciation is to be secured by selling to another investor at a higher price securities that he buys at a lower price. That other investor must have an object in purchasing the security. His object too may be capital appreciation, but the basic assumption behind the purchase for capital appreciation is that somewhere at some time there will be an investor in search of security and of income who will buy the shares and hold them. The ultimate buyer in a chain of transactions is a payer of so many years purchase for the share's expected dividend. This analysis demands that dividend should be one of the factors that control share prices.

It is not of course the only factor. We have already seen how dividend maps out afterwards a course that corresponds very roughly to price, although in the post-war period downturns of dividend for the market as a whole have so far been slight. Formerly, when we came to peaks of price, dividend generally turned down soon after price but when we were in a trough it turned up long after price. But the correlation was bad and the amplitude of the oscillations is much greater for price than for dividend. The lag of dividend behind price is not constant; and there have been plenty of occasions in recent years on which price has turned down but dividend has done no more than flatten out (and in 1947/49 it did not even do that).

It has long been thought by some investors that price was controlled more by earnings than by dividend. In recent years it has become fashionable to lay great emphasis on earnings and to stress the importance of the Price: Earnings ratio (popularly called the P/E ratio) which has come into fashion since the introduction of the Corporation Tax. The correlation of earnings and prices is fairly good if you plot your chart showing the earnings at the time when they were earned, not at the time at which they became known. Earnings as a controlling factor are less helpful than dividend. The dividend that a company pays is a figure declared by the directors and ultimately paid into the shareholder's bank. Everybody who is interested is agreed what it means to him. The figure that a company has earned for its ordinary shares is an accountant's figure; if the company had used a different firm of auditors it might well have been advised to show different earnings. In the case of a manufacturing company there may be big differences between earnings calculated on a FIFO or a LIFO basis. And who is to tell which is right? FIFO means that the stock is valued on a 'first in, first out' basis and LIFO on a 'last in, first out' basis. There are items, both of income and expenditure, which may be classed as normal or as non-recurrent. If the item is not likely to recur, its relevance to future earnings is small and the earnings may look quite different to two analysts, one of whom is calculating the margin by which they covered the dividend, the other of which is looking at the earning power of the company in order to make his estimate of the next year's dividend. Nor will there be agreement which items are normal and which are non-recurrent.

Dividend is something precise but earnings are not precise, even if they are now somewhat more precise than when the first edition of this book was written. Therefore we can use dividend as a basic known factor in the shaping of ordinary share prices much better than we can use earnings.

A second factor that is known is the rate of interest and the level of prices of fixed interest securities. These two are, of course, different aspects of the same thing; when the London & Cambridge fixed interest stock index was declining from 1896 to 1920, the rate of interest was rising; when Consols rose from 1921 to 1946, the rate of interest was falling. This factor is certainly known; the price of Consols appears daily in the Official List and the *Financial Times* calculates and publishes each day its fixed interest stock index. Does this known factor influence share prices?

There used to be no question about this; some people might now answer 'No'. In the first edition of this book the table that appears on page 18 showed British Funds alone accounting for more than 50% of the total value of the list; in this new edition the total for all the 'Government' section is only 14%. There are of course fixed interest stocks quoted for various companies in the rest of the list. There is still a very active market in Government stocks, and there are many investors who find it convenient to hold fixed interest stocks. Although one knows so many investors who insist that in no circumstances will they ever hold a fixed interest stock, it is assumed by many that the fixed interest stocks are always in competition with the variable dividend investments. This is especially true of the institutional investor. The manager of a fund other than a unit trust, who has to make regular investments every day, week or month, ought to ask himself on each occasion whether at the current level of prices fixed interest or variable dividend securities are the better investment for his fund. There is acute competition for the investor's money between the two classes of stock, and the competition is expressed in price. When the rate of interest was rising before 1914 and fixed interest stock prices were falling, this must have exerted a downward pressure on the prices of ordinary shares. It was almost certainly one of the strongest of the reasons why share prices did not rise between 1900 and 1915. When fixed interest prices were rising and the rate of interest falling between the wars, the pressure was exerted in the opposite direction.

Let us take a modern example. Between 1946 and 1951 we saw Consols 2½% varying in price from 100 to 60. When the investor could buy only £2·5 per annum Consols interest for £100, he would expect to buy smaller variable dividends for £100 than when he could buy £4·1 Consols interest for £100. In other words, it was natural that there should be some connection between the prices of variable dividend and of fixed interest securities. One could put the matter confidently in the early fifties; in 1970 ideas are not so simple. The table below shows various Low and High levels for the *Financial Times* industrial ordinary share yield, corresponding with high and low levels of the *Financial Times* industrial ordinary share index.

Low points of Yield			High points of Yield		
Jan.	1947	3·35%	Sept.	1947	5·5%
Dec.	1947	4·1%	Jun./Nov.	1949	5·5%
May	1951	4·4%	June	1952	6·5%
July	1955	4·3%	Nov.	1956	6·6%
May	1957	5·3%	Feb.	1958	7·1%
Dec.	1959	3·7%	Dec.	1960	4·95%
May	1961	4·2%	June	1962	6·2%
Jan.	1964	4·5%	July	1965	6·4%
June	1966	5·2%	Nov.	1966	6·8%
Jan.	1969	3·6%	July	1969	5·2%

This is not a simple table to interpret. It can be argued that the British Share Price and Yield cycle is normally not simple but compound, consisting, if we start from the top of the Share Price cycle, of an initial decline, a rally, a final decline and then a new rise. If we are looking at Yield instead of Price, we see an initial rise, a reaction, a final rise and then a new decline. This series was broken in 1951/52 when the decline of yield from 1949 to 1951 was compensated by the rise from 1951 to 1952 after which a new phase of decline began.

So the important low points of yield on which we must keep our eyes are those of 1947, 1951, 1955, 1959, 1964 and 1969; the important highs are those of 1949, 1952, 1958, 1962 and 1966 (at the time of writing the status of the 1969 high has not been determined but if the normal compound cycle works itself out there should be a higher point of yield established in 1970 or 1971). In the series of low yields, the lowest was recorded in 1947 when the yield of Consols was close to its lowest point. By May 1951 the Consols yield was higher; and so was the yield on the *Financial Times* index. But in July 1955, with the Consols yield still higher, the *Financial Times* yield was 0·1 lower and in December 1959, with the Consols yield considerably higher, the *Financial Times* yield was very substantially lower. When we look at the high points of yield, the important dates are November 1949, January 1952, February 1958 and June 1962. The parallelism between Consols yield and share yield here persisted as late as 1958, but by 1962 a very much higher yield on Consols was not matched by a higher yield on shares. There was a very large change in the normal relationship of variable dividend and fixed interest yields in the fifties and sixties. Up to 1959 it was the rule for the yield on Consols to be lower than the yield on the *Financial Times* industrial ordinary share index; after 1959 it was the rule for the yield on the share index to be the lower. But this change in the relationship does not prove that the influence does not exist. We should have been wrong to expect a perfect correlation between the yields on the two sorts of investments. The rise of shares from 1926 to 1929 owed something to dividend and nothing to fixed interest. The fall of 1930 was much steeper than the decline of dividend in that year and during the period from the beginning of 1930 to the middle of 1931, in which share prices fell very heavily, the thrust of fixed interest prices was not downward but upwards. The evidence requires that we must either reject interest rates as a factor controlling share prices or admit the existence of one or more other controlling factors. The second course is far the easier.

It is very much easier to isolate this other controlling factor than to decide, when it is isolated, what it is. The assumption that there is one simple other controlling factor appears to have no obvious validity. There may be one; there can just as easily be two. There seems no reason why there should not be three, or four, or as many as you please. But they can all be lumped together into one residual factor and because it is residual, of composition unknown but including all the factors that affect share prices other than dividend and interest rates, it shall be called for the present, quite simply, R. R's existence is proved, like that of an unknown planet, because it influences share prices, and it is quite simple to evaluate R by mathematics.[1]

---

[1] Our unknown R consists of all the elements in share prices other than the fixed interest element and the dividend element. Its mathematical evaluation presents no difficulties, even to the tyro, until you try to investigate the mathematical nature of what you have evaluated; and that is a task best left to statistical experts in search of doctors' degrees. All one needs on this occasion is the equipment of a non-mathematical grammar school child who proposes to study the subject no further than O level.

Let us take an average of share prices and call it P and the average of their dividends, D. Then we need an average of fixed interest stock prices, F. In order to eliminate the dividend and fixed interest elements from P, we must divide it by D and F; what we have left is our residual R. Our formula is

$$\frac{P}{F \times D} = R$$

We can, if we like, break down the left hand side of the equation into two separate expressions

$$\frac{1}{F} \times \frac{P}{D}$$

and these two can be examined separately.

If we were to substitute for our expression F a single exemplar of a fixed interest stock, like Consols 2½% or War Loan 3½%, and replace the figure 1 in the numerator by the actual interest rate applicable to the stock

$$\frac{£2\cdot5}{\text{Consols}} \qquad \frac{£3\cdot5}{\text{War Loan}}$$

we should then have, by substituting for the name of the stock the price at which it happened to be standing, the yield given at that particular price by that particular stock. But the actual numerator, as long as it is a constant, does not affect the proportionate changes of such a fraction as the price alters.

$$\frac{1}{\text{Consols}} \qquad \text{or} \qquad \frac{1}{\text{War Loan}}$$

is not the yield on Consols or War Loan; but it always varies proportionately to that yield. In the same way we may treat

$$\frac{1}{F}$$

as varying proportionately to the yield on fixed interest stocks.

Now let us turn to the second expression

$$\frac{P}{D}$$

The yield of an ordinary share is its dividend divided by its price. In our case that would be

$$\frac{D}{P}$$

and our expression $\frac{P}{D}$ must always vary as the reciprocal of the Share Yield.

So now we are able to rewrite our equation in two forms

$$\frac{P}{F \times D} = R = \frac{\text{Fixed Yield}}{\text{Share Yield}}$$

These are the two ways of looking at R; experience has shown that the ordinary investor who considers the matter finds it easy to use one or other of them. Either he treats R as what is left in ordinary share prices after the changes imposed by alterations in fixed interest prices and dividends have been taken out, or he thinks that ordinary share prices are controlled partly by their dividends, partly by the level of fixed interest prices, and partly by the relationship of fixed interest yields to ordinary yields. Many investors were accustomed to noting, each morning as they read their *Financial Times*, what was the difference between the yield on the industrial ordinary share index and that on Consols; from that difference it is not a long step to move to the ratio of the Consol yield to the industrial ordinary yield.

R, then, is something that can be worked out from day to day and its course can be plotted on graph paper just like a price or an index number. We can examine its behaviour just like that of the other indices and stocks that we have already charted;

The name which Investment Research gave to its version of R was 'Confidence'. Its original purpose was to look at what was actually happening to equity through the smoke screen of Dr Dalton's manipulation of the gilt edged market. Very soon, in the early months of 1947, a steep down trend of Confidence appeared, pointing, it appeared, to a level for equities by September horribly below that ruling at the time. When the market collapsed in July and the *Financial Times* index fell from round 130 to 105 by early September, Confidence seemed to have proved its worth.

If one had been using a curve of this sort between the wars, one would have seen it decline in advance of the downturn of shares in 1929 and turn up in advance of the new rise in 1932. It turned down very early in the rise of the thirties and again in the rise of the forties, while it turned up at the same time as shares in 1940. In 1949 it turned up in June while shares came down to a second bottom in November, but it has not since acted as a leading indicator. Before 1949 the movements of dividends were sufficiently violent to compensate the movements of the long term interest rate; for example in the first half of 1947, when the gilt edged market was weakening, there must have been a very strong rise in dividends for Confidence to have declined. Contrarywise, in 1949, the abnormal decline of gilt edged at the time when shares were working out their bottom was responsible for the upturn of Confidence. Since 1949 Confidence has not acted as a leading indicator.

Changes of the level of Confidence have very potent effects on the prices of shares. You have seen on Chart No. 7 how the share index rises and falls much more than the curve of dividends; part of this difference may be attributed to changes in the long term rate of interest while the rest reflects changes in Confidence. Chart No. 8[2] shows how there was established in the years up to 1958 what appeared to be a normal range of fluctuation for Confidence. Then in 1959, when the yield gap was reversed (*i.e.* the yield on the *Financial Times* industrial ordinary share index began to be lower instead of higher than that of Consols $2\frac{1}{2}\%$), Confidence

from its behaviour we may, perhaps, be able to make some decisions about its nature and about its value to investors in making investment decisions.

Investment Research of Cambridge, where the author (as proprietor of the firm) was studying this relationship in an attempt to 'dedaltonise' the indices in the autumn of 1946, calculated R weekly back to the middle of 1944 and later daily with the formula

$$\frac{100,000}{\textit{Financial Times} \text{ fixed interest stock index} \times \textit{Financial Times} \text{ ordinary yield}}$$

The numerator in this case has no significance; it was selected in order to give the market the three figures and one decimal point that are liked in numbers of this sort.

[2] The basis of calculation was changed in 1967 from the *Financial Times* indices to the F.T. Actuaries series. This gives a possibility of more than ten times as many changes of dividends during a year.

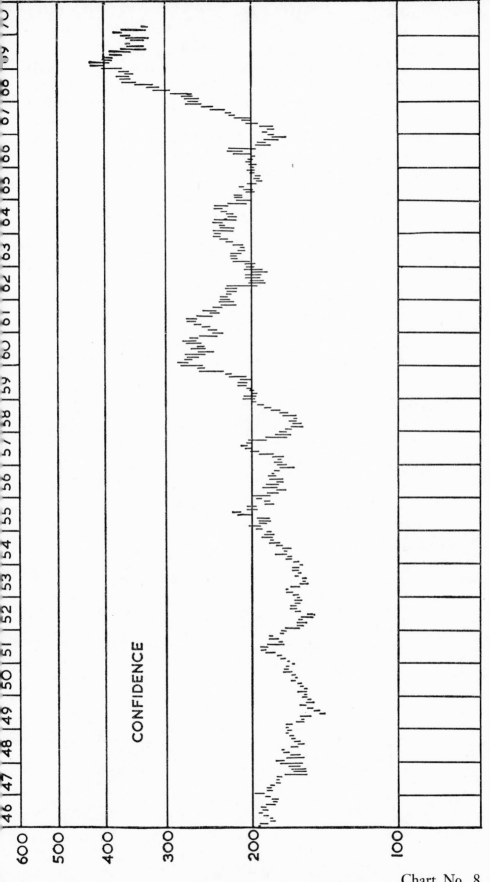

CONFIDENCE

Chart No. 8

moved into a new range through which it drifted uneasily downwards in the fluctuations of 1960/66 and out of which it broke upwards in 1968.

What is Confidence? Technically it shows the changes in the investors' preference between fixed interest and equity investments. More simply, it shows the state of the investors' liver. Put it whichever way you like, it is a major influence on prices and you are not likely to be a successful investor if you ignore its fluctuations.

CHAPTER SIX

The Investment Cycle

The wave motion of share prices, which is generally called the investment cycle, can be traced in the charts we print from their first year, 1886. There is little doubt that the same features could be traced much farther back, probably to the very first transaction that ever took place in the stock of the East India Company. The railway boom of the eighteen-forties was an exuberant peak in the early part of the nineteenth century; and the South Seas Bubble is recognisable, from its descriptions, as a fantastic stock exchange boom of the eighteenth century.

Our own experience of the years between the wars confirmed everything that we had been told about the close relation between the trade cycle and the investment cycle. When security prices declined in 1920, 1929 and 1937, unemployment rose in 1921, 1930 and 1938. The records showed that the same thing had happened in 1900 and 1907. We had been shown the reasons why a coming decline of trade should bring in front of it a decline of securities, and more reasons why a decline of securities should bring in its wake a depression of trade.

In the period 1946–48 the rules seemed to have been changed. In America there was a comparatively slight decline of industrial and rail common stocks in the autumn of 1946, a decline quite severe and sudden enough to look like the first phase of a deep bear market. It appeared to be the cyclical counterpart of the rise from 1942 to 1946. It is difficult to associate it with any fluctuation of trade. It came after the high industrial activity of the war period had run down; by two simple tests, those of industrial activity and of dividends declared, 1947 was a better year than 1946, and 1948 a better year than 1947. Common stock prices did rally in the spring of 1948 and decline again in the autumn, and after that decline in 1948 there was a mild recession of trade in 1949.

In Britain the pattern was slightly different. Prices fell from January 1947 to June or November 1949; here too there was an interval in 1948 during which prices were well above the low points of 1947 and 1949. This fall was trifling in comparison with those of 1920, 1929 and 1937, but it was substantially larger than those which began in 1900 and 1907, both of which were associated with cyclical depressions of trade. In the

1947–49 period the depression of trade failed to make an appearance in Britain.

The evidence of this period shows quite plainly that the investment cycle can continue unaccompanied by a trade cycle. Further, the analysis that we have made suggests that we could go on having investment cycles without cyclical fluctuations of trade. This analysis shows that the investment cycle is the product of three other rhythmic variables, interest, dividend and a third residual, R, which comprises all the other factors that influence markets and to which we have given the name Confidence (we must be careful at times to distinguish 'Confidence', our name for R, from confidence with a small 'c', which is used for the normal meaning of the word).

The investment cycle of 1949–52 was, in the author's reckoning, the shortest of the post-war period. The upward phase was about the same length as that of 1962–64, but the decline that followed was completed, if we treat the summer and autumn highs of 1951 as a 'double top', in a single stage, while all the other investment cycles of the post-war period, at least up to that which began in the autumn of 1966, showed two stages of decline. The fall in prices of 1952 was accompanied by a brief, and by post-war standards severe, depression of trade. Excessive stocks had been built up in the preceding boom and the liquidation of these, especially in the textile trades, was a painful business. In this period, also, the Government returned to the use of monetary policy as a means of controlling the economy. Bank Rate was raised for the first time since the outbreak of war in 1939, and a forced conversion of Treasury Bills, which are counted as a liquid asset for the banks, into short-dated gilt edged stocks, which count as investments and not as liquid assets, produced a sharp contraction of liquidity. By the middle of 1952 the market began to look forward to better times, and a new major rise of equity prices began. This culminated in the summer of 1955, after the Bank Rate had been raised twice. The initial stage of decline was completed in the autumn of 1956; after this a rally developed and there was considerable enthusiasm generated in April and May 1957. But shares could make no further progress, and when New York began to slide in the third quarter, London followed. Our difficulties were growing fast and in September Bank Rate had to be raised punitively to 7%. The second stage of decline ran from the summer of 1957 to February 1958. The subsequent rise, from February 1958 to the end of 1959, was notable for the disappearance of the old 'yield gap', the amount by which the yield on the *Financial Times* industrial ordinary share index exceeded the yield on Consols, and its replacement by the 'reverse yield gap', which is the excess of the Consols yield over the share yield. This change, and its great extension in 1967–68, of course appear as bold rises in the long-term chart of Confidence (Chart No. 8). A new development appeared in the decline of 1960–62. After the initial stage in 1960, the share indices rose into new high ground, a feat achieved again, but with the barest margin only, in the 1964–66 decline. In the sixties the bear market has worn an entirely different shape. It has been a period of highly irregular fluctuations which succeeded many months of a regularly fluctuating rise. But both in 1960–62 and 1964–66 the irregularity started with the peak of industrial bargains marked (*Financial Times* industrial activity index 5-day mean), and it finished when the lowest level of prices was reached at the end of the second stage of the decline. But in both bear markets the secondary rally which succeeded the initial stage of decline carried the index as high as or higher than the peak of the bull market. As these words are written in the spring of 1970 many investors must be hoping to see this happen again in the months ahead of them.

These declines of share prices were associated with diminished industrial activity and accompanied by measures aimed at 'reducing demand'. The measures tended to reduce the demand for shares and to increase the supply. But the same applied to gilt edged securities; and when these began to fall too fast the Bank of England, in the interest of 'orderly markets', used to instruct the Government Broker to buy. This took securities out of investors' hands and put money in their pockets; and thus the demand for securities was increased, especially for ordinary shares, as the investors who had sold gilt edged were most unlikely to buy them back being likely to prefer ordinary shares in their place. This may have been one of the reasons for the strength of the secondary rallies in 1961 and 1965–66.

In the short term the rate of interest is generally moved by the Government (or in an open economy possibly by some other government). But the long term movement is more mysterious. What strikes the student of the British experience is the similarity between our movement since 1946 and the previous great decline which ran from 1896 to 1920. Thus the first of the factors which control the price of ordinary shares has been generally depressing since the end of 1946. When we have discussed this with analysts from many other countries they have looked blank; in their better regulated countries the long term interest rate did not move and was not a factor in investment. In 1970 there was a conference of the Federation of European Financial Analysts' Societies; the long term rate of interest was not on the programme but the attitude of the European analysts had undergone a substantial change!

Dividends seem unlikely ever to become entirely stable. Stabilization could prevent them from going up, but only a Government guarantee could prevent some from going down. We might find a period in which directorial caution in increasing dividends could subsequently go a very long way towards preventing them from being decreased; but there would surely be some limits to that caution and some increases of dividend.There was a period of stabilization at the end of the sixties; at least increases were strictly limited. As a result a downward tendency in dividends appeared, because increases were limited and decreases were not.

We can look forward for many years, if not for ever, to moving interest rates and to changing dividends. Those changes are likely to be—for the student of the movements rather than for the holder of the securities—fairly orderly and regular and to persist in one direction or the other for a substantial period. But the movements will not be irreversible.

As for our residual R, the old rhythm we have learned to know is confidence, enthusiasm, panic, funk, confidence, enthusiasm, panic, funk. This rhythm of R is the rhythm of human experience. We all have our own rhythms of this sort, are all prone to be confident and then over-confident; when our confidence betrays us we lapse easily into panic and when panic has passed we remain for some time in a state of funk before confidence returns.

The investment cycle is controlled, to a large extent, by human hopes and fears. It is probably controlled, to some extent, by human habits of saving and spending; and these habits do not change rapidly. Their changes are slow, worked out through a period perhaps as long as a generation. The variation of hope and fear is somewhat quicker; the cycle is usually worked through in six years, more or less, more in the long cycles, 1921–32 and 1940–49, less in the more recent cycles, 1958–62 and 1962–66.

Up to this point we have confined our study to indices; we have looked always at the average and never at the individual share. As investment has to be conducted through the medium of the individual share it is necessary to study the individual share; it is necessary also to justify our method of illustration by indices. Are the patterns traced out by shares recognizably similar to those traced by averages? Or are the averages made up of shares whose individual patterns are utterly dissimilar?

The *Financial Times* at present records two main indices for British equities. One is the old industrial ordinary share index, an unweighted geometric mean of 30 shares. (Unweighted means that the share of the smallest company in the 30 counts for just as much as the share of the largest company. Geometric means that the average is worked out by multiplying the prices of the members together and extracting the 30th root of the product.) This index shows what would happen to an investor who at the close of business every day sold shares from the holdings which had risen in value and bought shares to add to those which had fallen in value till he had once again 30 holdings of equal value. The index certainly represents a most unlikely investor, but you can say in its favour that it is, perhaps not very efficiently, 'an imitation of things done'. The F.T. Actuaries covers a whole series of indices, for the British market as a whole, for British Industrials, and for many groups and subsections. We are concerned at this moment with the 500-share industrial index. These F.T. Actuaries indices are based on a weighted arithmetic mean (without going into the complications of this calculation, weighted means that a change of 1% in the price of a £500mn. company counts 100 times as much as a change of 1% in the price of a £5mn. company, and arithmetic means that the basic averaging is done by addition and not multiplication). This index represents an investor who holds the 500 different shares in blocks proportionate to the market capitalisations of the companies' equities on an appointed day, varied by subsequent issues. What it aims at imitating is the fluctuations in the value of the British equities in the Stock Exchange Official List.

Although the construction of these two indices is so different, their performances are remarkably similar, and the variation in the performances seems to owe more to the fact that Oils are excluded from the *Financial Times* industrial ordinary, on the sound ground that they are not particularly industrial, while in the F.T. Actuaries the monster companies, Shell and British Petroleum, carry very heavy weight. In general we prefer to use the *Financial Times* industrial ordinary, because we are mainly concerned with what is being done in the market, but in this particular case the F.T. Actuaries seems the more appropriate.

Chart No. 9 shows the course of this index for the years 1963–66. In 1963 we see a regular rise; it had started in June 1962 at 85 and, apart from a severe spasm of irregularity on the assassination of President Kennedy, progressed decorously upward to the first week of January 1964. Here it reached a high point which coincided with the highest level of Activity (the word used by the *Financial Times* for its index of bargains marked) and the lowest level of yield. The index stood at about 118. Slightly higher levels were reached, accompanied by lower activity and higher yield, in the third quarter of 1964 and the middle of 1966. But January 1964 is plainly the frontier between regular progress and irregular, and of the three successive low points in the winter of 1964, the summer of 1965 and the autumn of 1966, the last is the lowest. After the experience of 1960–62, where the decline was more severe, this looked like the model of a slight bear market of modern times.

This performance is what we want to compare with that of shares. In order to make up a panel of shares without any partiality, every twentieth share was taken from the London daily chart books of Investment Research; the only deviation from this strict rule was the selection of

75

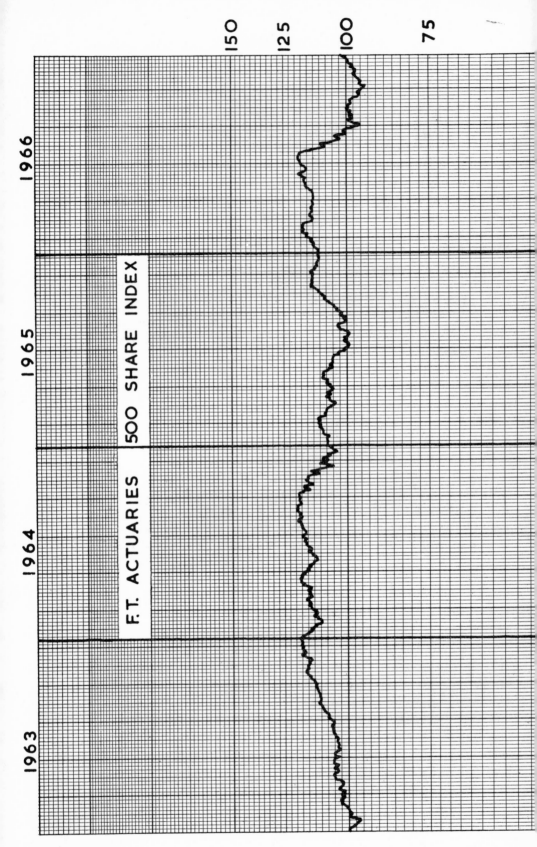

Chart No. 9

Associated Fisheries in place of Associated Fire Alarms whose quotation was suspended at one of the relevant dates. The dates selected were January 1964 for a high price, June–July 1965 for a low price, May–June 1966 for a high price and October–November 1966 for a low price. All prices are expressed as indices of their January 1964 high.

Share	J/J 1965	M/J 1966	O/N 1966
I.D.V.	51·5	78·0	58·5
Associated Fish	89·5	114·0	71·5
Birmingham Small Arms	130·0	215·0	136·0
Brooke Bond	91·5	118·0	94·0
Courtaulds	96·0	114·0	79·9
Elliot-Automation	50·5	61·0	40·5
Great Universal A	84·0	120·0	88·5
Hudson's Bay	83·5	116·5	92·0
Limmer & Trinidad	124·0	109·0	92·5
Herbert Morris	65·0	76·5	58·0
Pretoria Portland Cement	129·0	145·0	121·5
Royston Industries	52·0	71·5	54·0
Staveley	106·0	143·5	89·5
Transparent Paper	63·5	87·0	55·0
Wellman	50·0	50·0	28·0
Charterhouse Group	116·5	173·5	129·0
Royal Exchange Assurance	69·0	84·0	74·5
Dorman Long	109·5	100·0	84·5
Ayer Hitam	50·0	90·5	62·5
Buffelsfontein	124·0	159·0	141·5
Anglo-Ecuadorian	84·0	144·0	108·0
St. Martins Property	69·0	90·5	70·0
F. T. Actuaries 500	83·5	101·5	79·0

For the first column the median is 84·0 against 83·5 for the index, for the second column 111·5 against 101·5 for the index, and for the third column 81·75 against 79 for the index. In the first column seven shares out of 22 rose against the trend. In the second column one share fell against the trend. In the third column all the shares moved down with the trend. In this last column there are five shares which were higher at the end of our bear market than at the beginning; of these five, two are domiciled and operate in South Africa, and one, domiciled in Britain, operates in Latin America. On the other hand, operation overseas does not guarantee immunity to the attacks of a bear market; the operations of Ayer Hitam are entirely overseas and those of Hudson's Bay mainly in Canada.

There is a New York adage that Wall Street is not a stock market but a market of stocks. The meaning is that stocks do not move as a single herd but there are a vast number of different movements, and thus a knowledge of what the average is going to do is of very little value for the investor in individual shares. Against this it is possible to argue forcibly that the prices of shares in general follow more or less closely the main movements of the averages, like the rise from June 1962 to January 1964 and the steep declines like those of the autumn of 1964 and the summer of 1966. But in a period like the first three quarters of 1964, the first few months of 1965 and the last quarter of 1965 and first two of 1966, where the market has no strong and characteristic trend, some shares will go up and others go down. The adage is also more likely to be quoted when the next vigorous trend will sweep downwards than when it is going to be a benign upward movement.

One of the alarming facts that appears to emerge from the table on page 77 is that at the end of the initial decline of this bear market, in the summer of 1965, the bottom quartile of five out of twenty-two shares showed indices ranging from 52 down to 50. You cannot infer that this was the common experience of the market; while the 5% sample has a good chance of being adequate for conclusions about the market as a whole, when you come down to individual quartiles the sample is too small for drawing sound conclusions. At a later stage when similar statistics are required, use will be made of a 20% sample of the Investment Research daily chart book covering a total of 91 securities.

In the days before the Capital Gains Tax the inexperienced investor tended to take his profits on the way up. He replaced the good shares which he sold because they looked as if they had gone far enough with shares that looked cheaper and so appeared to offer more scope. But they were cheaper for the simple reason that they were worse. So as the bull market advanced the quality of his portfolio deteriorated and he tended to hold at the end of the rise the sort of share that finished up in the lower quartile instead of the middle or upper quartiles. One of the side effects of the Capital Gains Tax is the protection of the weaker investor against this particular fault.

One tends to think of success in investment as stemming from an ability to pick and hold the right shares through the rising phases of the market. This table suggests that it may be even more important not to hold the wrong shares through the falling phase. In fact, one can take to heart the lesson that through such a period as this the best thing to do is not to hold any shares at all. Any investor who sold in January 1964 or in the late summer, or in the final months of 1965 to the middle of 1966 and kept his money in the bank till the early months of 1967 would have made himself much richer.

PART TWO

CHAPTER SEVEN

Investment Strategy

Some of the American writers have treated Wall Street as a field of battle where the bulls are always routing the bears or the bears inflicting defeat on the bulls. This phraseology has established itself, and in any case it came naturally to a generation which had seen a war or two and had spent an important part of its life in the forces. Strategy in investment is very much the same as strategy in war; it is the formation of the broad general plan of campaign while the details lie in the province of tactics. The investor does not make strategic decisions every day; he makes them only when he feels that he must plan large changes in the constitution of his portfolio.

There are two main sorts of strategic decision, the first concerned with the nature of the war to be fought and the second with the method of fighting it. The investor's first decision should be strategic; what is his objective? He must make up his mind whether he is planning investment primarily for income or primarily for capital appreciation. It should be quite easy to form a clear opinion about the object of investment, but one of the causes of failure for many investors is that they never make this simple decision but hover between investment for income and investment for appreciation without making a clean choice for one or the other.

While this is the primary decision, it cannot easily be made without some knowledge of the markets in which he is to invest. We are going to argue that in the security declines which we know the fall of price is a percentage of capital value far greater than the net amount of the dividends paid by the securities in question through the period of depreciation. This implies that there may be at times a strategic case for complete disinvestment, the holding of all resources in the form of cash and waiting for the appropriate opportunity to re-enter the market.

It is our purpose here to study the nature of the market and the methods of campaigning to which the market is adapted; and our order of study will be the market first with its secondary strategy and the primary strategy second. This secondary strategy concerns itself with the sort of investments that the investor should be holding and the proportions in which he should be holding them. We distinguish seven main strategic groups whose characteristics are sufficiently different to justify very different distributions of resources between them at different stages of the investment cycle. These groups are:

(a) Cash or call
(b) Gilt edged—short
(c) Gilt edged—long
(d) Domestic equities
(e) External equities and commodity shares
(f) Gold shares
(g) Others.

'Cash or call' covers monies in the bank on current or deposit account, savings bank accounts (important for the small investor), Government securities that are callable at par like savings certificates, deposits and share investments in building societies, and money lent at call or short notice to a local authority. Gilt edged covers the securities issued in London by the British Government as its own direct obligations or under its guarantee (it is odd that you can buy on the Post Office Register stocks that are direct obligations of the Government but not those like British Electricity or British Gas which it guarantees). It does not include the stocks of our local government authorities, Dominion and Colonial governments and their local government authorities. At various times in the past ten years investors have been gravely suspicious of various African governments, and at the moment of writing Rhodesia, thought to be the most secure of them all, is not paying the interest on its loans. The investor should buy gilt edged for absolute security and should not diminish that security by a hair's breadth for the sake of higher income. People will tell you that our local government stocks are absolutely secure, because they are secured on the rate fund and the councillors can be compelled by law to raise the rates sufficiently to cover the service of their debts. But anybody who looks dispassionately at the finances of New York City can see that there is a point where the law of diminishing return operates, where higher rates drive citizens out of the area so that an increase in the poundage results in a decrease of the revenue. Say if you like, "It can't happen here". Ten years ago it could not happen with Rhodesia, and now it has happened. If you buy a fixed interest stock for security, the security must be absolute. Large institutional investors have a spread so wide that they can risk a default or two if they are compensated by a sufficiently higher income over the whole fixed interest portfolio. The private investor cannot afford this luxury.

Gilt edged stocks are issued in large lumps by the British Government; in 1969 £400mn. was the popular amount. For our strategy we have to consider two categories, short and long. If the stock must certainly be redeemed within five years it is short; note that the word 'must' is important. Twenty-five years ago it was generally expected that War Loan 3½% would be redeemed at the earliest opportunity in 1952, but before 1952 arrived interest rates had risen so much that the Treasury could not redeem War Loan and re-borrow the amount at a cheaper rate. War Loan and a certain number of other stocks, Conversion 3½%, Consols 2½% and Consols 4%, and Treasury 2½% have no final dates of redemption; the Treasury simply has the option to repay them when it wishes after the dates specified, like 1952 for War Loan, 1961 for Conversion 3½% and 1975 for Treasury 2½%. Other stocks have a single date for redemption or the Treasury has retained for itself the option of repaying between an earliest and a latest date. For example, the great 3% tap issues of the war were issued with a ten-year spread for maturity, like Savings 3% 1965/75 and have all, so far, been repaid on the latest date. But now the Treasury is issuing long stocks with high rates of interest, like 9%! If a long stock is issued at a high rate with a wide spread of maturity, the Treasury may wish when the time comes to redeem at the earliest possible date instead of the latest. If rates of interest fall as they did in the second quarter of the century, the Treasury will be able to borrow in the eighties at rates far lower than 8% and will want to repay at the earliest possible date loans on which they are paying so high a rate of interest. So short stocks are those which must be repaid within a very few years, and if their interest rate is low they stand invitingly under their redemption price and offer a capital gain which under the 1969 Finance Act is tax free. As the Government has issued many stocks in the period of low interest rates at 3% and rates not much higher, there will be a supply of low interest 'shorts' to buy up to the end of the century (there is a Funding 3½% which may be redeemed in 1999 at earliest and 2004 at latest). When interest rates are rising, the shorts fall least and the longs most; when interest rates are falling, the shorts rise least and the longs most.

The arguments raised against Local Government issues and Commonwealth stocks apply with equal force to debentures and preference shares. In times gone by these may have seemed to have merit as almost permanent investments. This book is not concerned with permanent investments; nor would it be easy to find, in times when the value of money has been falling at increasing annual rates, a reputable investment advisor who would favour holdings of debentures and preference shares. They do not share the advantage of gilt edged that capital gains are free of tax. They are not so easily negotiable, and the commission is higher and transfer stamp has to be paid. There are periods in the investment cycle in which gilt edged stocks rise, and so there may be a case, despite the popular argument about inflation, for buying them as comparatively short term holdings. But the best advice for the ordinary investor is part of a pithy sentence uttered by an American broker—"Never buy a bond". What he actually said was, "Never buy a bond over 20", wise counsel because large profits can be made from buying busted bonds which return to respectability, but that is a technique for making a fortune which lies outside the scope of this book. So there is nothing to be said here about 'Other Fixed Interest' which was treated as an investment category in the first edition. Nor is there any need now to discuss the possibilities of 'Self-liquidating Securities' a category which offered useful scope at a time when collieries and so on were being nationalised but which are now too rare to be of any general interest.

But before we leave the subject of fixed interest stocks it is prudent to remind readers that there was an inflationary rise of prices from the beginning of the century to 1920 and this was accompanied by a decline of gilt edged which began in 1896. Then there was a decline of prices for more than a dozen years and, although prices turned up again in the middle thirties and have not stopped rising yet, Consols turned at $43\frac{5}{8}$ in 1920 and reached $99\frac{13}{16}$ths in 1946. The lesson of history is that a large rise of the gilt edged market is not impossible.

Domestic equities are the variable dividend securities of companies whose operations are conducted mainly in the United Kingdom. The word 'equity' signifies that the holders are entitled to the whole surplus after all prior claims have been satisfied. A preference shareholder is entitled to a fixed and probably cumulative dividend; an ordinary share-holder is entitled to whatever dividend, large or small, the directors decide to distribute. The emphasis here lies on the variability of the dividend.

External equities are the shares of companies which conduct the bulk of their operations outside the United Kingdom. They may be producers of commodities like tea or rubber, or producers and distributors of oil, or they may be carriers who own ships, or they may be industrial concerns like the British-American Tobacco Company, or land-owners like the Australian pastoral companies and the Hudson's Bay Company. We include in this category all overseas mining, except for gold mines, which need a category of their own. There is some difficulty here with British companies. Clearly concerns like the British-American Tobacco Company, Shell Transport and Peninsular & Oriental are externals. But what about Unilever and Bowater? So many British companies have external interests that the British company sector itself is to quite a large extent external. Experience suggests that while Bowater and Unilever may technically be external, the shares react so vigorously to domestic stimuli that it may not be prudent to treat them very differently from normal domestic equities. We must also count among the externals all the shares of companies incorporated abroad and dealt in on our stock exchanges, whether officially like International Nickel or unofficially like General Motors or Poseidon. It is perfectly possible, within the rules of the Stock Exchange, London, to buy or sell shares through your London broker in Bayer, Pechiney, Mediobanca, Conzinc Rio Tinto of Australia or indeed anything which is officially quoted on any recognised stock exchange.

Gold shares used to be put in a different category. In theory, share prices and commodity prices fluctuate in the same direction. When commodity prices fluctuated, gold used to stay fixed. Thus, when commodity prices rose, the cost of mining rose and the profits of mining gold fell. When commodity prices fell, the cost of mining fell and the profits of mining gold rose. So gold share prices were supposed to move in a direction opposite to other shares. This is a short and crude expression of the theory, which justified the separation of gold shares into a separate class. Since the war it will be difficult to find two consecutive months in which the costs of mining in the Transvaal or Orange Free State have fallen. Further, since 1968 the price of gold has not been fixed, and we have too little experience at present to know whether it rises or falls with other commodities, in so far as other commodities do move together, or whether it pursues a contrary course. As demand for gold depends on the activity of industry and the prosperity of fairly primitive farmers, mainly in the East, it is possible that gold will rise in price, like everything else, when the world feels it is growing more prosperous and fall in price when prosperity dwindles. At the moment there is one school of thought which holds that gold is no longer a monetary metal, is just another commodity, and therefore has no right to be considered separately. Another school holds that the world is coming to distrust the dollar and that at some stage there will be a flight from the dollar. Perhaps the flight would be from the dollar into gold. Perhaps the flight would enforce a devaluation of the dollar and a higher price for gold. Clearly the position of gold is now very different from that at any time before the 'two tier' system was introduced in 1968; what is not clear is whether the position of gold now is better or worse.

There are three important sub-divisions of gold shares which must be mentioned. The producer is a company which has gained access to its source of ore and is working it; it has usually sunk shafts, erected a reduction mill, and is hoisting ore from a reef and is milling it. It should be making a profit and paying a dividend. The finance company is a concern which sponsors mining ventures and brings them, sometimes, to production. It usually draws some of its income from the dividends paid by the mines under its management and some from the profits of dealing in their shares on the Stock Exchange. This class of share was extremely popular in the late sixties. The third class is the developers, mines at any stage prior to the payment of the first dividend from the profits of gold production.

These, then, are our various groups whose behaviours ought to be different, one from another, in the upward and downward phases of the investment cycle. We can put them to the test by the record of prices and index numbers. We select as our dates first 27th June 1947, a day of

	Table A					*Table B*		*Table C*	
Stock or Group	*27th June 47*	*29th Aug. 47*	%	*11th Nov. 49*	%	*2nd Nov. 51*	%	*20th June 52*	%
Consols 2½%	89½	84½	94	70	78	64	92	55½	87
Savings 3% 65–75	106	100	94	90½	85	89	98	79	89
Funding 2½% 56–61	101	99	98	97½	96	97	99	89	92
Hotels and Rests.	163.9	110.5	67½	92.6	56½	96.9	104	83.5	86½
Boots and Shoes	176.6	151.0	85½	123.1	70	124.7	101	89.5	71½
Newspapers	166.2	126.9	76½	119.3	72	153.2	128	115.3	75
Rubber Manufacture	175.7	134.7	76½	117.0	67	152.5	131	110.1	76½
Breweries	146.2	122.4	84	89.1	61	90.7	101	79.9	88
Food	141.9	108.7	77	95.8	67½	100.8	105	78.1	77½
Electrical Equipment	129.6	108.7	84	94.4	73	119.9	127	91.8	77
Wool Textiles	130.1	113.9	87½	95.9	73	96.2	100	65.5	68
Retail Drapery	168.7	124.9	74	111.1	66	129.4	116	85.1	66
Collieries	165.4	151.6	92	169.0	102½	198.9	117	186.7	94
Cotton Textiles	123.6	111.3	90	90.6	73½	118.8	131	82.1	69½
Motor Accessories	124.3	93.5	75	86.6	69½	132.7	153	101.6	77
Housing	134.8	107.5	80	97.3	72½	128.3	132	99.0	77½
Paint	180.9	145.0	80½	110.1	61	170.7	154	128.9	75½
Tobacco	103.7	81.2	78½	79.4	76½	87.9	111	69.1	79
Rayon	134.1	110.7	82½	77.9	58	133.1	171	61.7	47½
Insurance	154.7	125.3	81½	106.5	69	128.2	120	100.7	78½
Bearings	124.2	110.7	89	108.9	87½	159.3	147	131.4	82½
Motor Car	114.8	84.0	73	75.7	66½	115.0	152	83.5	72½
Aircraft	144.6	118.3	82	134.7	93½	172.4	128	155.5	90
Roadmaking	122.7	98.1	80	84.9	69	89.9	106	74.5	83
Radio	88.5	64.0	72½	38.3	42	70.3	183	49.3	70
Consumer Goods	145.9	116.4	80	101.4	70	115.8	109	91.6	79
Industrial Equipment	130.2	111.8	86	97.7	75	142.3	146	107.8	76
Banks	128.7	112.5	87½	99.7	77½	98.7	99	79.0	80
Shipbuilding	158.2	131.9	83½	102.6	65	211.7	206	161.7	76½
Railway Equipment	140.4	127.0	91	109.0	77½	130.9	120	101.1	77½
Kaffir Development	139.8	145.8	104.5	132.8	95	92.0	69	82.4	89½
Mining Finance	119.7	123.5	103	97.2	81½	83.8	86	65.7	78
Lead and Zinc	152.7	144.6	95	170.8	112	261.4	153	190.5	73
International Trade	137.7	113.4	82½	105.3	77	167.8	159	134.1	80
Tin	128.6	125.3	97½	98.6	77	149.9	152	108.3	72½
Shipping	150.0	117.2	78½	95.9	64	136.0	142	107.1	79
Gold Producers	73.8	76.2	103	82.2	111	75.7	92	55.3	73
Rubber	88.0	85.5	97.0	64.9	74	102.9	158	62.4	61
Tea	109.8	99.7	91	71.7	65½	79.8	111	59.5	74½
Foreign Government	104.9	94.1	90	81.4	78	121.2	149	100.5	83
Oil	131.8	111.1	84½	81.2	61½	117.1	144	99.8	85
Copper	151.4	138.7	92	152.4	100½	286.3	188	255.4	89

comparatively high prices when the post-war boom was crumbling but its price structure was almost unimpaired, second 29th August 1947, when the first collapse was near its end, third 11th November 1949, near the bottom of the final decline after the 1949 devaluation, fourth 2nd November 1951, a day of comparatively high prices when the 1949–51 boom was crumbling but its price structure was almost unimpaired, and fifth 20th June 1952, when the collapse was near its end. We propose to call in evidence the prices of three gilt edged stocks and thirty-nine of the share group indices compiled by Investment Research.

These indices were unweighted geometric means, worked out for groups of ten shares each as far as possible. Their compilation was abandoned when the F.T. Actuaries series began to be published; but the F.T. Actuaries series, which are all based on weighted arithmetic means, do not seem suitable for this purpose. What we are looking at are shares that might be chosen for investment, and for this purpose a share is a share, any one as possible as any other, and Imperial Chemical Industries ought not to be counted one hundred times as often as a share whose capital was valued, on the appropriate date, at one-hundredth of ICI.

The percentage columns give in Table A levels of August 1947 and November 1949 as percentages of June 1947, in Table B November 1951 as a percentage of November 1949 and in Table C June 1952 as a percentage of November 1951. Thus Table A deals with a period of declining ordinary share prices, Table B with a period of rising ordinary share prices and Table C with a period of declining ordinary share prices. In the two declines Consols suffered less than most of the share groups, though over the period 1947–49 the comparison with the external groups is unfavourable. The 1965–75 Savings 3%, at that time a long stock, offered better protection than the optional redemption Consols and the medium Funding $2\frac{1}{2}\%$ fared better still. The differences between the three stocks were noticeably smaller in the shorter period from November 1951 to June 1952 than in the period from June 1947 to November 1949. All three stocks suffered some decline during the period of rising share prices between November 1949 and November 1951.

As this table goes back to the late forties and early fifties it is not surprising to find a group of self-liquidators in the list. Collieries are printed in italics as they are an animal of a rather different kind from all the other share groups in the list. They are not entirely different; in the sharp falls from June to August 1947 and November 1950 to June 1952 this group gave way in sympathy with the market. Over the longer period from June 1947 to November 1949 it showed some appreciation and thus gave better results than any other domestic equity group or any of the three selected gilt edged stocks.

Amongst the domestic equities the outstanding group is aircraft, which in November 1949 stood at 93½% of its June 1947 number and in June 1952 at 90% of its November 1951 number. Of course, these performances are due to the developments in foreign politics which were responsible for a reversion in 1948 from disarmament to rearmament, and the pace of rearmament was much quickened from the summer of 1950. It cannot be argued from the data presented here that aircraft shares are normally a sound purchase in declining markets.

The normal reaction of markets is well displayed in the August 1947 column. In declines where there is an early collapse and then a rally and a long delay before the main decline takes prices down again to the level of the early collapse, one can often see in the early collapse the expectations of investors and in the late decline the manner in which they were falsified. For example, breweries are believed to show a good resistance to depression; the August 1947 column shows that the market was then comparatively optimistic about the group which, by November 1949, was showing one of the heaviest declines.

Consideration of this table showing the performances of domestic equities suggests that the ideal strategy, when a decline is in force, is to hold none of them. Protection should be sought among the self-liquidators, if any are to be found, in short gilt edged, or in suitable areas of the cash or call category.

The external groups present a confusing picture. Look for the expectation in the August 1947 column. The three gold groups appreciated; all the others depreciated. Look in the June 1952 column; there you will see, the whole external category showed depreciation. But in the November 1949 column we find appreciation for gold producers, lead and zinc and, fractionally, for copper. This was due to the devaluation of September 1949; and if, as is to be hoped, we cannot rely on a devaluation every time the security market goes into a decline, we must not rely on this evidence. Let us revert to the low point of markets shortly before devaluation in June 1949. The picture which is then presented is shown in the table at the top of the next page.

The lesson of these figures is that a depression of security prices depresses security prices, except possibly self-liquidators (which are really cash camouflaged as shares). The figures are adequate for the equity groups; they may not be adequate for gilt edged. For we have suggested that the habit of gilt edged is to move in much longer cycles than equities. A downward half-cycle began in 1946, and this may be the factor responsible for the poor results of holding gilt edged over the period we have just been studying. If you will refer to Chart No. 1, you will see that a purchase of Consols 2½% near the peak of equities in 1920 would have

Group	24th June 1949 number as percentage of 29th August 1947	11th November 1949 number as percentage of 29th August 1947
Kaffir Developers	71·5	95·0
Mining Finance	66·0	81·5
Lead and Zinc	78·0	112·0
International Trade	67·0	77·0
Tin	63·0	77·0
Shipping	63·0	64·0
Gold Producers	78·5	111·0
Rubber	52·5	74·0
Tea	65·5	65·5
Oil	58·5	61·5
Copper	72·0	100·5

involved no serious loss by the time the low point for equities was reached in 1921; again, if you look at 1929, you will find that Consols stood far lower then than when equities reached bottom in 1932. But a purchase in 1937 would have involved a sharp loss by the time equities had reached their worst level in 1940 in the ninth month of the war. These figures do not disprove the case against Consols made by the figures of this first post-war equity cycle (and re-emphasised in every subsequent declining half-cycle up to the end of the sixties), but they do suggest strongly that in the gilt edged market the stage in the long gilt edged cycle as well as that in the shorter equity cycle must be taken into consideration.

Let us return now to our metaphor of strategy. The investor is a general who commands an army made up, not of men but of money. It may be a large army; Prudential Assurance valued its securities on 31st December 1951 at £520,518,000. But the vast majority of investors must count their resources in hundreds or thousands. The Prudential then carried about £278mn. in British Government securities and £66mn. in ordinary shares; the rest was spread between the lesser varieties of gilt edged and what we have described as 'other fixed interest' (ordinary shares, in this classification, will include self-liquidators and external as well as domestic equities). The Prudential's funds were increasing round 1950 by £20mn. or £30mn. a year. The changes of strategic grouping were controlled mainly by the direction of new funds, not by the transfer of funds from existing investments to new investments. With a portfolio of this size such transfer would seldom be possible on any large scale. But the company's general strategic planning can be detected from the following table.

Category/Year	1947 £m	1948 £m	1949 £m	1950 £m	1951 £m
British Govt. Secs	−11	+28	+13	+ 4	+ 3
Ordinary	+ 6	+ 1	+ 7	+ 3	+ 3
Total Portfolio	+11	+19	+35	+33	+22

The big differences between the sums of the two upper rows and the bottom row show how large was the interest of the Prudential in fields outside gilt edged and ordinary, mainly in the fixed interest stocks that give yields better than gilt edged, but the table also shows that the company's preference for gilt edged and for ordinary shares is subject to large changes from year to year. Those changes correspond to changes in the company's strategy. But at the beginning of 1946 British Government securities were $60\frac{1}{2}\%$ of the portfolio and ordinary stocks and shares $11\frac{1}{2}\%$, while the corresponding figures for 1951 were $53\frac{1}{2}\%$ and $12\frac{1}{2}\%$. The changes of grouping in a giant portfolio like this cannot be very large, but your small investor with a few hundreds or thousands of pounds, or your medium investor with tens or even hundreds of thousands, can, if he wishes, move swiftly from 100% in gilt edged to 100% in ordinary shares and a little time later to 100% in cash. The Prudential's power of manoeuvre is obviously much slighter than that of the small investor, but it can and does practice a strategic disposition of its forces.

The kind of disposition that an investor makes depends on two main factors, first his opinion about the object of his investment, second his opinion about the state of the investment cycle. The Prudential, in the years round 1950, was probably quite clear about the objects of its investment; its object was to earn, with the least possible risk, the income which its actuaries told it that it required. Income was the object and capital appreciation hardly entered into the calculation except where it was assured, *e.g.* in the purchase at a price below par of a stock with a fixed date of redemption. Ordinary shares were bought in comparatively small quantities 'to sweeten the yield'; in those days ordinary shares usually carried yields higher than gilt edged. Certain favoured shares whose yields were lower than gilt edged from time to time did thus recognise the possibility and scope of capital appreciation, but it was a period in which a very large quantity of investment was aimed mainly at security of income. This was the policy of many private investors; and 'performance' had not entered the vocabulary of the investment trusts. There was a distinction to be made between the permanent investor, who does not expect to sell what he buys and exercises his strategy through changing the direction of investment of a constant flow of incoming resources, and the trusts and individuals who look to their investments for income but who have no objections to making large changes from time to time in the stocks in which their funds are invested. The permanent investors are mainly the life assurance offices and the pension funds, and they, like the trusts and private investors, whose minds were of the same cast, were called at the time when this book was first written 'income funds'. There were other private investors, whose objects were quite different. To these, whom we called 'capital funds', income is a secondary consideration; in fact, they may be content to let their funds lie idle in the bank and draw no income at all, if they think that course the most advantageous. Their object is to increase the capital at their disposal, and they buy shares because they think that they will appreciate in value and sell them because they have appreciated or because they fear that they will depreciate. The actuarial funds have now a much better understanding of the mathematics of capital appreciation and have learned that money in their pockets is money whether it has entered their pockets by way of income or a rise in values. Their duty to their policy holders or their pensioners is to maximise the fund for those people's benefit.

But even when they operated as income funds, they still strove to buy securities when their prices were below their normal level. For example, in the instance of the Prudential which we gave, it bought its largest supplement of ordinary shares in 1949, a year of low prices. It bought its next largest in 1947, and in that year purchases made before July were made above the normal level but purchases made in August and September would have been advantageous. The managers of these funds did not overlook the fact that if they bought stock cheaply they received a larger income from the investment than if they bought it dearly.

The personal income fund must strive to hold during rising markets the sort of securities that have the biggest amplitude of cyclical fluctuation, those that rise most in rises and fall most in falls. On the contrary, in falling markets the income fund must strive to hold the securities whose amplitude of fluctuation is smallest, probably something in the 'cash or call' category. Of course, the fund is best served if it can find securities that rise when the majority are falling. (It is arguable that this is so difficult on most occasions that it is more prudent not to try to achieve so desirable a result.) The problem of what to do in a falling market has been enormously simplified as interest rates have risen; it is difficult for many to believe, though quite true, that in the period immediately after the war for a number of years you had to wait your turn before you could put money into a building society!

The capital fund too must strive to hold volatile securities in rising markets and to secure itself against falling markets by the best expedient available —and at one time that was a deposit account earning $\frac{1}{2}\%$! It enjoys a far wider scope than an income fund; it can play the part of a tramp going where it will in search for profitable freight while the income fund, like a liner, ploughs tediously through the same sea along well-worn routes. But the decision between income fund and capital fund is one on which little advice can usefully be given. This decision is one which the investor should be able to make for himself; we have already emphasized the importance of his consciously making it. What is much less easy to determine is the state of the investment cycle. About this too the investor must form a clear and certain opinion, and this is the difficult problem to which we shall turn in the next chapter.

CHAPTER EIGHT

Cyclical Timing

Our object in this chapter is to determine how we may decide that the primary trend has changed. Our answer to this problem lies in the use of various charts in combination, first charts of a share index and its three controlling factors (interest rate, dividend and Confidence), second charts of other aspects of the market which are not concerned with price levels. In this second group the first is called, wrongly, an Activity chart. In New York you can plot Activity, because the number of shares which change hands in each normal bargain is recorded. In various other markets you can plot Activity or turnover. But in London there is no figure for Activity and the turnover figure is released in arrear only once a month. What you can plot (and call Activity) is the number of bargains marked or an index based on that number. The fluctuations in the numbers of bargains marked in London reflect the participation of the investor in the market. When many bargains are marked, there is a large public participation in the market and when few bargains are marked the public is taking little part. The second chart is called the Advance/Decline Line. This curve represents the accumulation of all changes of quotation in the relevant columns of the *Financial Times*; if you start your curve at zero and on the first day the *Financial Times* shows 800 pluses and 300 minuses, you add 500 to zero and plot 500. If the next day the *Financial Times* records 500 pluses and 700 minuses, you deduct 200 from your total and plot 300. On the third day you may have 900 pluses and 250 minuses; you add 650 to your total and plot 950. The A/D Line is an import from America, like most technical tools. It originated there in a situation very different from ours. The Dow Jones Industrial Average was an arithmetic mean of 30 constituents while the total number of common stocks listed on Wall Street was well over 1000. It was argued that there might be quite a different performance by the shares of companies outside the DJIA, and in those days before computers there was no quick way of dealing with the price performance of say 1500 stocks. But the exchange officials recorded each day how many stocks went up, how many went down and how many did not change. So there began the plotting of price changes on the basis of how many advances or declines were recorded, not how much the prices changed. The Americans used this to investigate 'the breadth of the market.'

The situation in London is very different. There are several thousands of ordinary shares listed; but many of them are of smaller sized companies which in America would appear only on the American Stock Exchange or on the Over-the-counter market (deals are done by telephone all over America with members of the National Association of Security Dealers). Of these shares the *Financial Times* quotes a comparatively small number. But the number is quite large enough for it to be possible for the A/D Line at times to diverge from the pattern of the *Financial Times* or F.T. Actuaries indices. Some technical analysts plot also the number of Highs and Lows. Unfortunately these are recorded on a peculiar basis; from April 1st to March 31st the *Financial Times* reports daily the new highs and lows for the period beginning on January 1st, that is a minimum of three months at the beginning of the period and a maximum of fifteen months at the end. This is the American practice and many technical analysts make use of it, but it appears statistically unsatisfactory.

So the two additional charts that we wish to study, in conjunction with our share price chart and the charts of the factors controlling share prices, are what is popularly called 'Activity' and our 'A/D Line'. Charts for Activity are available for the whole period since the war; but we have got the A/D Line from 1960 only.

Let us accordingly discuss the Activity chart and its relation to the others first and then consider the more recent A/D Line at a later stage. If the primary trend has been upwards for some time and we see two of the controlling factors showing a down-trend and at the same time we detect a downward trend in Activity, then we should fear that the primary upward trend has been reversed; likewise, if a primary downward trend has been running for some time and we see two of the controlling factors turned upwards and at the same time we detect an upward trend in Activity, then we should hope that the primary downward trend has been reversed. In the first part of this chapter we must explain the primary characteristics of Activity, why we rely on them and how we use the Activity chart in conjunction with the share index and its controlling factors.

We assume as the basis of all our argument that the development of prices through their changes from day to day, week to week and month to month, is governed by changes in the relationship between demand for stock and supply of stock. This assumption seems unlikely to be contested and does not, in our opinion, require proof. We believe that there are comparatively long periods (the periods of the primary trends) in which the market is dominated by demand or by supply. In the primary upward trends the domination of demand is persistent and the trend of prices, of Activity and Advance/Declines is upward except for comparatively brief reactions. But in the bear markets—a better term because in the sixties we had new highs in the bear markets and this makes the description 'primary downward trends' inappropriate—the domination of supply is intermittent and often brief while the rallies are often long and powerful. But in the bear markets supply has dominated in the end and the lowest prices were usually recorded between two and a half and three years from the initial downturn (which may have been succeeded, as in 1960–61, by a subsequently higher price level). We believe that a study of this changing relationship between supply and demand is necessary for success in investment. We believe that security charts afford a very good way of studying the changing relationship between supply and demand.

How do these dominances show? When demand is dominant each secondary peak of price (or almost each) stands higher than its predecessor and each secondary trough (or almost each) fails to fall as low as its predecessor. When supply is dominant this pattern is reversed; the succeeding peaks each fall below their predecessors and the succeeding troughs strike into new low ground (at least, almost each one does; in Chart No. 13[1] the *Financial Times* industrial ordinary fails to fall lower in September 1947 than at any time in 1948 only because the chart is plotted to Friday's close each week and not to the daily closing levels). This is as true of Activity as it is of price; Chart No. 10[2] shows Activity in the industrial market from 1946 to 1952 and you can see how the pattern showed a dominance of supply from January 1947 to June 1949 and a dominance of demand thereafter to June 1951. A rather different pattern emerged in the sixties. There you have high levels of Activity at the end of 1959 and the beginning of 1964; each time Activity and price turned down. But price reached new high levels compared with 1959 in 1961 and compared with the beginning of 1964 in the later months of the same year and again in 1966. But the decline of demand appeared in the lower levels of Activity recorded in 1961 in comparison with 1959 and at the high points of price in 1964 and 1966 compared with the beginning of 1964. The lowest prices for the years 1959–62 were recorded in 1962 and for 1964–66 in 1966.

We must consider next the construction of an Activity chart. The American security exchanges publish every trade in every stock listed with the number of shares involved; this publication is made through the ticker at the time the business is transacted. Further, any investor can read in the appropriate newspaper not only how many shares were traded in the day's whole business but also how many shares of each stock in which business

[1] Page 107.
[2] Page 96.

was done. The British investor has no such wealth of data. The Stock Exchange publishes a Daily Official List which shows, in addition to the prices at which business has been marked, the total number of bargains marked during the day and the numbers marked in each subdivision of the list. Only one mark is printed at each price, but, if several bargains have been marked at the same price, they are all included in the number of bargains. So our information is far from complete. For example, the student can never know how many bargains were done by brokers who did not mark them. Again, when the list shows nine marks received in Diamonds and records one for Consolidated African Selection Trust, three for De Beers deferred (registered) and three for De Beers deferred (bearer), that is seven in all, he cannot know in which of the three stocks the two missing bargains were transacted. Our data are inadequate, but they are not hopelessly inadequate. The list gives very little information about the business transacted in any single stock; it gives much useful information about the amount of business transacted in its subdivisions and in the whole. It is on this information that we must concentrate our attention, especially on the numbers of bargains marked daily over the whole list and the numbers marked in the industrial sections. (Students of gilt edged will want to observe what is happening to bargains in their section.) The *Financial News* calculated the average number of bargains marked daily through the second half of 1942 and the *Financial Times* publishes index numbers using these averages as the base. Separate indices are shown for 'gilt edged', 'industrial', 'speculative' and 'total' and each index is published to show the index for the day and the five-day mean. The five-day mean eliminates the distortion caused by the British investor's habit of making his mind up over the week-end and doing his business on Monday (a distressing statistical aberration which does not appear in the transatlantic statistics, perhaps because a similar tendency among odd-lot investors is drowned in the recording by the round lots of one hundred shares or multiples of one hundred).

The five-day mean would be quite inadequate for a speculator wishing to profit from tertiary fluctuations, but it should serve adequately for the investor who is interested in a cycle that takes years to work itself out. The question that must be raised is whether fluctuations of Activity can show changes in the relation of supply and demand. Every purchase must involve a sale, every sale a purchase, therefore every bargain indicates supply and demand and if ten thousand bargains show twice as much demand as five thousand they also show twice as much supply. The theoretical answer to this objection is that you can determine by the direction of the price fluctuation whether the increased Activity shows buying pressure or selling pressure. This may be good theory, but it is not sound practice. Increases of Activity in practice represent increases of demand and only very seldom increases of supply. An insistent buyer can almost always find a seller, but an insistent seller cannot, in Britain at any rate, always find a buyer. The test of practice will show that prices are high when business is active, prices are low when business is dull. It is necessary to note that this is due in part to the jobbing system. On Wall Street sharp breaks in the market, as in September 1946, are marked by very high rates of volume, as high or almost as high as the boom volume which preceded them. Further, the correlation of low volume with low prices is not as high as the London correlation between low participation and low prices; New York volume was not much lower in 1947 and 1949, when prices were lower, than in August 1946, when prices were higher; and the constant decline of volume from the beginning of 1951 to the autumn of 1952 was accompanied by a rise rather than a decline of price.

Let us now turn from the theoretical to the practical, to Chart No. 10 of the *Financial Times* industrial Activity (five-day mean) which will show what happened to Activity in London during the period from 1946 to 1952. You have a high peak in May 1946 followed by a broad dip and a higher, thinner peak in January 1947. There was a steep rise of prices in April 1946 which reached a peak in the third week of June; prices fell in September and then rose to a peak in the middle of January. There was a sharp fall in February (one Friday afternoon Mr. Shinwell came down to the House of Commons and informed the members that there would be no electricity next week), but prices rallied in the spring and failed, only by a narrow margin, to reach in the summer the highest point of the previous winter. But in August prices collapsed, and so did Activity. There was a rally to the end of the year, a lesser collapse in February and then a succession of rallies and relapses of which the last carried prices to low levels in the summer and autumn of 1949. Prices rose and so did Activity through 1950 to a peak in the summer of 1951; here, as in 1946, the peak of Activity preceded the peak of prices by several weeks. Activity began to subside in the summer, and in the autumn prices followed. Activity in 1952 was back at the 1948 level; prices were lower than in 1948.

There is a clear downtrend of Activity through the years 1947–49. This trendline is broken, not very convincingly, by the upsurge of Activity in February 1950. At this point now, though not necessarily in February 1950, it is easy to draw in the uptrend from the low point of 1949. The downtrend was drawn across peaks of Activity; the uptrend is drawn on the other side of the curve across the troughs of Activity. The Christmas decline is ignored. The British investor inclines to inactivity on his summer holiday, but he anticipated the shift of the holiday to the end of August and in the fifties and sixties tended to be inactive late in the month

95

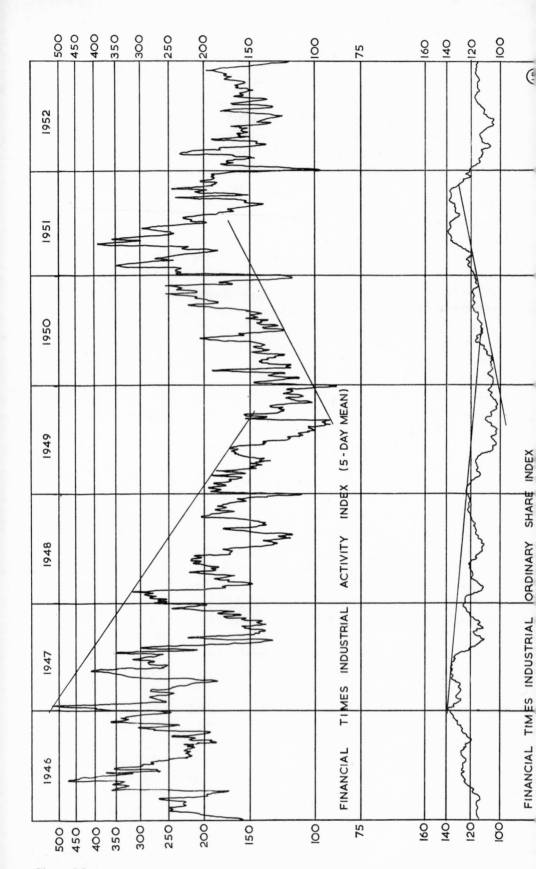

FINANCIAL TIMES INDUSTRIAL ACTIVITY INDEX (5 - DAY MEAN)

FINANCIAL TIMES INDUSTRIAL ORDINARY SHARE INDEX

Chart No. 10

rather than at the beginning of it. However this summer inactivity is a reasonable inactivity; he may take his summer holiday from the market in June or July or September if he feels so inclined. But Christmas is different, and it takes a nationalisation of the railways, as in 1946 and 1947, or a major boom as in 1959, to induce a high rate of investor participation on Christmas Eve and between Boxing Day and New Year. The Christmas decline must be treated as an irrelevancy, but the summer decline of 1951 was a portent, like the Easter decline of 1947. The trend of Activity had turned downwards in the spring of 1947 and this was evidenced by the decline of the Activity curve to the low levels of the previous summer. The downtrend was less clearly visible, except by hindsight, in the summer of 1951; what was important that year was the failure of Activity to ievive in the autumn when prices rallied to test the summer top.

The lesser peaks of Activity in 1947, over 400 in May and 350 in July, were associated with high points on the price index which fell short of the January top. The peak of Activity at the beginning of 1948 is of a different nature. The high point of price was touched at the turn of the year, the subsequent rise of Activity was associated with a subsidence and levelling out of the price curve until Activity soared on a sharp fall of price. This formation shows a large area of supply. Here it was supply, not demand, that was the dominant factor. This characteristic marked out this Activity peak as being of an entirely different nature from its predecessors in 1947; it is through this supply peak that the trendline is correctly drawn. The next contact is with the twin peaks in March 1949; these peaks of Activity were associated with a decline of the price index. So also was the peak of Activity in June.

If we look at another seven year period, 1958–64[1], we find the development of the patterns is not quite the same. The lowest point for the *Financial Times* industrial ordinary after the 1955 peak was reached at the end of February 1958, and the Activity curve went a little lower early in March. But by the middle of April a far clearer uptrend had appeared in the Activity curve than in the chart of the share index. After the Election in 1959 the Activity curve reached a fantastic level; for the rest of the year the share index ran up to new highs but the Activity curve swung down and rallied to a New Year's peak that fell far short of the level reached in October. This was a significant divergence and heralded a substantial change in the character of the market. In 1960 the two curves worked substantially out of gear; they moved down together in the spring, rallied together in the summer; then the Activity curve suffered a seasonal lapse

---

[1] Chart No. 11 on next page.

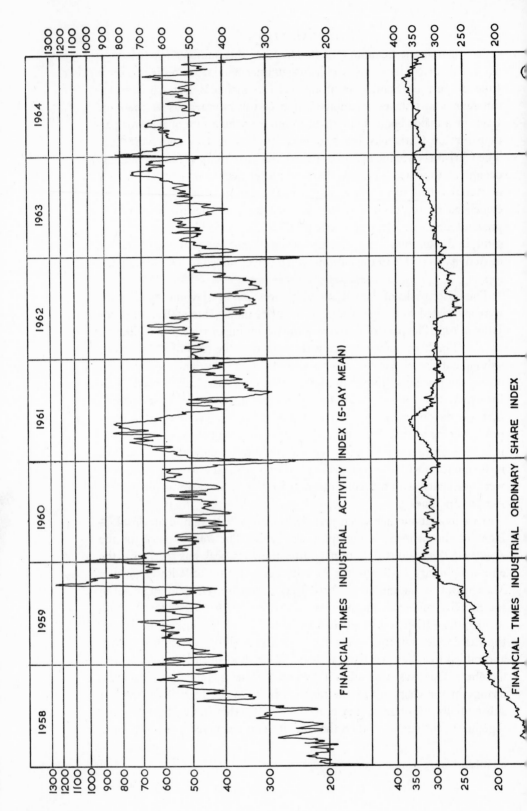

FINANCIAL TIMES INDUSTRIAL ACTIVITY INDEX (5-DAY MEAN)

FINANCIAL TIMES INDUSTRIAL ORDINARY SHARE INDEX

Chart No. 11

and then rallied strongly against the trend of the price index which was by that time suffering a secondary decline. In the autumn the share index fell while Activity held its high level, but after the fall of the share index, the Activity curve entered its Christmas decline through which the price curve persisted blithely upward in what developed into one of the strongest secondary rallies the London market has seen. It is probably right to treat this movement as an exceptional rally in a bear market which took the index to a new high level rather than as a continuation of the 1958–59 bull market; the 1961 peak of price was accompanied by lower Activity, a lower level of Confidence and a higher yield than the peak of 1959–60. The Activity curve reached a peak in April and fell back and rallied, almost to its April high, when the price index was reaching its peak in mid-May. Here again there was a slight divergence between the two indices at a critical point. From mid-May both declined precipitously; Activity bottomed first and was well above its worst level when the price index reached a low level in October. Here it looks as if buyers were coming out to meet the sellers. The market then showed some recovery, and in April 1962 the Activity curve rose strongly while the share index refused to follow. This turned out quite differently from the example discussed in 1958; in April the American market went into a steep decline; and the London price index dropped in June to its lowest level after the 1959–60 peak. Activity reached its low point for 1962 after the price index, but at no time did it fall as low during the summer of 1962 as it had twelve months earlier. By November both curves, Activity and price, had established upward trends. The curves rose through 1963, and each shows peaks at the beginning of November 1963 and the beginning of January 1964; the small seasonal drop of Activity at Christmas, however, turned out to be unduly encouraging. January 1964 saw the lowest point for yield and the highest point for Activity after the bottom of the bear market in 1962 until these levels were exceeded at the end of the decade. The divergence between the Activity and price curves that was manifest in the charts by the autumn of 1964 was evidence that the bull market of 1962–63 had shot its bolt, and though very high levels were reached again at the end of the second quarter of 1966, the share market never seemed to enjoy strong support after the peak of January 1964 till it was purged by the collapse which followed Mr. Wilson's measures of July 1966. The bear market of 1964–66 was singularly innocuous; it conditioned investors to believe everything they were told by the missionaries of the 'cult of equity' and left them hideously unprepared for the savage treatment which they suffered in the collapse of 1969.

We had a pattern in 1947–49 of peaks of Activity falling short of the trendline when they were associated with rises of price and rising up to the trendline when they were associated with downturns of price. Making allowance for the descending angle of the trend, the prominent peaks were associated with supply and the less prominent with demand. This does not always happen; it was not a prominent symptom in the 1960-62 bear market, but there is a good example in October 1964. There is no universal rule here, only a symptom which it is worth while watching for. In markets other than industrials there is little scope for it. The gilt edged market should be sufficiently large and flexible, but the behaviour of Activity there is somewhat different from the industrial market, because there are three parties in the gilt edged market, the public, the institutions and the Government Broker, while there are only the institutions and the public in the industrial market. If the Government Broker, since money supply theories became fashionable, has changed his practices, it is difficult to see how Activity can rise far on declines, because the institutions and the public, both trying to sell at the same time, will find no buyers to absorb their stock. No buyers means no Activity! In less elastic markets, like Kaffirs, excess of supply implies disappearance of demand. The excess of supply cannot express itself in bargains, as the buyers cannot be found to take what the would-be sellers are offering.

The characteristics of the rise are quite different. When one looks at Chart No. 10, one is given the impression that the 1949-51 rise moved through five phases. The first phase is the upsurge of Activity in February; this is a very narrow and spiky peak which appeared to have little weight behind it. The occasion was odd; the 'radio doctor' had made a party political broadcast for the Conservatives in the General Election. Mr. Morrison was furious that the Stock Exchange should respond with rising prices. How wrong Mr. Morrison was! If he had been experienced in the interpretation of charts he would have seen that a rise of Activity up to the levels of selling pressure recorded eleven months earlier could not bear the construction that he put on it; he should have claimed that this was the investors' vote of confidence in the measures taken by the Labour Government to bring the country out of its crisis. For what is significant here is the sudden emergence of enough buyers to carry the Activity index to such a level. Investors are ready enough to shout for the Conservatives, but they buy much more cannily than they shout. Most of the buying in 1946 should be traced ultimately to stimuli supplied by Mr. Dalton. The investors did not approve of Mr. Dalton, but they bought because his activities argued higher prices. The 'radio doctor' supplied the occasion for the buying in February 1950, but its volume was related to the investors' opinion of the economic prospects. The next rise of Activity in June was triggered by a similar irrelevancy, the end of petrol rationing. This was a much broader movement, and the share price index, which had been rising quietly, appeared to gather a considerable momentum. Unfortunately, at this point, the Korean War broke out. Activity came down with a run, but it climbed quietly through the time of the normal summer doldrum and soared in the autumn into the third phase of the rise. This rise was checked by the entry of the Chinese into the war, but early in 1951 we find Activity at a new peak as investors hurried to buy ordinary shares before the nationalization stock was issued to the holders of steel shares. Once again there was a subsidence for Easter and the Budget, and then we get the fifth and final burst of Activity.

In our study of Activity so far we have paid most attention to the upper side of the Activity curve. But it can be argued that it is really the under side of the curve that is important. The turn at the top in 1947 was signalled first by the Easter dip to the low level of the previous summer; if the trend had still been upwards there should have been more demand in a dull spot in the spring of 1947 than in the summer of 1946. It is after this preliminary signal that the rallies of Activity in the summer fail to reach the peak of the previous January. We get a similar pattern in 1951; the decline of Activity that summer fell very much farther back from the peak than any previous decline of Activity since the rise had begun. That was a preliminary signal, and it was followed by a signal from the top side of the curve when the election rallies failed to lift Activity to a new high point.

If you look at the under side of the curve from 1946, you will see that the summer doldrum in each year to 1949 was lower than its predecessor. Then in November, when share prices fell to a new low level, Activity did not. This was just a vague hint; after all, the previous low point belonged to the summer doldrum and was not strictly comparable. Then comes Christmas, an irrelevant interlude. Then there is a low point of Activity in January, above November's. There is a low point in March; it is above January's. Then comes a low point in April; it is above March's. Look back over the decline and try to find a gradual climb of this sort; there is no pattern like it. Something new was happening in the market, and the simplest explanation was that each time the market became dull there were more buyers looking for stock than there had been at the previous dull point. The demand-supply relation had changed; the dominance of supply from January 1947 was dead and some time in the second half of 1949 a new dominance of demand had been born.

We must now turn back to Chart No. 10 which covers two complete cycles, high prices in 1947 and 1951, low prices in 1949 and 1952. At the tops the pattern is what we shall later learn to describe as a 'double top'; the index rose to a high level, retreated and then rose almost as high as before. In each case Activity reached a high level at the first top of the share index, fell away heavily through its rising lower trendline, then rallied with the share index but fell far short of the previous top. (This double top pattern for the share index did not recur till 1968–69, and then Activity also made a double top, but the beginning of the final upsurge of Activity was accompanied, most suspiciously, by falling prices for shares.) At the first bottom in 1949 Activity traced out a pattern the reverse of that described at the top; the share index made a 'double bottom' and Activity was lower at the first of the pair of bottoms than at the second. In 1952 Activity reached its lowest level a week after shares. There followed a period of indeterminate movement which ended with a lead upwards from the Activity curve. Good upward trends were then established for Activity and for the share index, but from the end of 1954 the Activity curve failed to reach upwards to its top trendline. The first set-back of 1955 was savage and both curves came down to their lower trendlines which had been long unvisited. Shares recovered in the summer to their upper trendline; but Activity only just exceeded the previous highs of 1954 and early 1955 and fell far short of its trendline. The share index peaked in July, four weeks after Activity. Share prices declined to November 1956; Activity came down with them. In the rally of 1957, big enough for one to describe it as a 'calf market', Activity failed to participate; it rose no higher in the big flurry of the spring than it had in the recovery from the lowest levels the previous autumn. But it did not abdicate its functions; the share index rose to 205 in the spring with Activity up to 515 and to 205 a second time in July when Activity climbed no higher than 460. Here you have again the pattern made familiar by 1947 and 1951; down came prices to a bottom in February 1958. The bottom of Activity is obscured by the seasonal dip at Christmas. By the end of March the trend of Activity appeared to have turned upwards, and by the end of April it was clear that both the share index and the Activity curve were in new uptrends. The top of 1959–60 was an extraordinary performance. In October Activity reached the highest level established since the present rules for recording bargains were introduced, but shares did not reach the top of this cycle till the turn of the year when Activity had recovered from its Christmas dip to a level far below its October peak (and far above anything recorded since). In 1960 the heavy decline of Activity was not accompanied by an important decline of share prices, and a strong rally developed at the end of 1960 which took the *Financial Times* industrial ordinary share index to a new high level in 1961. This high point for shares was accompanied by levels for Confidence and Activity lower than those of the end of 1959 and beginning of 1960, and it was succeeded by a heavy fall in prices to the middle of 1962. Activity did not, however, fall as low in 1962 as in 1961 and a new rise developed. Activity reached its peak, just below the 1961 top, in January 1964. Shares then retreated only a little of the way with

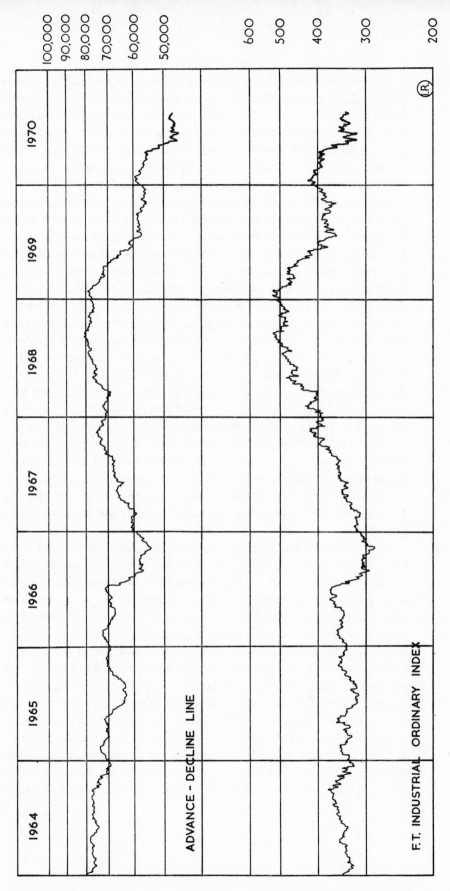

ADVANCE - DECLINE LINE

F.T. INDUSTRIAL ORDINARY INDEX

Chart No. 12

Activity and went on to a new high level at the end of September (this new high level was not significantly above the top of 1961). Prices see-sawed through 1965 and were up to their best levels again at the end of June 1966, while Activity continued to show how far from whole-hearted investors were about the price level. The tops of Activity were 830 in January 1964, 690 on falling prices in October, 610 in April 1965, 505 in February 1966 and 435 on steeply falling prices in July 1966.

The Advance/Decline Line has not been plotted, or at any rate not been published, over any great length of time in Britain. Investment Research has charts that go back to the beginning of 1960; at first the figures were determined by a daily count of the pluses and minuses recorded in industrial sections of the market by the *Financial Times*. Later the *Financial Times* began to publish a count; at first this used a very broad classification and Investment Research had to count a number of sections and deduct their total from the *Financial Times* omnibus classification but more recently the *Financial Times* has published daily figures of pluses, minuses and no change for the strict industrial classification which Investment Research had used from the beginning. But there is a sad statistical defect for which allowance must be made in using the early figures; when Investment Research started counting in 1960 the population was 994 and it did not reach 1700 till late in 1965. The figure in February 1970 was 1734, while in June 1968 it was 1661; so figures after July 1965, when there was a total of 1685, are comparable one with another. In the earlier period when the population was rising succeeding swings must tend to be exaggerated. Thus, in this period, comparisons between June and July 1962 are valid, comparisons between May 1961 and January 1964 are probably not.

Up to the beginning of 1962 there appears to be little significant difference between the two curves, but in the summer of that year, after both reached a low point in June, the *Financial Times* industrial rallied and lost two-thirds of its rally before it resumed its uptrend. The A/D Line, however, lost all its rally; and in this case the A/D Line appears to have been a laggard at the bottom. Both curves reached a high level in January 1964; the share index recovered to the same level in April and stood higher in October; the A/D Line was lower in April and lower still in October. The population increased from 1414 in January to 1558 in October and this was certainly a period in which distortion of the curve was possible. But as it was a period in which the market seems to have been rising for a longer period than it was falling, the A/D curve, if it was distorted, should surely have been distorted upwards? It seems fair to accept this as an instance where the A/D Line was a leading indicator at a top. The share index stood higher in May 1965 than in March and the A/D Line higher in March than in May; both fell in July to levels below the preceding December. Both then rallied to November and on to February, but between February and July 1966 the share index went higher and the A/D Line failed to follow. There was a substantial period of disagreement between the share index and the A/D Line in 1964/65; this ended in the summer of 1965 but disagreement broke out again after February 1966.

From the downturn of the share index in July 1966 the A/D Line moved in step through the bottom and up to the autumn of 1967. Then a puzzling and deceptive divergence appeared. The share index dropped sharply and the A/D Line subsided gently. The share index rallied and went above its previous peak just after the turn of the year. There was only the slightest recovery in the A/D Line. The share index dropped but its worst point in March 1968 was well above its lowest of the previous December. The A/D Line fell below its secondary bottom of January. A clear divergence was established here, a divergence that apparently signified nothing, because the rise was renewed and both share index and A/D Line went on to new high levels in September. Both fell back in the autumn and rallied at the turn of the year; but the January top of the *Financial Times* industrial ordinary share index equalled its best of 1968 while the A/D Line fell significantly short.

A very substantial divergence emerged in the second half of 1969. Both moved down together to a low point at the end of July; both then rallied but the recovery of the A/D Line was feeble. Both declined in the autumn to a low point in November, for the share index just above the worst of July, for the A/D Line lower. A substantial rally of the share index took it well above the best point reached between the bottoms of July and November; the A/D Line just succeeded in getting above its best level for the same period. By the Budget in April 1970 the share index had twice tested the support laid down by the secondary top of September and October, but the A/D Line had worked through its lowest level of the previous winter. This divergence was followed by a second phase of liquidation which carried the indices well below the worst levels of 1969.

The chart of Consols $2\frac{1}{2}\%$ [1] is possibly the simplest indicator for the trend of the long term interest rate. As it pays its dividends four times a year the stock never becomes very 'full of dividend' in the way that this happens to War Loan $3\frac{1}{2}\%$. The stock moves in fairly long trends and the reversals of these trends are often closely associated with reversals of trends for the share market.

Let us look first at the behaviour of Consols in relation to share market tops. Consols turned down only a few weeks before shares in 1947, a few

---

[1] Refer to Chart No. 2 on page 38.

months before shares in 1950–51, roughly the same interval before shares in 1954–55 and rather more closely before shares in 1959–60. Consols turned in the second half of 1963 while the share index faltered significantly in January 1964 and made little further progress. But in April 1967 Consols turned down a year and a half before the peak of 1968 and a year and three-quarters before the peak, at approximately the same level, of 1969. At the bottom Consols turned up in 1949 a week or so after the second bottom of shares, in 1952 a single week before the bottom of shares, in 1957 nearly six months before the bottom of shares in 1958, in 1961 nearly a year before the bottom of shares in 1962. In 1963 Consols started a decline that ran to September 1966; shares, which had collapsed in July 1966, turned up soon after Consols in November. We must also look at the ineffective rallies of Consols, in 1947 and 1957. Each of these was accompanied by a rally of shares, short-lived in 1947 but quite substantial in 1956–57. However, neither of these rallies, unbacked by a persistent rise in Consols, developed into true bull markets. The big rise of share prices that started in December 1960 was accompanied from the start by a declining trend of Consols, and this rise, like its predecessor in 1957, came to a bad end. There was a quite long rise of Consols from May 1948 to May 1949 which was not followed by any significant rally of shares. The record of the post-war period suggests that Consols generally lead shares at tops and bottoms, though this was not true at bottoms immediately after the war, and that rises of ordinary shares that are not backed by Consols come soon to a bad end, although this signally failed to happen in any short time after the downturn of Consols in 1967. Generally in the bear markets for shares Consols have been going down and in the major phases of accumulation in bull markets Consols have been going up, though this was not true in that part of the major phase which extended from April 1967 to September 1968.

In this chapter we are concerned partly with ancillary indicators, Activity and A/D Line, and partly with components, which we discussed in the previous chapter. In Chart No. 13 we trace out the course of a share index and set of components for the period 1946–52. At the top is a curve called 'dividend', plotted from the product of the *Financial Times* industrial ordinary share index and the *Financial Times* industrial ordinary yield. You calculate the yield of a share by dividing its dividend by its price; you can therefore calculate its dividend by the reverse process of multiplying its yield by its price. In the same way you can calculate the notional dividend of a market average; and this is what we have done here for the *Financial Times* industrial ordinary share index. The next curve is called 'Confidence' which covers the residual elements in share prices when the dividend and interest elements have been removed. This was

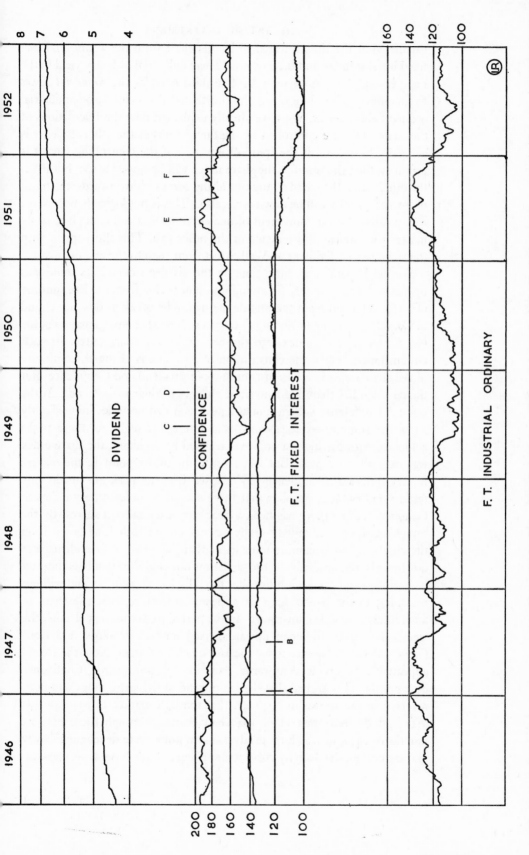

Chart No. 13

calculated at the time referred to in this chart from the *Financial Times* fixed interest index and the *Financial Times* industrial ordinary yield in the manner explained in Chapter V. The third curve is the *Financial Times* fixed interest stock index and the fourth the *Financial Times* industrial ordinary share index. We have already explained how the fluctuations of the share index are controlled by the fluctuations of the other three. It is generally likely that if the trend of any two of the controlling curves is upwards, then the trend of the share index will be upwards too, but if, on the other hand, the trend of any two of the curves is downwards, the trend of the share index will be downwards also. (This is not logically necessary; it is possible for the movement of one curve to be steep enough to over-master the opposite movements of the other two. This did happen with the steep rise of dividend on Wall Street from 1949 to the end of 1950.)

We need spend very little time on the dividend curve. Its trend was upwards, except possibly for an unimportant period from the late summer of 1947 and again from the middle of 1952. The break in this curve (and in Confidence) at the beginning of 1947 was due to the amalgamation of the old *Financial News* index into the new *Financial Times* index. In such circumstances, when the constitution of an index is changed, continuity of the share index involves discontinuity of dividend and Confidence. But the curves other than dividend show changes of their main trends. At the point A Confidence is high (not at a peak as it had been declining slightly since the summer of 1944) and fixed interest is high. As these peaks coincided with the highest point yet reached by dividend, the share index was naturally at a peak. But when you come to the point B, the picture is very different. Confidence has relapsed from its peak and made only tertiary rallies. It is peculiar that there should be only tertiary rallies of Confidence when there has been a clear secondary rally in shares. By the time Confidence had failed to rally beyond 180 on 20th June (point B on the chart), it was becoming most likely that the trend of Confidence was downwards, not upwards. At the same time one could see that fixed interest had rallied from the March low, but the rally had come to an end without returning to the winter high. It appeared, therefore, that the trend of fixed interest was also downward. In the period from the 1945 election the trends had been: dividend upwards, fixed interest upwards, and Confidence downwards, except for the last quarter of 1946. Now the trends appeared to be dividend upwards, fixed interest downwards, Confidence downwards. This argued that the main trend of the share index had been reversed in the winter of 1946–47, that the bull market of 1940–46 was over and the bear market of 1947 had begun. Through these first six months of 1947, in which these adverse symptoms were developing slowly in these curves, the Activity curve was spelling out much the same message.

At the time of the fuel crisis, in February and March, it was beginning to suggest that demand was wilting. The failure of demand to expand to its former levels when prices rallied in the second quarter was another warning. By the middle of summer there were plenty of danger signals. It was hardly arguable that the trend of Confidence was still upward. Fixed interest had rallied and failed to regain its old levels; the clinching movement would be a penetration by the fixed interest index of its secondary low level of 141·2 recorded on 25th March. It sank to that level again on 16th July and subsided no lower on 17th and 18th. But the week-end brought sellers; the number for 21st July was 140·7. The share index reading was 132·1, 8·5 below the peak level of 140·6. The final signal was given with shares a shade worse than 6% below the peak.

The signals that we have used at this primary reversal, signals that gave their warning long after the turn but still in good time, were changes in the trends of our controlling factors confirmed by a change in the trend of activity. How do these signals work at the reversal of 1949?

At the point C in the middle of the summer the trend of dividend was up. Confidence and fixed interest, whose primary trends had apparently been downward since January 1947, were in steep phases of decline, and it is interesting to note how the secondary phase of fixed interest continued downwards when Confidence, and to a lesser extent shares, were rallying (this was the last time up to the date of writing that fixed interest turned up late). Activity at this stage was receding from a burst of selling pressure; the decline seemed to be in full spate. Now let us advance to D in the autumn. The trend of dividend is still up. The trend of fixed interest is probably, though not quite certainly, down. But the latest reaction of Confidence has been checked far above its low point of C. The trend of Confidence looks as if it had changed; there is certainly a divergence of Confidence from shares, more strongly marked than the significant divergence which we noted at the top in 1947. It is certainly open to argue that the bear market is ending and a new primary rise beginning. A few more weeks showed that the trend of fixed interest had been downwards; the fixed interest index went to its lowest point reached so far on our chart. At this point it is necessary to turn to Activity for confirmation. For, if a bear market is ending and a bull market is beginning, the reign of supply must be terminated and a new dominance seized by demand. This might be argued from the rise of the Activity curve through the descending trendline on the occasion of the devaluation in September. On the other hand, the very low level of Activity at Christmas pointed in the other direction. Both these items of evidence are very tenuous. More solid witness comes from the upsurge of bargains in February and the rising trend of the underside of the Activity pattern. By March it still appeared that the Confidence trend was upward; it appeared also that the Activity trend was upward. Dividend was neutral, last indication upward; fixed interest was neutral, last indication downward. The majority appeared to be on the side of a rising market; it was time to spend the cash, acquired by realisations in 1947, and to buy promising shares. Again our timing is months past the turn; again we are late and in plenty of time.

The third set of signals comes in 1951. At E the fixed interest index has been in a decline for six months; dividend is rising strongly and Confidence and shares are at a peak. Move on to F; dividend is held steady by the limitation proposals made by the Labour Government; Confidence is below its peaks of the early summer and farther below them than shares. The warning divergence is there again, although it is small. The trend of fixed interest shows no sign of reversal; it must be presumed to be still down. The signals then read: dividend up, fixed interest down, Confidence probably down. If Confidence is truly down, then a bear market has begun. It is therefore necessary to turn for confirmation to Activity. The large decline of the summer and the anaemic rally of the autumn both suggest that the trend of Activity has been reversed, and the dating of the Activity peak earlier than that of shares is another of the divergences which sometimes appear at reversals (this divergence was notably absent from the reversal at the top in 1968–69).

This double top pattern of the *Financial Times* industrial ordinary share index did not reappear at primary reversals of bull markets till 1968–69. A divergence of Confidence is not likely to be discernible in a 'Head & Shoulders' type of reversal like that of 1955 (peaks in January and December with a higher peak in the summer between them) nor in the single peak of 1959–60, but it was very plain when you set 1960 against 1961 and it showed up in the series of tops for the share index from 1964 to 1966. Confidence was generally more useful (or would have been if it had been invented) in the period between the wars when strong rises of dividend continued through the price tops and steep declines of dividend persisted beyond the bottoms. In the post-war period persistent rises of dividend at the top have been offset in Confidence by the weakness of gilt edged, and the strength of gilt edged at the bottoms after 1952 has been quite as potent a factor as any slight decline of dividend. When the Government limits dividends stringently, Confidence is crippled and unable to signal, (in 1951 the signal must have been in the pipeline before the limitation was imposed).

Of the three reversals studied in conjunction with Chart No. 13 that of 1951 was undoubtedly the most difficult to detect. The decline of the summer, both in price and Activity, seemed so obviously due to dividend limitation. The autumn rally and its curtailment seemed so obviously due to the General Election. These were not circumstances in which one could expect increases of Activity or new high levels of price. This is one of those occasions to which the devoted chartists point when they advance their theory that the future of the market should be interpreted from the chart alone without any consideration of external factors. Such students of investment are quite exceptional; the ordinary human investor is much more frail and he wants his decisions supported by evidence which springs from something that seems more solid than a curve on a chart. It is not much use arguing whether he is right or wrong; in any case he will go on demanding evidence external to security charts. All we can point out is that security charts did their duty and gave their warning—and were right.

CHAPTER NINE

Policy for Individual Shares

The problems that we have been considering in the previous chapter were general problems, what is the direction of the primary trend, how are we to tell in time when it changes? The actual investor always finds himself concerned with a set of particular problems, the individual shares which he holds and might sell, or alternatively which of the various securities which he does not hold he should select when he wishes to invest.

Let us take the case of an investor who is holding variable dividend shares and who decides, from evidence of the sort that we described in the previous chapter, that the upward trend has come to an end and the new trend is down. It follows from what we have just said that such an investor is a believer in the shares which he holds. If he had not been believing in them, he would already have sold them; if he had not been believing that the trend of the market was upwards, he would have realised his holdings earlier. What he is now deciding is that he is wrong, that the market which he thought was rising is really falling. We may presume that he is holding the shares which he thought likely to show the best rises. In short, he believes in his shares. Now the charts are telling him that his general judgement is wrong. He is abandoning his own judgement in general and deferring to the chart. But the chart cannot select; it can indicate the main trend of the market, not what shares will behave as exceptions to the main trend. The question arises whether the investor should retain any shares when his charts signal a reversal from uptrend to downtrend, or whether he should obey blindly and sell them all. The answer surely is that he must obey blindly and sell them all. In doing this he may well err; some of his shares may more than justify his hopes. But however sound it may be to trust to his judgement when he believes his judgement is sound, it is almost certainly unsound to trust to his judgement when he is taking a decision because he believes his judgement to be unsound. The moment, when the decision is taken that the upward trend is finished and the downward trend has begun, is a moment of abdication of judgement; the new decision should be a decision to sell the lot.

The belief had been growing up that the declines of the post-war period were not sufficiently deep to justify so drastic a policy. The first two declines of the post-war period, 1947–49 and 1951–52, were not very large but seemed large enough, because the pattern at the top gave an opportunity of selling when the decline had made little progress. Their declines from the top amounted to 29% and 26% respectively. The next decline, from the top of 1955 to the bottom of 1958 was bigger, 31%, but the difficulties of making sales close to the top were much larger. After that the difficulty of timing sales grew. The top appeared to have been reached in the first few days of 1960, or at least in the autumn, and the recovery of 1961 looks like a secondary rally in a bear market rather than a part of the primary rise that started in 1958. (Early writers on the Dow Theory acknowledged that secondary rallies in a bear market could regain more than 100% of the ground lost). The drop from the 1960 tops to the 1962 bottom was about 23%; the descent from the top of 1961 was bigger— and also steeper—so that the chances of selling at good prices were correspondingly smaller. That decline was 39%. The next top was again very difficult; the bear flags were flying after January 1964 but the top of the market was reached in September and equalled again in June 1966, only five months before the bottom. This experience made the policy of selling the lot even less profitable. Then came the experience of 1969. The *Financial Times* industrial ordinary share index reached 520 twice in the winter of 1968–69, and by the late spring of 1970 it had dropped 37%.

It is also argued that however profitable this policy may have been in the past, it is no longer worth pursuing now that we have to cope with the Capital Gains Tax.

In both these arguments there appears to be an underlying hypothesis that the investor holds the right shares at the top of a bull market and should want to hold the same shares through its successor. The contention of Hargreaves Parkinson in 'Advanced Hatch' was that the investor should sell on the Hatch signal and should then start thinking what he should buy when the next Hatch signal put him back into the market. The advice was that you should plan all your switching in the period in which you were out of the market. This unfortunately is a counsel of perfection; the selection of shares is a business so difficult and chancy that nobody will choose a portfolio full of strong runners which needs no adjustment when the bull market is under way. But it is obvious that different times need different shares and that portfolios which were successful in the fifties were very seldom equally successful in the sixties. So, if changes are to be made—and they surely are—it is quite a good idea to try to get out near the top of one bull market and defer the selection of your new portfolio till you think you are moving into the next primary rise.

The same arguments apply to the plea about Capital Gains Tax. If you sacrifice 30% of your profit on share A, sit on the cash for a year or two, then buy share B when prices are generally lower, share B has not to do much better than share A in the next primary rise for you to be better off with your new choice after tax than you would have been with your old untaxed. It is true that 30% sounds a high proportion, but it is a proportion of your profit, not of your price; we took a random 20% sample from our chart books for the period January 1964 to November 1966 and 40% of the shares dropped 30% or more in price during the period. Investors seem eager enough to take losses nowadays and minimise their tax; they would probably fare much better if they preferred a policy of selling as near the top of a bull market as they could and thus maximising their tax!

The normal sequence at a reversal of a primary uptrend is for dividends to go on rising (something with which governments can interfere). Thus yields will rise, not only when prices are falling, but also between two dates at which prices are equal. Shares, in fact, are by this test appearing to be cheaper. There are also other more violent changes in the market's yield structure. Fixed interest securities at such a time are normally falling; so their yields too are going up. In this process the differential between fixed interest yields and variable dividend yields narrows—the word was 'widens' in the first edition, written at a time when the yield on the share index was normally higher than the yield on Consols. This change on the yield gap is a counterpart to the fall in Confidence; the trend of Confidence should always be watched closely but at the top it is pulled in opposite directions by the rising yields on gilts and the rising yields on shares. It is therefore important to watch also the behaviour of the yield on shares; when yield starts going down markedly less than shares go up, the market is obviously becoming less willing to discount a happy future and this is an important warning signal.

If you see the market making a top and decide to go on holding a particular share, you are making a judgement that the favourable expectations which you hold for that share will be so well fulfilled that they will compensate the ill-effect of the deterioration of the general market which you see beginning to unfold before you. Further, you are making this judgement when you ought to reckon that your favourable expectations are probably widely shared and are, in that event, already in the price of the share. In many declines we have seen the special favourites of the previous rise suffer the severest falls. The investors who held them may have believed that these were the shares which it could not be right to sell, but their judgement was proved fallible.

Thus the principle that it is right to sell everything, as the top of the general market trend develops, is easy to enunciate and to defend. The opposite principle, that it is right to buy everything at the bottom of the general market trend, is advice that cannot be carried into practice. At the top 'everything' is all the different variable dividend securities that an investor holds. At the bottom 'everything' is all the variable dividend securities that he does not hold, several thousands of them. May we substitute 'anything' for 'everything'? Not with much conviction. The investor at the bottom ought to believe that some securities will rise more than others, and he ought to set about selecting them, or rather he ought to have a list of selections in readiness, prepared during the months during which he was out of the market. This is the moment of accession; here judgement is enthroned. Charts can tell you when to go into the market and buy, but when they tell you to go into the market they do not tell you what to buy, although many charts of individual shares may be indicating that if you want to buy a certain share this is the time to buy it. We examined the charts of shares which scored the biggest rises in the 1949–51 bull market; we did not detect any common characteristics which were not equally present in shares that enjoyed quite subnormal rises. We also made a study on different lines of shares which did well in the 1966–69 bull market. We went through the Investment Research daily chart library and took out all the shares which rose in 1969 to over 400% of the initial entry on the chart made in November 1966. The mining sections of the chart library were excluded. There were, in all, 43 shares. Of these eight were newcomers which had not existed, at least not in the same form, in the previous bear market. So there remained 35 shares which did very well and had gone right through the previous bear market. Of these nine, or 26%, had a good bear market and finished at 100% or better of our arbitrary starting point, ten did badly and finished at 50% or less of our starting point and the remaining 16, or 45%, all fell short of 100% but did better than 50%. This looks quite interesting against our bigger sample of 91 shares, which produced $17\frac{1}{2}$% finishing at 100% or better and 13% at 50% or worse. Clearly the shares which did better than average by a wide margin or worse than average by a wide margin in the previous bear market threw up a higher proportion of big winners in the next bull market than the shares whose bear market performance had been nearer the average. But this statistical approach is not, by itself, going to make anybody's fortune. In our sample of 91 shares the good performers of the old bear market put up very average performances in the new bull market, and exactly the same is true of the bad performers. If you concentrate on buying good performers or bad performers or both, you are likely, even if you do get some winners, to secure a very average performance.

The investor looking for high performance is thus thrust back on hard work or intuition. Probably these are best combined. It is reasonable to guess that a certain share, solely on account of what the company does and with little reference to the company's financial position or recent record, is likely to attract glamour in a new bull market. It is also reasonable to argue that certain shares, in companies which have a good past record but have experienced bad fortune in the bear market period but are likely to return to good fortune when conditions change, can give the bold investor, who buys the shares while they are still under a cloud, most satisfactory results. Such a study of companies and shares requires time, a commodity of which the professional investment analyst may have enough for the task but the private investor is usually lamentably short.

Can the use of charts help here? It is clear that shares which are going to quadruple themselves in a bull market must rise more steeply over the period than shares which are going to do no better than double themselves. It is possible by inspection of charts to select shares which are rising exceptionally steeply, but not, alas! to be sure that such shares will continue to rise steeply. So it should be possible for an investor who read the market well to buy shares with steep uptrends at an early stage in a new bull market, prune his portfolio after six or nine months, ejecting shares whose uptrends are no longer steep and moving into shares whose steep uptrends are persisting. The process might be repeated when the bull market is twelve to fifteen months old, but after that it is too late, if recent experience is a guide, to go looking for new shares; it is the shares bought in late stages of a bull market that cause investors most trouble when the primary trend turns down. (It is not certain that there is any reason why British bull markets must go on being as short as they have been since the war; in the twenties we had a bull market that ran from 1921 into 1928 or 1929 and in the thirties its successor ran from the middle of 1932 to the winter of 1936–37. If the politicians can master the art of winning an election without wrecking the economy, we may have primary uptrends which persist unbroken for much longer periods than we have known since 1947.)

The methods to be adopted for choosing shares to buy at the bottom differ in detail more than in principle from those applicable to purchases at any other time. At most times one chooses a share to buy because there seem to be new and strong reasons for buying it; at the bottom one chooses to buy because there seem to be new and strong reasons for buying shares. The factors controlling the ordinary share market were analysed in Chapter Five; and it is, of course, these same factors which control the movements of individual ordinary shares. At any time the movements of gilt edged and the fixed interest market are a general factor; a 10% rise of War Loan exerts just as much influence on Imperial Chemicals as on Vickers or Lesney Products or any other British share. Changes of dividend rates, on the other hand, are strictly particular. Ask a stockbroker and he will probably tell you that an increase of dividend for Allied Breweries may well provoke a sympathetic rise in Bass, Charrington. This is true, but it does not disprove our contention. We have in reserve our third factor, Confidence. This is the factor which causes a sympathetic rise in Bass, Charrington. It is a particular much more than a general factor; a Confidence ratio can be calculated for each individual share and these ratios change with the expectations concerned with the individual shares. When Allied Breweries declare an increased dividend, investors argue that the beer trade is better and accordingly expect better results from Bass, Charrington. The peculiarity of Confidence, which makes this paiticular factor into a general factor, is that Confidence, while it is particular, like measles, is also, like measles, infectious. You cannot have my measles but you can catch my measles, and Confidence can spread, in this infectious way, from one share to another. But Confidence persists only if it is justified in the event, and unless the increased dividend is in due course declared the hopes of investors are likely to wilt and the price of the shares to slip back as the Confidence ratio relapses.

What do investors want from their shares? The answer used to be 'rising dividends' but more recently it has been fashionable to say capital appreciation or rising earnings. The first of these fashionable choices is reasonable; what the investor ought to want and what the institutional investor does want is the maximisation of the net receipts from the investment, both those that come in the form of taxed or untaxed dividends and those which stem from the ultimate sale. Rising earnings are fashionable because they are thought to point the way to higher net receipts, perhaps because dividends do increase, perhaps because the rising earnings make other investors willing to pay higher prices for the shares. But earnings and P/E (Price:Earnings) Ratios are not important in themselves. Analysts used to talk about earnings and earnings yields before the Corporation Tax made the P/E Ratio fashionable instead. They also used to point out that a dividend yield could find its way into the housekeeping but that you could not live on an earnings yield. Before Corporation Tax most analysts used to think about earnings, even if they did not talk about them much; now it must be feared that too many analysts talk about earnings without thinking about them enough.

So let us get back to hard cash and stick to the phrase used in the first edition 'what the buyer of shares wants is rising dividends'. Considerations about gilt edged and Confidence are invaluable in telling him when to buy in general, but when he wants to know what to buy he must begin to make judgements about the future dividends of particular shares. How is he to look for bigger dividends? These can come from two main sources, either from the company's making larger profits from which the directors can declare larger dividends, or from the directors becoming more generous and declaring larger dividends from the large profits that the company seems, on the evidence of recent balance sheets, to be making.

There seems no obvious manner in which one can diagnose which board of directors will feel more generous at its company's next dividend meeting and which will feel less. Every company balance sheet shows what outstanding commitments for capital expenditure exist and this may be some guide, but they do not tell you what plans for expenditure exist in the directors' minds. Directorial generosity can be estimated by guesswork. But an improving stock market seems to make directors feel more confident and be more generous in their declarations; so it is usually sound to buy at the bottom a share which has recently been showing a large margin of earnings over dividend.

The alternative is to seek out companies that will make larger profits. The making of profits depends partly on the management of the company, partly on the assets that the company controls, and partly on the climate in which the company is working. The appropriate image seems to be a cricket eleven, where we equate the management with the captain, the assets with the other ten players, and the economic climate with the state of the wicket. Good management finds it hard to make adequate profits from poor assets, and the best management with the most ample assets may fail if the economic climate is adverse. A stage coach company would be on a very bad wicket in the later stages of a railway boom.

At the moment we are considering purchases of shares near the upturn of the cycle; this assumes that there is in progress a general change of wicket in favour of companies. We do not suggest that investors at this stage should give no consideration at all to the wicket on which the company will be playing, only that more consideration should be given to management and assets. (If the wicket does look bad, that is a factor which may have been discounted very heavily in the preceeding bear market.) Just the opposite applies in later stages of the cycle—then one should consider first the changes of wicket which at such a time are likely to help or hurt one company more than another, while considerations of management and assets, which are likely already to have exerted considerable influence on the price, should take second place. If one decides early that the main trend has changed from down to up, it is very difficult to make any judgements about the state of the wicket for various companies, but there is ample evidence about management and assets. If one makes the decision later, more details of the various wickets may have come into view, but the evidence about management and assets is available just the same as before.

When the first edition of this book was written in the early fifties, it was sufficient to look for shares with a consistent record of high earnings and you could find them. Shares were valued mainly on their dividend yields; shares with high dividend cover commanded lower yields than shares with poor cover but the differences were not large. Now the market has learnt its lesson; and a search for cover high enough to compensate for the lowness of the yield is not likely to be found. Shares have come to be priced more on earnings, especially on maintainable earnings, and the cheap earnings bargains available in the early fifties can no longer be found. For success one has to find growing earning power, and this is a matter of judgement or intuition. The successful investor gains not as in former times by seeing what the market could see but does not, but by guessing right what the market will see when it rounds the next corner or climbs to the top of the hill.

If this analysis is correct, what courses are open to the independent investor? The easiest is to follow the advice of his broker, but his success depends on his choosing a broker not necessarily who found winners in the last bull market but who is going to find winners in the next. The second method is to back his own judgements and intuitions, taking care to check by charts whether the actual performance justifies the faith put in the share. If performance fails, the judgement or intuition and the share must be rejected. The third method is to study the charts carefully, pick out the good performers which appear and then look for the judgements or intuitions which are moving the share. The difficulty here is that the facts seldom appear in the early stages of a rise and the rise has generally gone too far for the man who waits for the data that ultimately confirm the wisdom of the early buyers.

You can check what your broker says by looking at the charts of the shares he recommends. This is likely to be a more successful tactic than listening to what your broker says if you ask him about shares whose charts have suddenly turned good. It stands to reason that when a company is turning round this appears plain to new converts to the share while the conventional wisdom may stick to old attitudes and condemn on its past performance a share which other brokers are buying for its future. If you see a share which appears to be behaving in a promising way you should check with your broker, if he has the knowledge and the time, whether the promising behaviour comes from the buying of one or two brokers or is instigated by a tip in a journal or newspaper. A broker is likely to be buying quantities of a share because he thinks it is good for his clients, and his reputation depends heavily on the wisdom of his choice. When a share is recommended by a newspaper, you should ask yourself who told the newspaper about it and why. Sometimes financial journalists are following up good performances and most valuable information is then printed, but the broker who has ferreted out a promising situation is not likely to talk about it to financial journalists till he has bought for his clients all the shares that he thinks they want.

The great advantage of using charts is that you base your judgements on what you see. Investors do the truth to the best of their ability and you see in charts what investors are doing; their purposes in what they say and write may be far divorced from truth. What they say and what they write is meant to influence their hearers and readers; what they do is meant to profit themselves. So when you are looking for shares to buy, eyes must be open, ears are better kept closed. What songs the sirens sang may have been a difficult question (though he thought not too difficult) in the days of Sir Thomas Browne; had he lived another forty years through the South Seas Bubble he would have known that the sirens were financial journalists.

CHAPTER TEN

Why Price Charts
help in Forecasting

It is probably true that the majority of investors in Britain and a minority
in America believe that a price chart, whether it records the movement of
a share or that of a market average, is nothing more than a historical
record. They say, "That's the past; what I want to know is the future."
They are probably unwise in despising the past from which it is usually
possible to draw useful lessons, but the point on which we disagree most
strongly is that the chart is only a historical record. It deals not only with
the past but with the present; in addition to providing a historical record
it offers a current commentary as well.

The value of a current commentary depends on two factors, the authority
of the commentators and the audience's ability to understand the language
in which the commentary is spoken. The points that we have to make are
that the chart speaks with authority, and that it speaks in a language which
we can learn to understand. In its best form the chart records business
which has actually been transacted, a bargain marked at such and such a
price in the Stock Exchange Official List. In some cases it may be necessary
to plot quotations, the prices at which or near which a bargain could have
been done. Where active securities are concerned the difference between
quotation and actual bargain is generally small; with inactive stocks it
may be large and there the authority of the chart is admittedly much less.
All bargains originate from changes of mind; either an investor who holds
a stock decides that he wants money in its stead or an investor who holds
money decides that he wants a stock in its place. Each stock has its own
crowd, which consists of the investors who hold it and of those who have
the resources necessary and may have the desire to buy it. The crowd of a
share like Imperial Chemical is large; the holders number round 575,000
and almost all those with investible funds have heard of the stock and may

give it consideration when they feel that an investment should be made. At the other extreme we may take a small company whose headquarters were near Cambridge, Pest Control (since absorbed by Fisons). The ordinary capital amounted to £550,000, or 2,200,000 5/- shares. The number of ordinary shareholders probably did not exceed a thousand or so. What about the other side of the crowd, the people who might have bought the shares? They comprised the suppliers, mainly of chemical and engineering materials, the staff (entomologists, plant pathologists and economic botanists sometimes have money to invest), and the customers, who were farmers, growers, plantation companies, and growers' associations. To these we must add their friends and acquaintances with resources available for investment. Advice from this side of the crowd may provoke direct investments, or it may filter indirectly into a broker's office or the financial column of a newspaper and thus bring new recruits to the crowd. Obviously the crowd here was of no great size; equally obviously, where a share does not develop an excessive popularity, the crowd is likely to be in many ways well informed. If the supply of materials to such a company is increasing or diminishing, if the use of its goods or services is expanding or contracting, these changes come to the notice of members of the crowd and are likely to cause holders to sell or to refrain from selling and other investors to buy or refrain from buying.

At any time the sales of those who have got to sell influence the price; they may not be related in any way to the prosperity of the company. They may be dictated by outside circumstances, but it is a matter of great importance to investors whether the number of those who must sell is larger than usual or smaller, whether it is increasing or diminishing. Such factors do alter the shapes of charts and represent comment by uninformed opinion; yet it is comment of value. In a single stock it may be most misleading; the liquidation of a big line of shares might depress a stock while its company was expanding its profits. Prices may be depressed and raised by factors that are relevant or irrelevant to the profits; for example the Great Plague of 1665 is likely to have killed some holders of East India stock and forced their executors to realise while it drove potential buyers out of London. As the plague continued for some time and the factor probably persisted, we may suggest that in this half-imaginary example uninformed opinion supplied authoritative comment. While uninformed opinion is sometimes of value, it is more important that changes in the circumstances of a company are likely to be detected by members of its crowd who act on their observations and buy or sell in accordance with them. But we may consider the whole question from another angle. Let us look at the market for fixed interest securities, the gilt edged market in its broadest sense and the debentures and preference shares that are generally looked on as being almost free from risk. Here opinion may be well informed, badly informed or uninformed, but if the supply of investible savings destined for fixed interest stocks is less than the offerings of stock, old and new, the prices at which the stocks are offered must fall or the volume of offerings contract or the supply of savings increase. The fall in price may tend to reduce the offering of stock and increase the supply of savings destined for this field of investment, but the fall is likely to continue until supply and demand are brought into balance. The chart records this progress towards equilibrium together with all the oscillations of opinion that occur while it is going on. It may record false and temporary equilibria and unjustified movements in the wrong direction—there may be justified movement in the wrong direction. The chart should be a record of bargains done, and it is the flow of bargains that influence the price and it is the effect on the price of the flow of bargains with which we are concerned. The chart records what people are doing, and that may be the same as or quite different from what they are saying.

We hope that we have now settled the question and established the chart as a current commentary in addition to being a historical record. The chart speaks with authority, but does it speak in a language which we can understand? There are really only three things that the chart can say, and there are three tones in which it can say them. The first is 'More buyers than sellers', the second 'More sellers than buyers' and the third 'Buyers and sellers in balance'. In short, the chart must record movement up or down or sideways. We have already discussed the three different sorts of movement, primary, secondary and tertiary; these are the three tones in which it can speak. It speaks in all three at once, but the clear and certain tertiary tone is often loud enough to drown the less certain secondary, and when the secondary is certain it may blot out the dubious primary. When the chart speaks it tells us most clearly what we least want to hear and least clearly what we most want to hear. But despite the obscurity of its articulation and the limitation of its vocabulary, speak it does, and its messages are of value to those who can understand.

In Chapter Three we discussed the nature of the price movement and the classification of individual tertiary movements, the compounds of tertiaries which are secondary movements, and the compounds of secondaries which are primary movements. Tertiary movements count their duration in days or weeks, secondaries in weeks or months, but primaries persist for months or years. During the first half of this century there have been three primary rises of ordinary shares of less than two years, those of 1904–06, 1909–11 and 1949–51. Since 1951 the primary rise at the end of the fifties clearly started in February 1958, but when did it end? If you choose the secondary top that immediately succeeded the peak of Activity, the end was at the beginning of January 1960 and this was a primary rise of less than two years. There is a strong case for putting the end of the primary rise from June 1962 in January 1964; even if you extend it into the autumn this rise overran the two year span by only a small margin. And the great rise which began in November 1966 made its first top in September 1968 and its second in January 1969; it again exceeded the two year period, if at all, by only a small margin. All these short primary rises occurred in periods in which the rate of interest was rising. The long bull markets, with one exception, at least began in periods in which the rate of interest was falling, the primary rise that terminated in 1900, and the rises that ran from 1921 to 1929, from 1932 to 1936 and from 1940 to 1947. There remains the one exception, the rise from 1952 to 1955 (and in that case Consols $2\frac{1}{2}\%$ turned up in June 1952 and down as late as November 1954). Readers of this book, if there are any, in the next long decline of interest rates, may do well to remember that it studies mainly a period in which interest rates were rising. The declines that lasted less than two years were those of 1920–21 and 1951–52; at the time of writing the duration of the decline that started in 1969 has not yet been determined. Despite these shorter primary trends it is fair to say that in all recent experience the primary trend, once it is established, is a comparatively long trend which persists for a long time. We have already mentioned the peculiar structure of the bear markets of 1960–62 and 1964–66, and as this chapter is being written the bear market that sprang from the double top of 1968–69 is pursuing a decline of ferocity unexampled since 1929–30.

The main purpose of reading charts must be to decide what is the direction of the primary trend and to determine, as early as possible, if it has changed. The investor who determines, early enough, that the primary trend has changed can then make dispositions of his investments which should, for the duration of the new primary trend, be much more profitable than the old. We have discussed in Chapter Eight how these primary changes may be detected. The reader of charts bases his forecasting on his knowledge of the habits of trends. Trends go on till they stop. Tertiary trends are likely to stop today or tomorrow in most cases. Secondary trends are likely to stop this week or next. But primary trends go on and are likely to go on still further. The speculator never (well, hardly ever) can find out in time that the tertiary trend is changing. The short-term investor may be a little luckier with the secondary trend. But the longer-term investor who is interested in the primary trend can decide one day that his trend changed some weeks or months ago and still be in time to operate profitably on his decision.

The primary reversal is characteristically slow. We have already seen how ordinary share prices are controlled by three component factors: fixed interest prices, dividend, and Confidence, and that the peaks and troughs of these components are not synchronised. Your primary reversal seldom happens all at once. Usually the fixed interest component leads, and up to the second war dividend generally lagged. In 1921 Consols had turned up eleven months before ordinary shares. In 1928–29 ordinary shares made a broad top of twelve months duration. The bottom of 1931–32 was a broader version of 1921; the main decline terminated in May 1931, Consols began to rise at the beginning of 1932, but there was a subsidiary extension of the ordinary share decline to a new low level in June 1932 (dividend went on falling nearly to the end of 1933). The next peak, the double top of November 1936 and January 1937, was perhaps the swiftest and most deceptive of the reversals before 1952. The top was very narrow, a matter of no more than three months. The peak of Consols had been reached two years earlier, and the significance of the downturn of Consols in January 1937 when ordinary shares were rising for the second time to their boom peak could too easily escape the observer's notice. But the nature of the movement should have been obvious, in a month or two, from the downtrend of Consols and the failure of a compensating rise of Confidence to develop, and also from the decline of Activity. It might not have been possible to determine the reversal in January or February 1937, but the fact of reversal could have been determined in time. March or April or May would have been in time. In 1939–40 we have the familiar phenomenon of the upturn of Consols preceding the final collapse of ordinary shares. In 1947 there is a comparatively broad top from January to June; by June it should have been obvious that Consols had reached their peak in the previous November. In 1949 the ordinary shares indices made two low points, one in June and one five months later in November; it was somewhat misleading that Consols made their low point after the second bottom of ordinary shares. But here again there was plenty of time. Again in 1951 there was plenty of time at the top; we had high levels in May and June and again in September and October. Primary reversal is often slow, and in most of the cases where it has been fast it has not come without adequate warning (the summer reversal of 1952 was exceptionally difficult).

What are the most reliable charts? The fashion has changed since the first edition when choice fell on 'broad market averages', like the *Financial Times* fixed interest stock index (20 stocks representative of the gilt edged market and the leading industrial debentures and preferences), and the *Financial Times* industrial ordinary share index (30 leading industrials). Computers have made these indices now look much less broad, in comparison with those based on hundreds or even thousands of shares which are now fashionable. The F.T. Actuaries series runs two broad market indices of about 500 and 600 shares, and in America there are two indices available covering all the common stocks listed on the New York Stock Exchange. One of these last is an unweighted geometric mean, the same method of construction as the *Financial Times*. This is a strange swing of fashion. The *Financial Times* indices were set up in 1935, the Indicator Digest Average (IDA) in the middle sixties. In between the fashion was for weighted arithmetic means, not of prices but of price relatives; that is to say you started all the shares off at 100, weighted them for market capitalisation, and adjusted the numbers from day to day by their percentage changes of price. Averages of this sort are meant to simulate the changes in value of all the equity shares quoted in any given market, and this is a job which they no doubt do excellently. Yet we have turned away from these excellent and fashionable indices back to the primitive and comical *Financial Times* industrial ordinary share index because it is unweighted. Issues worth five million pounds count for just as much as issues worth hundreds of million pounds. The index may be representative of leading industrials; it is almost certainly not representative of the market as a whole which comprises thousands of issues which are not leading industrials (hence the need to check its performance against the Advance/ Decline Line). But while these disabilities should make the index unsuitable for use by politicians, or by statisticians who want to measure the movement of the market, they do nothing to vitiate its merits for the purposes of forecasting. The constitution of the index at July 1970 appears on the next page.

An index of this sort has a crowd, just as each single share has a crowd, but in this case the crowd must be of startling dimensions. Imperial Chemical accounts, we guess, for about one quarter of our share investors. Many of the other shares in the table are of substantial, if not of that gigantic, size. When Hargreaves Parkinson examined the registers over twenty years ago the total number of shareholdings (not shareholders) in his somewhat different list of 30 companies was 819,577. If we make a reasonable allowance for some names appearing on several registers we may hazard a guess that the investors who hold these shares number between a third and a half of all the British share investors. Further we may reckon that a large number of the remainder must be included in the crowd too, on the other side of the fence among those who might wish to buy the shares. When journalists observe a rise in the *Financial Times* industrial ordinary share index and write 'better feeling in the market' they are not often wrong (sometimes there is a different direction of movement for this index, the F.T. Actuaries and the Advance/Decline

Line). The movements of this index do represent any except the smallest changes of feeling among the investors as a whole.

The business transacted in these 30 shares over all the stock exchanges of Britain must amount to several hundred bargains a day. These bargains are the results of decisions made about shares in companies engaged in a wide variety of industries, most of the important industries of the country. Some of these decisions arise from regrettable necessities that have no direct connection with the prosperity or progress of the industry; if one business man is selling his Courtaulds to pay his son's school bills, or one widow is sacrificing her Imperial Tobacco to bridge the gap between her income and her expenditure, these are just the normal flow of necessary sales, but if an increasing number of fathers are selling their shares, or an increasing number of widows sacrificing their holdings, these are not merely a flow of necessary sales but also a commentary on the future prospects of British Leyland Motor and House of Fraser whose customers

---

Financial Times Industrial Ordinary Share Index

Allied Suppliers	Grocery wholesale and retail
Associated Portland Cement	Cement manufacturers
Beecham Group	Pharmaceuticals, toiletries, soft drinks
Boots	Manufacturing and retail pharmacists
Bowater	Pulp and paper products
British Leyland Motor	Cars and lorries
British Oxygen	Industrial gases, plastics and welding
Courtaulds	Fibres, textiles and paints
Distillers	Whisky, gin and industrial alcohol
Dunlop	Tyres and other rubber manufactures
Electric & Musical Industries	Entertainment and electronics
General Electric	Electric and electronic engineers
Glaxo	Pharmaceuticals
Guest Keen & Nettlefold	Engineers
Hawker Siddeley	Aerospace and electrical engineers
A. Herbert	Machine tools
Imperial Chemical Industries	Chemicals and metals, fibres and fertilisers, petro-chemicals, paints
Imperial Tobacco	Tobacco manufactures and foods
London Brick	Bricks
Marks & Spencer	Chain store
Peninsular & Oriental	Shipping
Plessey	Electronic and hydraulic engineers
Spillers	Flour millers
Tate & Lyle	Sugar refiners
Tube Investments	Engineers
Turner & Newall	Asbestos, insulation and plastics
United Drapery	Multiple stores and tailors
Vickers	Engineers
Watney, Mann	Brewers
F. W. Woolworth	Chain store

are losing their buying power. If investors decide to sell London Brick because they think the outlook for building is deteriorating and to buy Electrical & Musical Industries because they think the prospects for entertainment are improving, the rise of one offsets the decline of the other and the index number remains unchanged. But if investors think prospects are improving here and there and not deteriorating over yonder, then buying orders flow into the market and prices have to be bid up to elicit compensating sales. The index rises because people think that the outlook is better, and, if the buying is not informed buying, there are so many informed investors among the shareholders that it will provoke informed selling. The Dow Theory maxim 'The averages are always right' has much truth in it. If the position of the country is changing, the change is observed by some of the million investors who hold these shares and the other million who do not but might. The change is missed by some, but it will be observed by the large number of investors who are well placed to see it. Let us start in the City (or in Edinburgh) where the biggest investors are the insurance offices, whose directors are generally leading men of business. Take, for example, the Royal Exchange Assurance at the time when the first edition of this book was written. The Governor was chairman of Morgan Grenfell, City bankers, and a director of Associated Electrical Industries and of Yule Catto. The Sub-Governor was one of the managing directors of Lazard Bros., merchant bankers, was on the Court of the of the Bank of England, deputy chairman of British Match and a director of the Bank of London & South America and of Rolls-Royce. The Deputy Governor was again a merchant banker and on the boards of Cunard, Dunlop, Martins Bank and *The Times*. We need go no further through the list; the point is proved. There is a formidable concentration of informed opinion behind the investment decisions of the insurance offices, the merchant bankers, the industrial pension funds. There is also much informed opinion behind the investment decisions of private investors. A purchase of Alfred Herbert may be inspired by the experience of an industrialist who notes that the delivery of machine tools which he is planning to buy is lengthening, a sale of Distillers by a chemical buyer who notices that his need for industrial solvents is declining. Every day people who are in a position to have a good view of some part of the picture are making investment decisions inspired by their observations; all these decisions take the forms of orders to buy or to sell and the result each day is a change, or no change, in the level of the index. The movements of the index reflect the daily balances of some hundreds of investment decisions, decisions based on information or necessity. The market may be controlled by the information or by the necessity, but in either case it is responding to a large number of investment decisions.

On the other side of the Atlantic the Dow Jones Industrial Average seemed to serve the same purpose well enough up to the end of the fifties, although thirty common stocks are unlikely to give so wide a coverage of the American investors as the thirty British shares do here. Unfortunately during the sixties the Dow has seemed less and less representative of the general behaviour of Wall Street and it has lagged very substantially behind much broader indices like Standard & Poor. At the beginning of the sixties the *Financial Times* industrial ordinary too seemed to be suffering from this defect; but in recent years it has not diverged very substantially from the F.T. Actuaries 500 (much of the difference grows from the inclusion of heavily weighted oil shares in the 500 as these, which are not British Industrials, are rightly excluded from the *Financial Times* industrial).

The Dow has a coverage which, if not very wide, would be wide enough, were it not for the fact that its constituents are mainly corporations that have been in existence for a very long time. The *Financial Times* industrial ordinary has been kept much more up to date. However, the Dow stocks are widely held in all the populous states of the Union and informed opinion is expressed through them on the New York Stock Exchange in much the same way as it is through thirty British shares in London.

The study of smaller groups, like Brewery shares or Composite Insurance shares presents some unexpected difficulties. In the first edition use was made of the Investment Research indices, to which reference has already been made on page 85. These consisted of groups of ten shares, or less if ten suitable shares could not be found, chosen to represent the groups which Investment Research wanted to study. This is an important point; the shares were chosen to fit into the groups and if they fitted well, in they went. There was no objection to treating Goodlass Wall (now Lead Industries) as a Housing share, because it was closely concerned with the building of houses and also as a Paint share because the company made paint and sold paint making materials to its competitors in the paint trade. So Goodlass Wall went into both groups, just as Dunlop appeared in the Rubber Manufacturing Group and also in the Motor Accessories group. The production of these indices was a commercial venture; it withstood the publication by the *Financial Times* of a panel of groups with indices based on six member companies, possibly because the Investment Research groups were planned with more precise objectives. There were, for example, three Textile groups, Cotton Textiles, Wool Textiles and Rayon. There you have three branches of one trade which come under very different market influences. Nobody who had worked in the textile trades would expect similar stock market experience from the Manchester trade, the Bradford trade and the rayon manufacturers; so three separate groups were required. Again, there was one group for Motor Manufacturers and another for Motor Accessories; important decisions were at that time to be made for the investor intending to put money in the motor industry, whether there were better prospects of profit through buying the car manufacturers like Austin or Morris or Ford, or through a purchase of Accessories shares like J. Lucas or S. Smith. In 1962 the *Financial Times* produced, with the co-operation of the Institute of Actuaries, the F.T. Actuaries series of indices. First they published in April 1962 an index for the Industrial market and an All Share index which comprised the Industrials and another hundred shares of companies engaged in financial activities, with which were included Property shares. Then in November they began the publication daily of Group and Sub-section indices, all started at 100 in April 1962. At this point Investment Research withdrew its indices and began to work on the F.T. Actuaries groups and sub-sections. These, however, are rather different animals from the Investment Research groups. Investment Research used unweighted geometric means and thus produced an instrument for comparisons in which each share counted equally. F.T. Actuaries rely on weighted arithmetic means and have thus produced an instrument for comparison in which each share counts according to the market value of the company.

If you want to measure the changes of value in certain groups, there is nothing to beat your weighted arithmetic mean except working out the actual changes in value of all the shares that your sub-section is meant to represent. But this is not at all what the investor wants. He wants to know what investors are doing, not what is happening to them. Let us suppose he is interested in Tobacco or Chemical shares. There are three Tobacco shares in the Tobacco sub-section and 19 Chemical shares in the Chemical sub-section. He is thus probably interested in chosing one or two out of 21 shares, or possibly in deciding not to choose one of them. When he looks at the F.T. Actuaries Tobacco sub-section he finds a record of the changes in value of a unit trust which holds Imperial Tobacco, Carreras and Gallaher in proportion to the market values of the respective companies in April 1962. The same objection applies to the Chemical subsection which must reflect in the main changes in the price of Imperial Chemicals which could be inertly holding the sub-section index almost steady while some of the smaller shares in the group were hurtling up or down.

If you want to use a sub-section to help in the making of investment decisions, it must be homogeneous, like Shipbuilding or Breweries (the separation from Breweries of the six Wines and Spirits shares was a great improvement) and it must contain a number of shares that are not too unequally weighted. But the whole utility of the group and sub-section idea has been weakened by the tendency towards diversification, of which the outstanding example in this context has been the removal of Reed Group, one of our two largest paper manufacturers, from the Paper & Packaging sub-section to Miscellaneous (unclassified)!

If you turn back to page 18, you will find a table showing the breakdown, into the Stock Exchange's own groups, of the Official List. Commercial & Industrial accounts for 43·5% of the total. The next largest group is Oil, covering 16·1% of the total valuation; there are 59 'lines' of the List but the F.T. Actuaries sub-section comprises only two shares, British Petroleum and Shell Transport, and those two, plus Burmah Oil and Royal Dutch, must account for more than 90% of the total value. Thus we have here a group which is homogeneous but which represents directly only two large crowds. Compare that with the Property sub-section, which represents directly twenty-seven different crowds and indirectly 367; there are 394 quoted Property shares and they comprise 1·1% of the total value of the list. The F.T. Actuaries All Share index is aimed at representing about 65% of the total value of the Stock Exchange Official List. The Oil sub-section covers about a quarter of the total index in value and is represented by only two shares, of which B.P. has at least two very large and completely idle holders, the British Government and Burmah Oil. All the other groups and sub-sections are very much smaller, and it is plain that all must speak with less authority than the 500 and the All Share. One of the possibilities which must be faced is that a sub-section can be overtaken by a fit of madness, which may be a case of exaggerated enthusiasm alone or of exaggerated enthusiasm combined with a complete misjudgement of the future. At the time of writing the 500 share index stands round 128, the Financial Group at 96. The reason for this discrepancy is the boom of 1962 in which a number of Financial sub-sections, accompanied to a lesser extent by Stores, recovered strongly from the setback of 1961 and soared into new high ground. The lowest reading for the other main groups since the F.T. Actuaries series were started is round 80; that for the Financial group is under 70. And Life Insurance, whose boom was exaggerated but not entirely unjustified, now stands at 101, while Composite Insurance, whose boom was wholly misconceived, stands at 69. So when the series were started on 10th April 1962, the Financials stood at comparatively high levels while most of the others were far down the bear market of those days.

Let us start by looking at the Merchant Banks for a period some time after the disaster of 1962. Chart No. 14 covers the period 1965–68, which includes an important part of the formation of the base for the boom of 1967–68 but none of the development of the subsequent decline. The

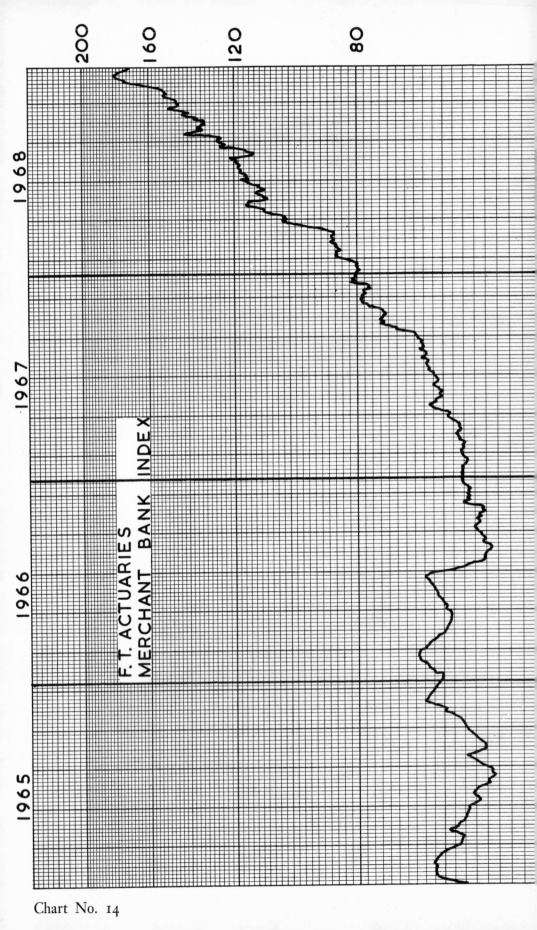

F.T. ACTUARIES
MERCHANT BANK INDEX

200

160

120

80

1968

1967

1966

1965

Chart No. 14

spring and summer of 1965 were a period of secondary decline; then came a secondary rally into the autumn, followed by several months of horizontal trading past midsummer of 1966. Then the market collapsed in July and Merchant Banks came down with the rest. But the decline was stopped in September above the bottom of 1965, a beginning of better than average performance, and no new low was made in November, further better than average performance. By this time the sub-section had worked out a substantial base, of which only the latter part appears in our illustration. The premature uptrend of September/November 1966 was continued gently and as the general primary uptrend was established these shares accelerated their climb, which continued at a better than average rate right through the first top of the market in September 1968 to a peak in December. The sequel was sad; after the second peak of the market in January, the Merchant Banks continued to run strongly and equalled their previous peak late in February. But the theory that they could run on independently of the rest of the market then received a shock. The sub-section index declined beneath the lowest point recorded between the December and February peaks and a new primary downtrend was established for these shares. Here we have a group which was wisely prophetic at the bottom and over-optimistic at the top. (Of course, by definition, all primary movements, which are right in their beginnings and their persistent middles, turn out to be wrong in their final stages). Do not be led by what we have written above to believe that a share group which forms a good base and then does better than average in the initial stages, especially by diverging upwards from the last bottom of the main index, is therefore bound for high success in the next bull market. The Composite Insurance group, with an almost identical pattern to Merchant Banks in 1965–66, fared somewhat better than average to the first quarter of 1968 and thereafter performed much worse than average to the end of the year. The Merchant Banks tripled their value over the course of the bull market, the Composite Insurances increased by only two-thirds.

If we look at Oil shares in Chart No. 15 we are considering something of a different kind. The *Financial Times* industrial ordinary includes no representative of Oil in its thirty shares; and much of the better performance of the F.T. Actuaries 500 over the old *Financial Times* index is due to the heavily weighted oil component. Our chart shows at the bottom the course of this index for the years 1963–66 and above for 1967–70 (it is not possible to show the full 1962–66 cycle because the primary rise started in June and the F.T. Actuaries groups and sub-sections are available only from November). The Oil shares carried their 1963 rise through to October 1964, with a markedly better than average performance in January–March 1964. They then fared much worse than average to May

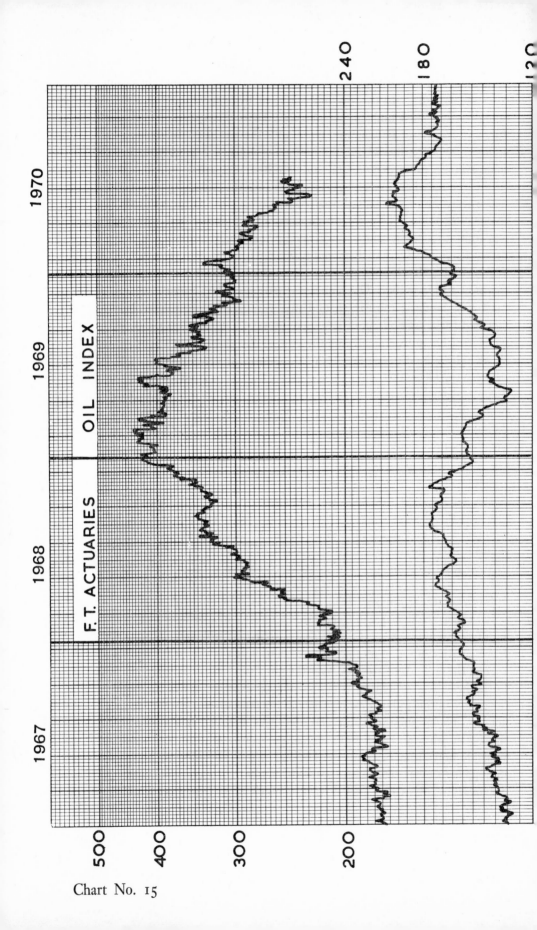

F.T. ACTUARIES   OIL   INDEX

1967   1968   1969   1970

500   400   300   200

240   180   120

Chart No. 15

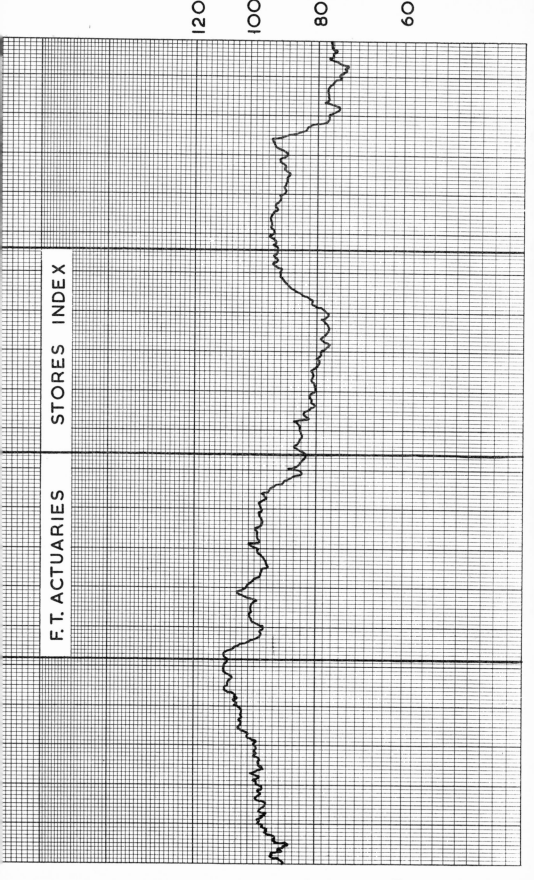

Chart No. 16

1965, failing to take any significant part in the general rally in the first months of 1965. This pessimism turned out completely wrong; the Oil index turned up in May while the rest of the market was sweeping down to a low point in the summer, and the Oils went on rising, reaching new high ground early in 1966 and continuing upwards to April. No further progress was then made for three months and after this steady period the shares fell in sympathy with the rest of the market to mid-September. Then the decline, which continued in the general market to November, stopped for Oils. But nothing came quickly from this better than average performance. For a whole year, from November 1966 to the devaluation twelve months later, Oils did worse than average; then in November 1967 they leapt ahead into a better than average phase of performance. This continued, most deceptively, to May 1969, when an upward movement, prompted by the British Petroleum discoveries in Alaska, challenged the three previous tops of 1969 and suggested that the downtrend, which had seemed to be established, ought to be reversed. The suggestion was wrong and imposed heavy penalties on the buyers who accepted it. The rise was simply a secondary rally against the main trend of a bear market.

A primary top is not usually formed by all stocks going up before the top and all coming down after; rather it consists of two or three phases in which some groups top out early, some with the main body of stocks, and others late. We can see this in the performance of the Stores group in 1963–66 (Chart No. 16). The index reached its high level in the autumn and early winter of 1963–64, a time when the market reached its peak of enthusiasm but not of price. Although the earnings of the Stores group went on rising, allowing for the interruption and drop when the Corporation Tax came into force in the summer of 1965, the price index for the sub-section declined from the beginning of 1964 to the middle of 1965. This was an early reversal; for the broad indices did not turn down till a little before the autumn Election of 1964. Nor did the group succeed in 1966 in coming near its high levels of 1963–64, although the main indices returned at that time to their best previous levels.

It is worth looking at the Tobacco sub-section index for 1967–70 (Chart No. 17). This group had done better than average in 1968 despite a sharp decline after the devaluation (the market may have remembered rather late the overseas interests of Carreras and the large shareholding of Imperial in the British-American Tobacco, which is not a member of the sub-section). It made its 1968 top rather early and declined, on a worse than average performance, to the end of October. Then it rose very strongly to a top at the end of January 1969. At the end of a bull market the buyers are flagging because shares are beginning to seem dear, and they go round the market looking for something that is still cheap. It may well be a case

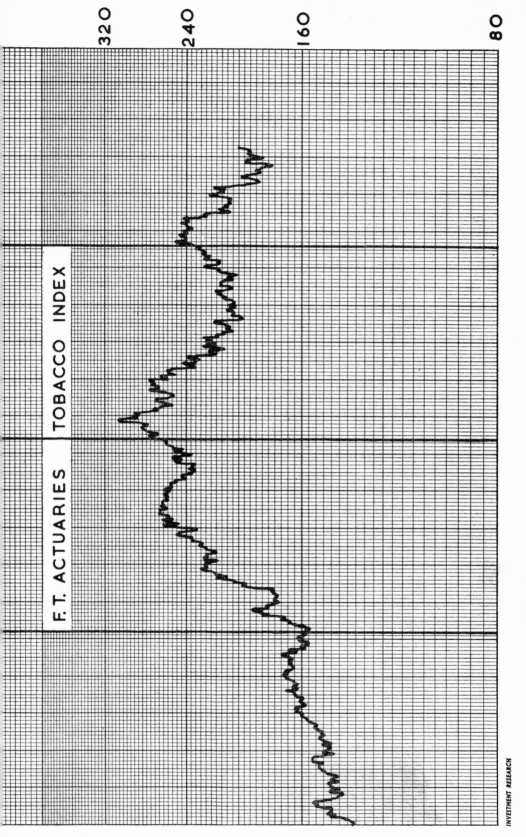

F.T. ACTUARIES   TOBACCO INDEX

Chart No. 17

INVESTMENT RESEARCH

of this symptom that we can see in the chart of the Tobacco index in January 1969; the buying immediately preceded a peak in published earnings which turned to a decline in May.

There are two important deductions to be made from this study. The first is that these group indices, with their relatively small crowds (and, in the cases of Aircraft, Tobacco and Oil, among others their relatively few crowds), are less reliable in their evidence than the indices which cover broad markets with many and large crowds. They are liable to fits of depression, for example Merchant Banks and Properties after the collapse of 1962, and to spasms of mania, like the Insurance groups in 1961–62, and Toys in 1968 (these were not plotted as a separate sub-section till January 1970). The second deduction is that the reliable evidence of the large crowds is made up of the less reliable testimonies of the small. In the large crowds the buoyancy of some groups which produce the late tops of a particular primary rise are counterbalanced by the different development of others which produce early tops. Each of the small crowds is able to see only a part of the whole; to comprehend the whole you must combine all the testimonies which cancel out much of the error and leave behind much of the truth.

Just as the broad average excels the narrow, so does the narrow excel the single share. The individual share generally, but not always, has a smaller crowd than a group. Of course there are a number of companies whose capitalisation exceeds that of many small markets. There can be hundreds of thousands of holders on a register; shares such as Distillers, British American Tobacco, Imperial Tobacco, Imperial Chemical, Shell Transport and Woolworth, among others, have really large crowds. (Large capitalisation need not imply a large, much less an influential, crowd; round the end of 1968 the market capitalisation of Lesney Products exceeded £100mn.). On the other hand a very large number of shares will have crowds of only a thousand or so.

The movements of individual shares are more erratic than those of group averages. Their crowds see a comparatively small part of the whole picture and fall much more easily into error. They attribute a high importance to factors which will carry little weight and they ignore other factors which will turn out to be of the highest importance.

With individual shares we must consider also the question of manipulation. This term covers a wide range of activity. If Mr. Brown becomes possessed of the idea that Jones & Robinson Ltd. are going to double their dividend and he goes about the country telling his acquaintances this out of the goodness of his heart, he is likely to influence the price of the share without any intention of doing so. But his activities are just as much manipulation as those of the philanthropist who, after laying in a stock of a certain share, sent anonymous circulars to likely investors advising them that he wished them well and could assure them that this share was shortly going to enjoy a useful rise. Enough of them bought to ensure the useful rise; and the philanthropist took a useful profit. Then there may be cases where a large holder wishes to dispose of his shares and finds that it is much easier to sell them if the market in the share is active; he therefore conducts his dealings in such a way that the market always is active until his holding has gone. Then the activity disappears and the price may collapse. Manipulation, in short, may be involuntary, it may be deliberate, it may be criminal. Recommendations in the press and in brokers' circulars lead to abnormal buying of individual shares and thus to manipulation of the price. The share of small capital is liable to manipulation; the group and the share of large capital is much less liable. The market as a whole out-weighs any normal manipulation, but the market may meet abnormal manipulation from the Bank of England or the Treasury. (One school of thought attributes enormous influence on the price indices to the money supply, which is of course manipulated by the Bank of England). The biggest manipulation of all was seen after the second war. The rise of Consols—and with Consols of almost everything else—from the third quarter of 1945 to the last quarter of 1946 was manipulated by the Treasury. An excursion of this kind may not recur in our lifetime, but changes of the Bank Rate and the operation of an open market policy by the Bank of England are perfectly legitimate transactions. Manipulation of this sort must be allowed for, but its scale is not likely to be very large nor its persistence very long. There are limits to the market powers even of the Treasury. Consols stopped rising in November 1946 but the manipulation went on with less and less effect until a new Chancellor came to the Exchequer and the policy was abandoned.

When we look at the behaviour of a really broad market average, we can estimate what a really large number of investors are doing and can trust that the sum of their transactions represents, more or less closely, what is right. When we look at a narrow market average, we can estimate what a much smaller number of investors are doing but we can have much less trust that they are right. When we look at the course of an individual share, we can estimate what is being done by its particular crowd, but we must reckon that this crowd can be as easily possessed of error as of the truth and must attach a correspondingly smaller weight to the evidence given by the single share.

CHAPTER ELEVEN

Activity Charts

Changes in the relationship between supply and demand are revealed in the fluctuations of price curves; a rise in price reflects an improvement of demand over supply, a decline in price a deterioration of demand against supply. What is shown by fluctuations in the Activity curve? These cannot be changes in the relationship between supply and demand because every bargain represents a sale to a buyer just as much as a purchase from a seller. Bargains reflect both supply and demand, and we must treat fluctuations of the Activity curve as representing fluctuations in something we must call supply-and-demand. In general we must expect activity to be high when prices are high. Prices are high because the demand for stock is strong, and there is a large supply because prices are high. It is generally admitted that the higher prices go, the more holders are willing to sell. It is very often true that the higher prices go, the more people are willing to buy. Rising prices attract attention to the stocks that are rising and thus increase their crowds. If prices are rising over a large sector of the Stock Exchange, public interest in investment increases. Investors who have not bought or sold a share for years get in touch with a broker; investors who have always bought property or put money in building societies think that this £100 might try its luck on the Stock Exchange.

While we talk of Activity in London, where our statistics are based on the numbers of bargains marked (a bargain in £10 War Loan counts equally with one in £100,000), in New York they talk of volume and their statistics are based on the number of shares traded (100 American Power & Light at 2½ count as much as 100 American Telephone at 159). The American statistics are more impressive because the marking of bargains in London is optional while the recording of every trade on Wall Street is obligatory. It is from New York that we derive the folk-lore of volume, and the best thing that we can do is to study a period of trading on Wall Street to see how prices and volume fared together.

But before we proceed to examine an actual piece of the market, we must record something of the great changes in its structure that have happened in the past twenty years. (Similar changes have altered the character of important sectors of the London market, but the prevalence of the small company in London's Commercial & Industrial sector has left the character of this major sector comparatively unaltered, although in other sectors the changes in character are very strongly marked). The Wall Street market of 1929 was still the market that Bernard Baruch knew at the beginning of the century, although the small private investor had moved into it on quite a large scale. In the thirties the Securities & Exchanges Commission worked hard to clean the market up and eliminate abuses, and the old buccaneering type of tycoon largely disappeared. The post-war market of the late forties was very much like the market of the thirties with the Dow Jones Industrial Average and the general level of volume below those of 1929, in the case of volume very far below 1929. Volume expanded in the sixties but the appearance of frequent eight figure volumes has been quite recent (and the return to seven figure levels may be a new and important symptom of changes in market conditions). The great feature of the sixties has been the expansion of large-scale institutional dealing and the working out of techniques by which very large lines of stock, worth many millions, could be quickly acquired if a large institution wanted to buy a block or sold if one wanted to sell. The large institutions were increased in number as the big mutual funds (in English, Unit Trusts) grew in size and became more active and aggressive in their dealing. But one must not think of Wall Street as being entirely dominated by eager young mutual fund managers bent on performance; New York has its insurance offices and pension funds just like London except that they are more and bigger. But through the sixties the cult of performance grew and with it the activity of the market. The small investor, as in London, tended to abdicate his judgement and buy mutual funds; 'odd lot' activity took a smaller and smaller proportion of the daily turnover.

It seems best to consider as large and as recent a chunk of Wall Street history as we reasonably can; so we have prepared a Chart No. 18 to cover in rough detail the whole of the sixties. The basis for price is the Daily Close of the Dow Jones Industrial Average; the daily fluctuations are naturally much compressed by the reduction necessary to bring the original drawing down to a scale that will fit our page. For volume we have taken the daily averages week by week; but the volatility of volume is high and to make the chart easier to read it has been plotted with a damping down proportionate to a square root reduction.

There appear to be four market cycles on the chart. Wall Street turned up in the autumn of 1957 and what we see on our chart in 1960 is its entry into the 'soaring sixties' which appear to have begun with a bear market that ended in October (it is possible but less plausible than in Britain, to

Chart No. 18

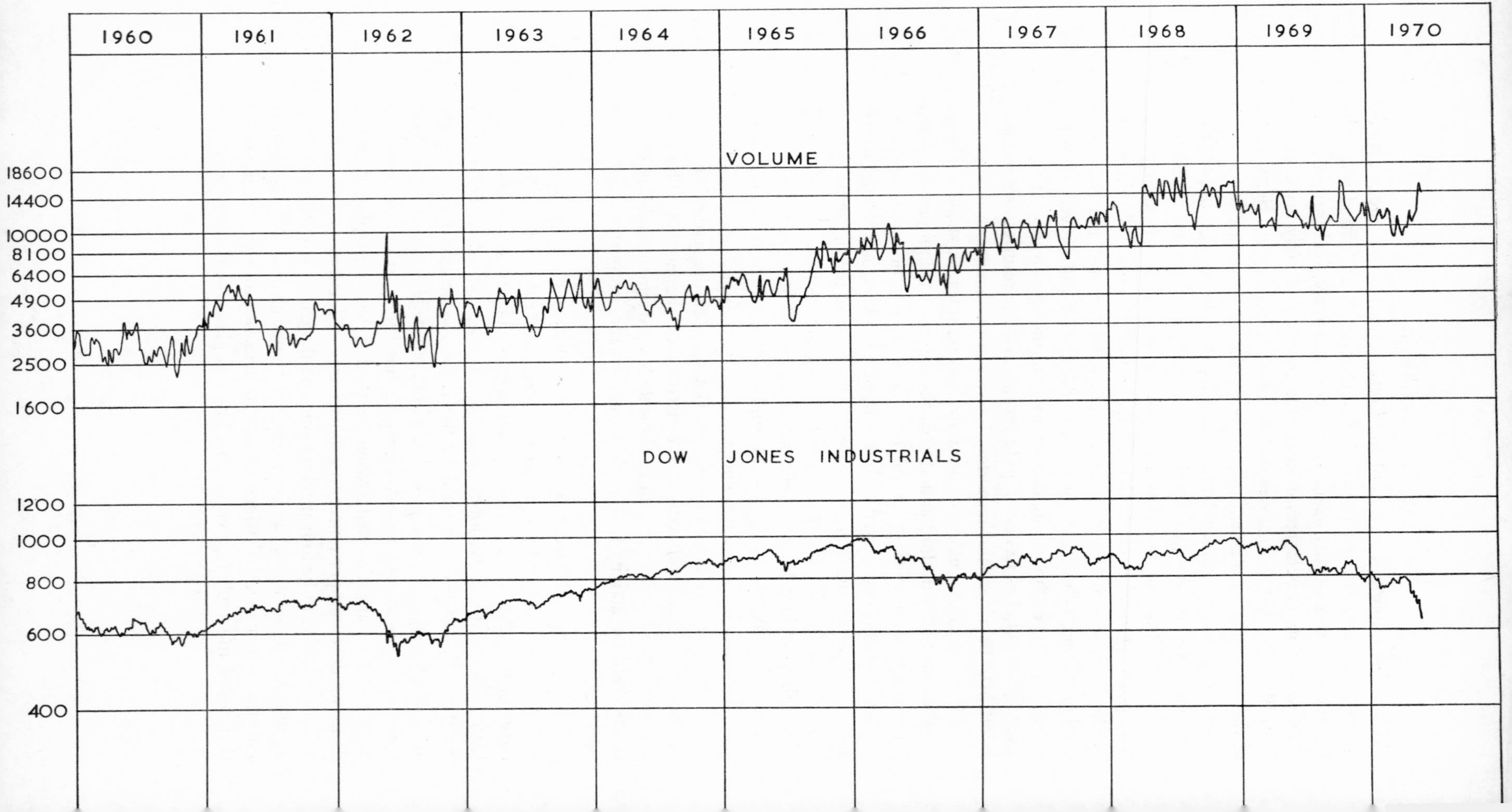

1960	1961	1962	1963	1964	1965	1966	1967	1968	1969	1970

VOLUME

DOW JONES INDUSTRIALS

18600
14400
10000
8100
6400
4900
3600
2500

1600

1200

1000

800

600

400

argue that 1960 gave us merely a technical reaction and that the cycle started in 1957 was not completed till 1962). Next we have a second short market cycle, from October 1960 to June 1962. The third cycle lasted longer, from June 1962 to October 1966, and the fourth, again a longer cycle, from October 1966 into 1970 or beyond. As these words are being written in May 1970 just after our markets have reversed their steepest decline for years, it is interesting to note that in 1960, 1962 and 1966, the peak of volume at the end of the decline was small in 1960, very large in 1962 and modest in 1966 and on each occasion accompanied the rally from the penultimate bottom. Volume for the last week of May 1970 enormously exceeded that for the top week of June 1962, but the June 1962 week carried a volume bigger by an enormous margin than any week in the preceding bull market (or in the records kept by Investment Research since 1945) but the May 1970 biggest week was a little less than the biggest of the summer of 1968.

Volume bottomed out for the 1960 bear market in the week ended October 14th and the lowest point for the Dow Industrial was reached in the next fortnight. Volume then climbed from a 2½mn. share daily average to between 5mn. and 6mn. in March and April 1961. That, for some time to come, was the peak of volume; prices advanced into late summer, reacted mildly, went ahead a little in the autumn accompanied by a strong recovery of volume that fell well short of the peak earlier in the year. Prices reacted slightly in January 1962, then rose and failed to reach the previous peak; and this failure was accompanied by a marked decline of volume. The market then went into a steep decline which was to carry the Dow Jones Industrial Average well below its worst levels of 1960. There was a very steep drop in the last week of May accompanied by a rise of volume that gave the week a 10mn. day average; this stands out like the Eiffel Tower in the first half of the chart. The rally that followed did not last long and the low point was reached, on steeply declining volume, in the last week of June. The decline of volume, partly seasonal, continued to the second week of October; and later in the month the Dow, which was declining in a secondary reaction, turned up into a major phase of accumulation. (The London market generally shows a well-marked seasonal decline at Christmas but this does not appear in New York. New York's slack season normally lies between Independence Day on July 4th and Labor Day on the first Monday in September, though it may stray beyond these limits—London's summer slack season is also mobile). Up to the summer of 1965 volume generally ranged between 3mn. shares and 6½mn. but in the autumn of 1965 it moved up to the 6½mn. to 10mn. range. The peak was reached in the week of April 15th 1966 although the Dow had topped out in February. Volume dropped to a 5mn. to 8mn.

range with a move up towards 8½mn. for the rally from the penultimate bottom. The bottom of volume came in the third week of September with days round 5mn. shares; and the Dow Industrial turned up in the first week of October. Volume then resumed its upward trend with more and more 10mn. share days through 1967. The peak of volume came at the end of July 1968 at a level close to 18mn. shares a day; the Dow Average was bottoming out from a mild secondary reaction and moving into its final climb to the end November peak. (This was the top of the market, but the Dow had become so laggard that it fell significantly short of the previous top in the first quarter of 1966, a landmark that the newer indices had left far behind).

What can we get out of this? Volume sometimes tops out well in advance of stock prices, but it did not do this in 1966. It runs up to a comparatively high level on the rally from the penultimate bottom, but this high level was not very easy to notice in 1960; however that was a very gentle decline. It generally falls to a very low level after its high performance on the rally from the penultimate bottom[1], and its upturn from that low level sometimes precedes the upturn of stocks, but not in a way that is in the least helpful. High volume no longer comes, as it did in 1946, after the breaking of a Dow Theory vital level; in 1946 volume showed what the public were doing as they were the largest factor in the market (the American investing public included some pretty large investors) but the market has become a mainly institutional market, dominated since 1966 by the pursuit of performance. It is now being more thoroughly understood that the achievement of performance in one year may be the prelude to disaster in the next, that American mutual funds are going to aim at appreciation over a much longer term and that their change of mind will be reflected in a very much reduced turnover.

Our conclusion must be that volume on Wall Street is not a very sound prophet, which is exactly the same conclusion as in the first edition where we studied the market of 1946–49. Perhaps we should be thankful that the Council of the Stock Exchange will not substitute accurate and clear volume statistics for its unscientific record of bargains marked; the markings in what the *Financial Times* calls the 'industrial' sections seem so much more helpful to the technical analyst than Wall Street's volume.

Before we turn back to the London market we must recall that the characters of the two Stock Exchanges are very different. Wall Street specialises in the common stocks of mighty companies with large numbers of shares issued. The shares are traded between broker and broker,

---

[1] In 1970 the peak of volume appeared on the rise from the bottom, or at least the bottom for 1970.

usually through the medium of a specialist who charges a small brokerage for his services (this brokerage is so small that it is absorbed by the commission broker and not passed on to his customer). Let us imagine a case. The share is priced about $50. It is not at the moment changing hands at 50; but the specialist has orders on his book to buy at 50 and to sell at 50⅛ and so he can meet the needs of any broker who comes to his post to deal in a normal amount of the stock; big blocks in New York are handled in a different manner. Of course, this ideal picture does not always apply. When stocks are moving fast, as in the decline of May 1970, the margin between bid and offered prices widens. The stock may be 48–50⅛ and a broker may come in with an order to sell at best. He may sell 200 shares at 48 and be left with 100 to sell; if the next highest bid is 46, the stock is now 46–48, unless the selling broker decides to take 46 for the balance of his stock (and, if his order is to sell at best, that is what he must do). Thus the specialist is not a principal (except in some special cases) like the jobber in London; he is a part of a trading machine whose purpose is to find sellers for buyers and buyers for sellers. The price of any stock is dictated directly by the investors who are willing to deal in that stock. If the investor wants to sell 1,000 shares of a stock, provided that there are bids on the specialist's book for 1,000 shares, there is nothing to prevent him from selling. Those bids may be 100 at 50, 200 at 48, 200 at 45½, 300 at 43 and 200 at 41. If his broker reports 100 at 50 and says there are 200 at 48 and the customer refuses to sell, another seller may come and there may now be 200 at 45½. This is a system in which prices can move swiftly, and the brake which exists in our jobbing system does not exist in New York. Nevertheless, the decline of the Dow Jones Average in 1946 was smaller than the decline of the *Financial Times* industrial ordinary in 1947. Wall Street may, over very short periods, show steeper falls than London, but a comparison of the post-war records will suggest that London is the more treacherous and speculative market, that London falls farther and faster while New York excels on the quiet and long rise.

The Stock Exchange is far more catholic than Wall Street. Issues are given quotations whether they are large or small. Our big companies are not so big nor so numerous; International Nickel, which is a giant company in London, is comparatively small on Wall Street. Wall Street trades in fewer stocks but they have larger numbers of shares in issue. London trades in more stocks and their share issues are of all sizes. Further, the London jobber, unlike the New York specialist, is a principal. He is expected to deal in a reasonable number of shares with any broker who wishes; and his part is to quote a double price, for buying and selling, without knowing what the broker's intentions are. Naturally, when markets are difficult, he widens his price in order to reduce his risk. If widening his price does not serve his purpose, he may quote the stock 'buyers only' or 'sellers only'. This slows down the movement and inhibits turnover. It is said to protect the investor in panics and prevent him from selling his stock at false prices, but it must often happen that the false price of today is the real price of tomorrow when the sale is actually made.

These two differences between London and New York, the existence of the jobbing system and the much greater prevalence of the small issue, predicate for London a different character from New York. In New York heavy pressure to sell can bring an increase of volume, sometimes on a very large scale, but in London pressure to sell almost always causes a contraction of Activity and never an upsurge of Activity to record heights. This may not be true of the gilt edged market, where single issues of stock run into hundreds or thousands of millions of value. It is certainly true of the industrial market. Here in certain stages of the 1947–49 decline there were bursts of selling pressure accompanied by marked rises of Activity. But these rises of Activity soared not to record heights, only to current high levels at a time when the highest levels were already far below the earlier peaks. (There was a strange development in 1969; at the beginning of the year Activity began to rise as prices fell but then prices turned round and Activity continued to rise till both equalled the previous best levels of 1968).

There were some interesting performances in the rubber market in the late forties and early fifties. This may be of interest because the rubber market is a field in which the small investor, certainly at that time, was important, but the institutions were not. The numbers of shares in issue were at that time for most companies extremely small, and you would think that there was little room for this phenomenon of rising Activity accompanying falling prices. In the 1947–49 decline there is one occurrence in February 1948, when rising Activity through a six-week line continued its rise into the collapse that followed the line (at the same time the phenomenon was occurring in vigorous style in the industrial market). There is a better specimen in October and November 1951 and a quite remarkable expansion of Activity during the steep decline of February 1952. In short, it is possible in many markets for Activity to rise as prices decline, but in no case among shares that has come to our notice has there been an upsurge of Activity on selling that lifted Activity curves to their highest levels for the previous rise of prices. The position in gilt edged is different; there you may get peaks of Activity on a selling climax.

In the gilt edged market you have not only very large issues of stock but also very large differences of opinion. There may be one hundred marks in War Loan where ninety-nine are sales (or purchases) by private investors and one is the compensating purchase (or sale) by an insurance company or the Government Broker. The institutions and the general public approach the gilt edged market in very different frames of mind, and the occasion that frightens the small man out may be the chance, for which the institution has been waiting, to invest some money at so much per cent. Here the difference of opinion between two classes of investors allows a very large Activity to develop as prices fall. Something of the same sort may have occurred in the industrial market at the beginning of 1948. There had been a steep rise as holders of Home Rails bought leading industrials (mainly in the second half of December for settlement early in January) against the Transport stock that they meant to sell for cash at the beginning of January. It is probable that jobbers sold stock short; certainly the prices were marked down immediately after the New Year when this particular demand ceased. Then for five weeks Activity expanded and prices held steady. The sellers at this stage were investors who believed the 1947 decline was by no means finished. They pressed their sales while more hopeful investors bought and while jobbers replenished their books, but early in February the market was saturated with stock and a trifling incident in Paris precipitated a collapse, in which Activity at first grew and then rapidly shrank (see Chart No. 10).

There is a difference between the broad and loose markets like gilt edged, where a small number of issues covers a vast capital value, and where different sorts of investors approach the market with very different attitudes of mind, and other tight and narrow markets. The industrial market is in part broad and loose, where dealings take place in issues with a market capitalisation of fifty to five hundred millions, but in part it is a narrow and tight market full of issues worth half a million to five million. One cannot fruitfully study the brewery market; far the largest issue here is Distillers whose business has little relevance to questions of brewery investment. On the other hand one can learn something from the fluctuations of activity in the Kaffir market. Although the basic figures, the bargains marked in the 'South African Mines' sector, are not fully valid, the dilution probably does not generally produce large distortion. The foreign elements are of two sorts, the shares in mining companies engaged on metals other than gold (copper in the case of Messina, antimony from Consolidated Murchison and platinum from Potgietersrust and others) and the mining finance companies. The companies mining metals other than gold are comparatively small; the finance companies are large. All of them are striving to extend their operations outside gold mining; all are still heavily involved in gold and appeal to investors who seek an involvement in gold. Many of the mines and holding companies are heavily capitalised (the table on page 18 shows that there are 127 lines of stock quoted in London with an average market value of £24mn.). Here, you might think, there is a broad and loose market, but in fact you have a market which seems broad enough but, while it may be loose one week, when interest in Kaffirs is high, it can be horribly tight the next week if interest in Kaffirs has faded. There are such sudden fluctuations of interest, and in recent years the market has been notable more for its long periods of little interest rather than for the shorter spaces of time in which dealing was free and active. In this market interest grows and Activity expands; interest shrinks and Activity contracts. The differences of opinion are not strong enough for there to be room in the market for any expansion of Activity when prices are falling; the fall in prices and the contraction of Activity are so closely linked that it is hard to imagine circumstances in which urgent sellers could find the buyers to push the Activity curve up in a falling market. So what the Activity curve gives you is some idea of how many sellers can be found at high prices to accommodate the buyers, how many buyers can be found when prices are low to accommodate the sellers. Thus low points for price accompanied by rising bottoms of Activity, as in the 1950 industrial market, would be hopeful symptoms, but high levels of Activity imply, much more than in industrial markets, that a level of price has been reached at which there is a fairly free supply. In a strong Kaffir market Activity must be high at the level at which the finance houses feel it is right to supply stock freely. The investor in London is used to dealing in markets where the powerful institutions are mainly buyers; they are accumulating stock over the long term and find it difficult to acquire and thus make at least one of their problems more acute if they indulge in selling, even at market tops! When the London investor is tempted into the Kaffir market, he has entered a field where the powerful institutions have a problem of selling stock. A mine has limited life, and one of the main objects of a mining finance house is to find new mines to back. To back the new ventures they need money; and the money must come from selling the shares of the mines already floated. Eventually the mines which were once shining new ventures become senile and decrepit, and at that stage they may be attractive once more to the finance house which can see the shares as self-liquidating investments whose break-up will give them, at a profit, funds for the promotion of a new venture. No doubt the houses buy in on a decline some part of the shares that they have sold on the preceding rise; just like the Government Broker in gilt edged they have an interest in maintaining an orderly market. But just like the Government Broker their ambition is to sell more than they buy, and the mining institution, which is fundamentally a seller of shares, must be recognised by the shrewd investor as a different animal from the life office or pension fund which is fundamentally a buyer.

At this stage in the first and second editions there came a triumphant examination of the rôle of Activity on the Oil market over the seven years just after the war. More recent experience insists that this section of the previous editions must be scrapped. Sectional Activity seems very much less helpful at the end of the sixties than it did at the end of the forties and beginning of the fifties, and we suspect that the reason for this is that the markets have become much more institutionalised. The institutional factor has not been changed in the Kaffir market, and Activity there is still as helpful as before. It is still helpful for the industrial markets as a whole, but these markets are not fully institutionalised and there is a vast number of small companies whose shares can be 'marked' while the number, though not the weight, of the institutional shares is comparatively small. But the Oil market may provide the clue. In the first edition we looked at an Oil market with 57 lines of securities and a value of £746,545,042. In the second edition we looked at 58 lines and a value of £2,715,415,387 and in the present edition at 59 lines with a value of £21,272,244,764. In the earlier editions we worked on the Investment Research indices; and the composition of the index was:

Anglo-Egyptian	Shell Transport
Anglo-Iranian	Trinidad Petroleum
Apex (Trinidad)	Trinidad Leaseholds
Burmah Oil	Ultramar
Lobitos	Venezuelan Oil Concessions

Venezuelan Oil was swallowed up by Shell and replaced by Canadian Eagle, and that stock, too, in its turn disappeared into the maw of the Royal Dutch-Shell group. The position now is that Anglo-Egyptian has gone, Apex has gone, Lobitos has gone, Trinidad Petroleum has been bid for and only a rump is left, Trinidad Leaseholds has gone and the only remaining stocks, apart from Anglo-Ecuadorian, are Anglo-Iranian under the name British Petroleum, Burmah Oil, whose chief asset is a vast holding of B.P., Royal Dutch, which was excluded from the I.R. index as being a replica of Shell, Shell Transport and Ultramar. So what you have is three colossi and one giant, and two concerns of modest size; the rest of the lines are used up by preference or loan stocks of the giants or by companies of extremely little importance. The influence of arbitrage (share trading across national frontiers) has increased with the listing of Royal Dutch and Shell Transport on Wall Street, and it was increased again when B.P. got a listing on the American Stock Exchange. Europe has always been interested in Royal Dutch and Shell. So the Oil market has become a field where the small investor, whose behaviour is revealed in the bargains marked, has very little influence. In Property we have quite a different state of affairs. When the first edition was written there was no separate

149

Property section; what shares there were appeared in the Financial, Land section. In the 1959 list there were 262 lines for Property with a value of £316,449,187 and in 1969 394 lines with a value of £1,515,565,048. There are big companies, middling companies and small companies in plentiful supply, and while there are certainly many big institutional holdings, there are probably hundreds of thousands of small investors. In the Property section you could have the same sort of mix that you find in the industrial market; so there is a better chance for validity in the marks curve.

The hypothesis advanced here makes it necessary to choose all our examples for study from the most recent years in which the institutionalisation of the market, accomplished to a considerable extent by the rapid expansion of the unit trust movement, has reached its present peak of development. Let us start with the Oil market for the years 1966–69 (Chart No. 19). What is plotted here is the F.T. Actuaries Oil index, composed first of B.P., Shell and Alexander Duckham which of course was not an oil share in the sense that it sought crude petroleum or refined it into petroleum products but simply a manufacturer and distributor of lubricants. The index was not a homogeneous group, but as it was weighted, and Duckham, compared with B.P. and Shell, had no weight, this defect did not matter. The Activity is plotted in the form of the square root of total weekly marks, square root because Activity, on a single logarithmic cycle, is liable to go off the page. Taking the square root is equivalent to plotting on a paper scaled from 10 to 1000 instead of 10 to 100 and that treatment tames all but the most volatile stock exchange curves.

Oil share prices, as represented by this index, had moved up sharply from May 1965; so we have the bargains curve, at the beginning of our chart, rising steeply from its seasonal low point at Christmas to a peak in February. The price curve went ahead to a peak in May, the marks curve slipped back, rallied in May but fell far short of its February peak. This is the classical behaviour in front of a reversal at the top; the price curve drifted away to the end of June, the marks curve, in a steep down-trend, rallied ineffectually, and in July the bottom dropped out of the market. The fall was accompanied, in classical style, by an upswing in Activity. At that time, in 1966, the interreaction between prices and bargains was still normal in the Oil market. After Christmas 1966 the Activity curve turned upwards; but the response of prices was very sluggish and the year from November 1966 was a period in which the F.T. Actuaries Oil index was putting up a much below average performance. On the devaluation the Oil Activity curve shot up to challenge its 1966 peak, and the index ran into a phase in which it did better than average to the end of May 1969. The failure of the Activity curve in the

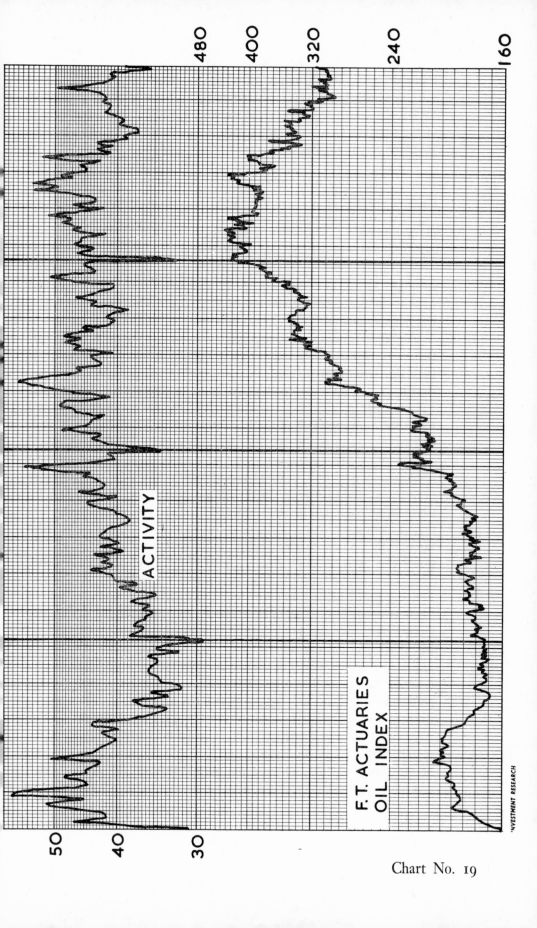

ACTIVITY

F.T. ACTUARIES
OIL INDEX

Chart No. 19

last quarter of 1968 to mount an effective test of previous highs was a warning signal of coming reversal, not badly timed for Shell but premature for B.P. In March and May the bargains figures rose to levels above those of the previous October. The signals in 1966 were splendidly clear; in 1968–69 they were not.

Next we turn to the record of Breweries. We get much the same helpful picture in 1966. In 1967 the two curves move in step up to about September; then the price curve turns down before the marks curve and we expect this to happen in the reverse order. By the first quarter of 1968 the trend of bargains seemed to have been turned down, and Breweries shares put up a worse than average performance up to November 1968. At this time the Activity curve correctly, but not very helpfully, forecast an improvement, but share prices rose steeply for only seven weeks and Activity did not signal the reversal till early April. The performance here was not very helpful.

The Property group, we have pointed out, is one of the less institutionalised markets and we can approach it hoping to find good indications from the Activity chart (Chart No. 21). The period covered is 1967–70. Activity moved up in step with prices up to the devaluation in November 1967 and fell away immediately afterwards. The price index then moved into a splendid specimen of the line formation, which will be dealt with in Chapter Fourteen; the Activity curve was shaped by the usual seasonal decline and its rising trend in the first quarter pointed to an upward resolution of the line, a development which was duly accomplished towards the end of March. In the second quarter of 1968 the Activity curve failed in a test of its 1967 peak and this would have justified holders in considering the shares with some suspicion. But the price level held through the second quarter, despite a dropping away of Activity; then prices went into new high ground, again with a lower peak for Activity. Then early in the fourth quarter prices took off almost vertically with Activity, a little belated, following enthusiastically. A splendid spearhead top developed; formations of this type are rare and investors are usually given a second chance, but a performance like this surely justifies selling. But those who did not sell got their second chance, and a very clearly indicated chance it was. The price index swept down to June, did not go lower at the end of July (thus establishing a much better than average performance and an early uptrend) and ran up strongly, confirmed by Activity after the normal summer seasonal low, to a top in February 1970. This top, which was moderately flat, equalled the sharp point of thirteen months earlier. What did Activity do? It rose in the autumn to the levels of the spring of 1968, suffered the normal seasonal fall at Christmas, struggled a little higher in the opening months of 1970 but lurked an

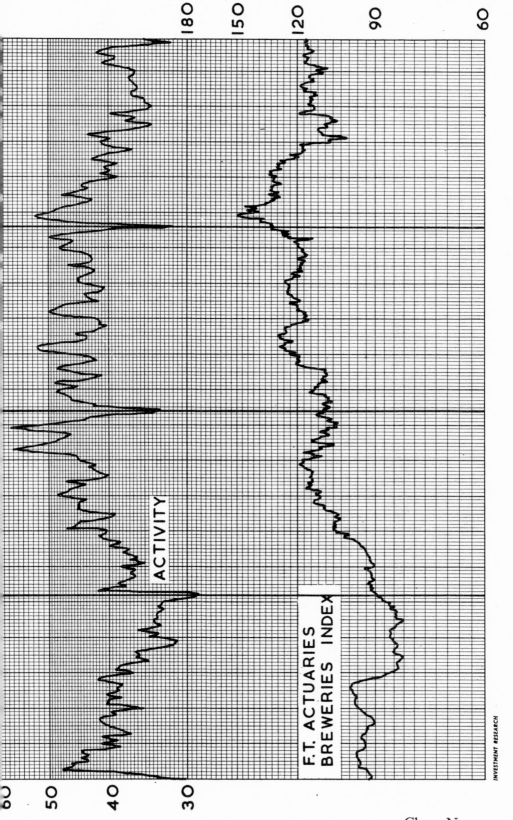

ACTIVITY

F.T. ACTUARIES
BREWERIES INDEX

INVESTMENT RESEARCH

Chart No. 20

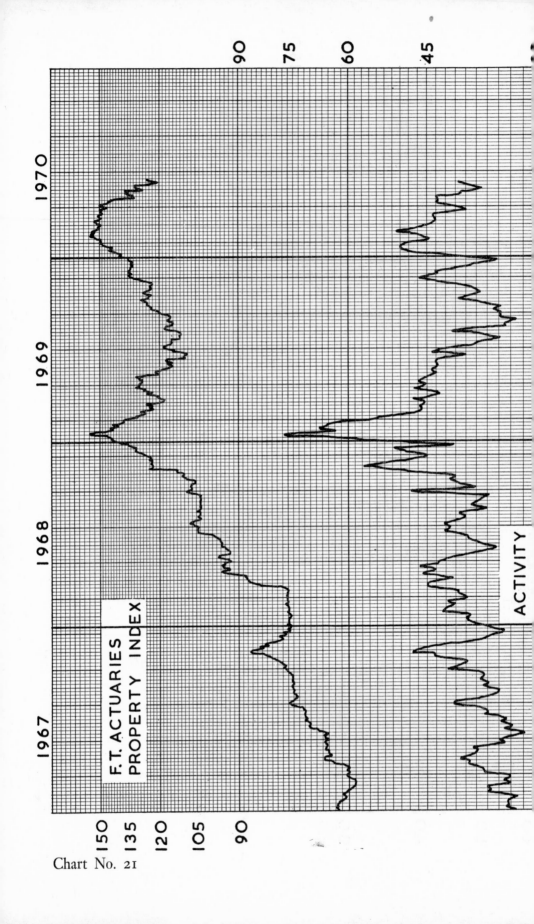

Chart No. 21

F.T. ACTUARIES
PROPERTY INDEX

ACTIVITY

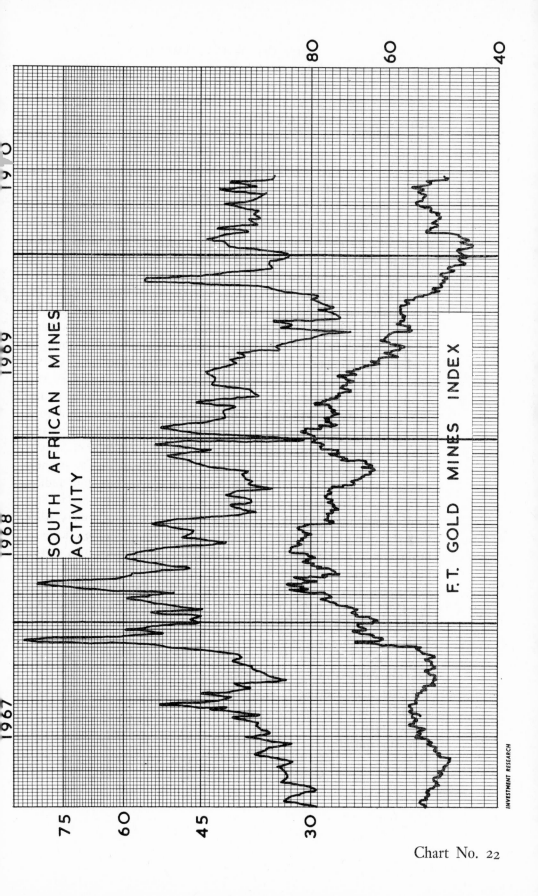

SOUTH AFRICAN MINES ACTIVITY

F.T. GOLD MINES INDEX

INVESTMENT RESEARCH

Chart No. 22

enormous distance below the best levels of January 1969. The message was clear; there was no real rekindling of enthusiasm, nothing to generate an upward urge that would push prices into new high ground, and as Activity began to ebb from this not very high level, the technically inclined holder of Property shares, if he had not got out at the beginning of 1969, received a clear message to sell at the end of the first quarter of 1970. Here you have a market in which the indications of Activity were not very clear and helpful always in the early stages of the rise. But at the top in January 1969 the Activity curve reinforced the dangerous and speculative nature of the rise shown by the price index, and at the second top of price in 1970 the failure of Activity to 'confirm' gave the traditional signal to sell. However, after a very substantial fall the index reached a new high later in the year.

Our last of these group studies deals with the Kaffir market in 1967–70. The Activity curve had risen over 50 in the share slide of 1966, presumably because frightened investors were taking refuge in Gold. Activity then fell very sharply in a belated seasonal decline and regained the autumn level at the beginning of 1967 after the normal seasonal decline at Christmas. Share prices were declining while Activity was rising in the spring of 1967. In the second quarter prices turned up and rose to the end of July. Activity went on rising. But it fell away in a normal summer doldrum, and prices came gently back into a line, or narrow band, which persisted through September and October. Recovery from the low point of Activity began in the second week of September and continued quite strongly despite the line traced out by the price index, and then both indices soared on the devaluation. At this stage the Activity curve reached its high point. Prices fluctuated in a fairly narrow range to mid-January when they moved into a new upward surge which culminated in the price peak in the middle of March. Activity too rose steeply but failed by a narrow margin to reach its level of the previous November. Here was a warning divergence. Prices then suffered a sharp setback, the most severe up to this point on our chart. The decline of Activity was less severe than that of the previous winter. The shares rallied in May within a hairsbreadth of their old high, and within a fortnight of this rise the Activity curve stood at the lowest level since the devaluation. The message should have been clear; however favourable the background for gold shares appeared there were not enough investors in the market buying the shares to push the price up. The party was over; it was time to go home. There was, however, a substantial rally in price in November and December 1968 but it came rather too quickly to be genuine, especially as the rally in Activity was not impressive. The price index declined through 1969; Activity surged up in the autumn on the rights issue by Consolidated Goldfields. When this rights issue had ceased to affect the curve the Christmas seasonal low was worked through at an unusually high level, and the chart now suggests that an uptrend of Activity had been established early in January before the price index turned up. From the middle of January to the time of writing the trend of Activity has been slightly downward, but it has not suggested that anything dreadful was likely to happen to Kaffirs, and in that period Kaffirs are about the only large group to which nothing dreadful has happened.

Our examination suggests that when one is dealing with sections of the market the Activity curve is less useful than when one is dealing with a really large corpus of issues and shares like the combination of Breweries, Commercial & Industrial, and Iron, Coal & Steel which is used by the *Financial Times*. The validity of activity indications may have been curtailed in some markets by their increasing institutionalisation, but there are still other groups, comparatively uninstitutionalised, in which Activity does give helpful indications. Great care must be used when the picture is blurred by a large rights issue or a major take-over bid. The tool was never easy to use; it is now perhaps more dangerously double-edged than it was in the early fifties, but if care is taken in handling it the results can be very good.

CHAPTER TWELVE

Ratio Charts

At this stage of the proceedings the notes, which the author prepared for the rewriting of this book, state quite simply 'Delete this chapter'. There is probably a lot to be said for this solution; we have not found ratio charts very helpful in the business of investment. But the fact remains that they can tell us things that we ought to know, also that a certain type of investor is likely to be very unsuccessful if he cannot make good use of ratio charts or some equivalent device.

A ratio is a mathematical comparison. It is easy enough to see from a series of prices whether Dunlop Rubber or Imperial Chemicals are going up or down. But suppose you want to determine whether Dunlop Rubber is going up faster than Imperial Chemical; then you should use the ratio Dunlop : ICI, which you obtain by dividing the price of Dunlop by the price of ICI. If Tuesday's ratio is higher than Monday's, Dunlop has risen proportionately more than ICI; if Tuesday's ratio is less than Monday's Dunlop has risen proportionately less than ICI.

This notion is important for the investor, especially for the investor who always holds equities and never escapes from the market when disaster is falling on it. This probably covers a high proportion of the investors, and the proportion was possibly increased by the behaviour of the market up to and beyond 1966. The experience of the sixties had, by 1967, convinced a very high proportion of the investors that bear markets, if such things really existed, were often short and always shallow. The experience of 1969 raised a little doubt; the fall from January to July had certainly been short and considering the few months it lasted it was a bit difficult to describe it as shallow. The experience of 1970, up to June when these words are being written, was nightmarish; the decline was extended and investors found themselves looking back over a fall that had lasted sixteen months, wiped out all the gain since devaluation and taken prices back to levels at which shares had been bought in 1964–66 and in many cases 1961. After this experience the proportion of investors who contemplate following a cyclical investment policy must increase (and of this increase only a small proportion will carry out their new intention), and there will remain a very large proportion of investors who will keep the bulk or the whole of their investible funds permanently in equities. Yet these investors will continue, as they always have, to look mainly at the prices of their shares and not beyond those prices to the ratios. They ought to be seeking securities which go up more than the average in times of rising markets and which fall less than the average in times of falling markets. The investor who holds ICI and sees the shares rise from 50/- to 55/- is fully conscious that his share has gone up by 5/-. He may be sophisticated enough to reckon that it has risen 10%. But how seldom does he ask whether over the same period the *Financial Times* industrial ordinary or the F.T. Actuaries 500 or All Share has gone up more or less than 10%. But that is what he should really be wanting to know.

The word 'ratio' has, since this book was first written, impinged on the mind of the investor because the investment analysts and journalists have seized on the idea of the Price: Earnings Ratio, in imitation of the Americans, since Mr. Callaghan brought in the Corporation Tax. It is difficult to see what great improvement was effected in investment analysis from giving up the 'earnings yield', turning it upside down and calling it a 'Price/Earnings Ratio'. There were flaws in the 'earnings yield' concept; a yield, in the phrase 'dividend yield' (although one usually wrote 'yield' by itself) referred to something that the investor received, while the 'earnings yield' consisted of something that the investor received plus something that the company did not let him have. In short, an investor could live on the yield of his investments but could not spend his earnings yield (and the bear market of 1969–70 refutes the argument that you can spend your earnings yield in the shape of a capital profit). Anyway, the P/E Ratio has caught on and is bandied about cheerfully by investors. It is of course a ratio; but in the context of this chapter the ratio to be considered would be the P/E Ratio ratio, that is the ratio of the P/E of a particular share to the P/E of its sub-section or group or to that of a main share index. You will find published in the *Financial Times* every day the P/E Ratio for the two main indices which that paper publishes; and a demand for P/E Ratio ratios certainly exists among investment analysts.

In short, the purpose of ratio is comparison. Comparison is essential in investment, and the use of ratios is the simplest and most effective means of making the comparisons that you want.

Let us start by looking at the F.T. Actuaries index of Oil shares for the years 1965–68. The share index was plotted initially on a weekly basis and later daily. It covered three Oil shares, Shell Transport, British Petroleum and Alexander Duckham, of which the last, a lubricant manufacturer, was engaged in quite a different business from the massive exploration, production, transport, refining and distribution of the two giants. But as the F.T. Actuaries series is weighted it makes practically no difference

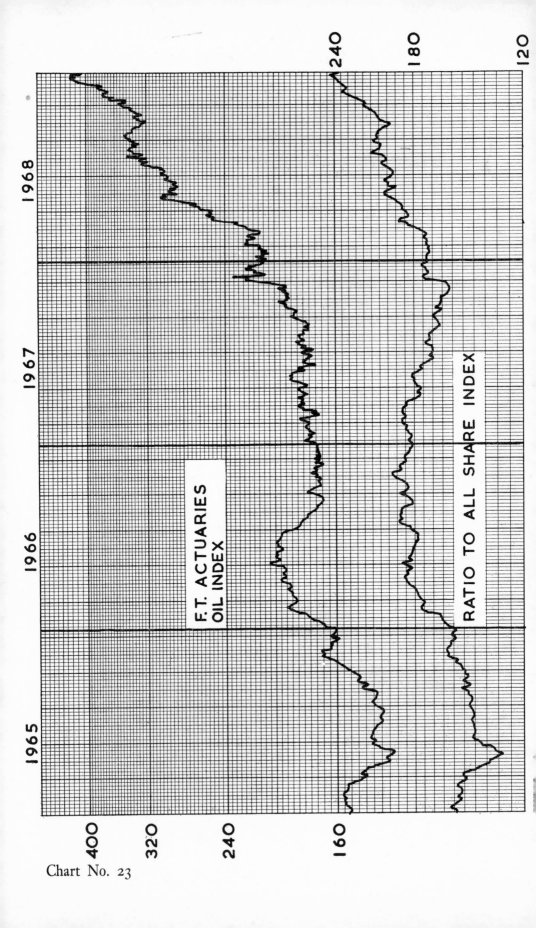

F.T. ACTUARIES
OIL INDEX

RATIO TO ALL SHARE INDEX

Chart No. 23

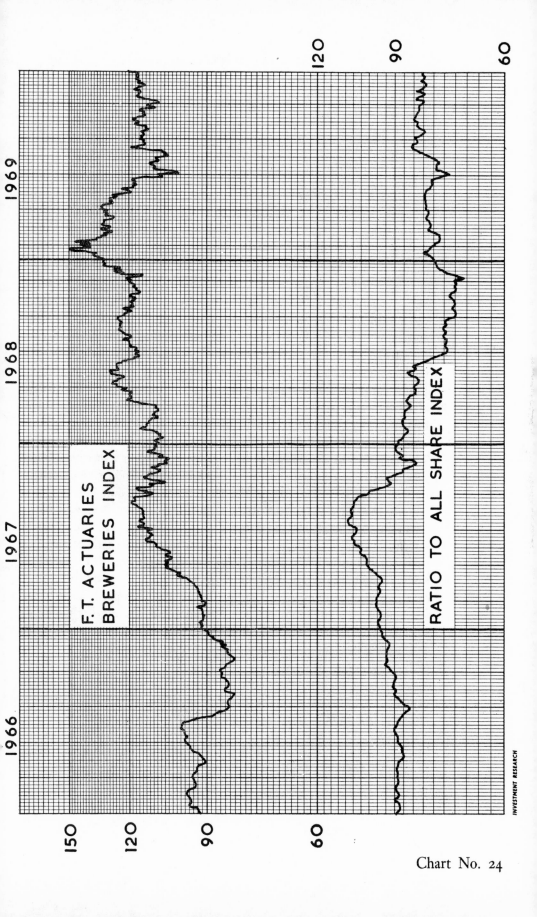

F.T. ACTUARIES
BREWERIES INDEX

RATIO TO ALL SHARE INDEX

INVESTMENT RESEARCH

Chart No. 24

whether or not Duckham is included with two giants like Shell and B.P. Once a week the ratio of the Oil sub-section to the All Share index is plotted in order to show the 'relative strength'. At the beginning of 1965 the Oil market stood in dire fear of the threatened Corporation Tax which was likely to be framed so that much of the giants' earnings abroad which fell outside the net of U.K. tax would be brought within it. Once the Budget had been introduced in April what had been feared had happened, but some temporary relief called 'overspill' was granted to the companies operating overseas and Oil investors could look back on, instead of forward to, this misfortune. Oil shares enjoyed the advantage that the bulk of their operations lay outside the United Kingdom where the Labour Government was then pursuing a rather unsuccessful course, and on the strength of these external operations the shares were favoured by investors and put up a better than average performance through the difficult summer of 1965, through the general recovery of the autumn, through the good market of the first half of 1966 and the bad market of the third quarter. Investors who bought the shares on the good showing of the ratio, say in the late summer of 1965 when its trend had manifestly turned up, enjoyed a good experience up to midsummer of 1966. Through the third quarter of 1966 their experience was better than average, but the investors who heeded the warning of the Activity chart and sold fared better than those who suffered the better than average experience of a fall of only 16%! This is one of the weaknesses of these ratios; a group or a share may show good relative strength, but in a really weak market good relative strength implies that the performance of the share is not good, only less bad. You will see that for a year, from April 1966 to April 1967, the Ratio shows Oils doing no better and no worse than average, but from April to the devaluation the ratio declined because the relative strength of the Oils was poor and investors in other groups were faring better. At the devaluation Oils shot ahead in price and the rise was accompanied by an upsurge of Activity. The climate had suddenly changed. External shares once again went to a premium because investors had become frightened of sterling. The uptrend of the Ratio continues right to the end of the chart and beyond into 1969 where it tops out only on the breaking of the news of B.P's Prudhoe Bay discovery in Alaska.

Ratio charts are not always as helpful as this. The chart for the Breweries group (Chart No. 24) shows a period of modestly good relative strength from the beginning of the 1966 crisis to the eve of devaluation a little over a year later, then a period of very poor relative strength up to near the end of 1968. In the last few weeks of the bull market the shares turned strong (was there nothing else left to buy?) but through 1969 the Ratio showed no significant trend either way. Obviously ratio charts, like the Dow Jones averages, do not talk all the time.

On the other hand the indications of these charts can be very helpful indeed. It is worth following the course of the Aircraft Index (Charts Nos. 25–26) and its ratio from the beginning of 1963 right up to the disasters of 1970. The ratio was in an uptrend from the last months of 1962 but nasty set-backs to the price curve, although they were reflected in the ratio, never impaired its primary upward trend between the beginning of 1963 and the early months of 1967. But from September 1966 to June 1967 the ratio ran horizontally with small fluctuations, and in July the curve was no longer horizontal but declining. Up to the autumn of 1968 the trend of the share index was upwards, but holders of Aircraft shares were faring considerably worse than average. Certainly the Aircraft share index gave its warning in due course; between May 1968 and January 1969 it traced out one of the best known of reversal patterns. But the ratio chart gave a much earlier warning at a time when there were good profits to be found in other sectors—and even if those profits have not been taken the subsequent experience of an alternative investment is most likely to have been happier than that of an aircraft share!

So much for the relative strength of share groups; now let us turn to a couple of individual shares. First let us look on Chart No. 27 at the performance of Marks & Spencer over two consecutive four year periods in the sixties. The earlier chart of the pair starts at the beginning of 1962. What is shown is the price, adjusted for a couple of scrip issues, and immediately below it the ratio of that price to the *Financial Times* industrial ordinary. Investment Research started plotting relative strength before the introduction of the F.T. Actuaries series of indices in 1962 and, partly for the sake of continuity, has continued to use the same standard ever since. At this stage the ratio was plotted only once every ten weeks. This is not often enough, and you will note that by the beginning of 1968 the ratios are being plotted every five weeks. In the case of Marks & Spencer a plot on the 24th April 1964 would have made a significant, but possibly misleading, difference to the shape of the curve. The ratio is not plotted direct as this would leave an inconveniently large gap between the price curve and the relative strength curve; instead a constant is introduced which lifts the ratio curve closer to the price curve. Through 1962 up to the autumn of 1963 there was no significant movement of the ratio curve. The best point in April 1962 was a little higher than any subsequent level, and this shows that, subject to the inaccuracies of our ten week intervals, Marks & Spencer was performing imperceptibly worse than average. But in the next year and a half the ratio number dropped 37%; over that period holders of Marks & Spencer were suffering a much worse than

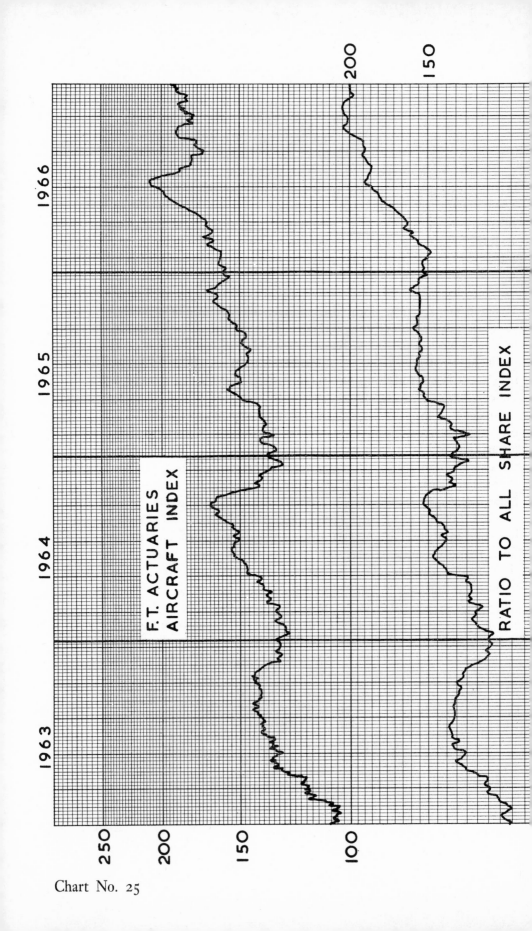

F.T. ACTUARIES
AIRCRAFT INDEX

RATIO TO ALL SHARE INDEX

Chart No. 25

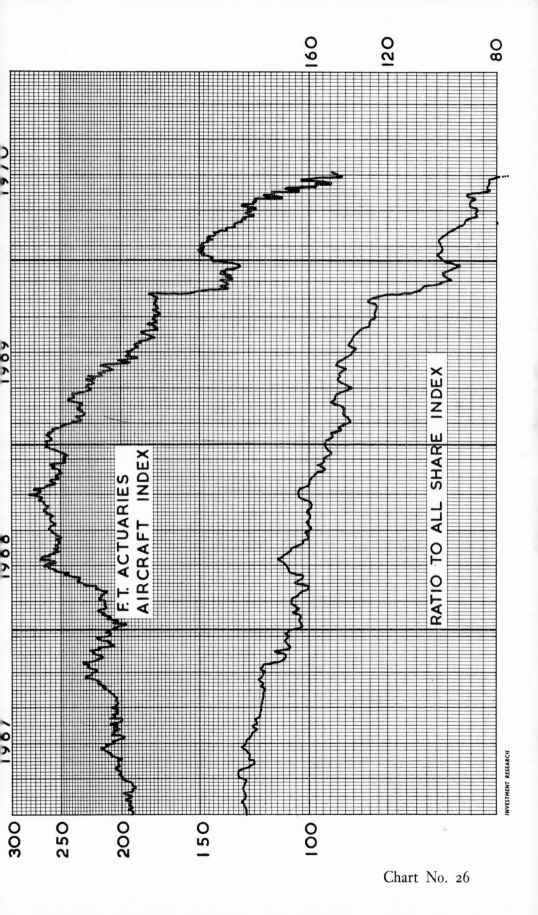

F.T. ACTUARIES
AIRCRAFT INDEX

RATIO TO ALL SHARE INDEX

INVESTMENT RESEARCH

Chart No. 26

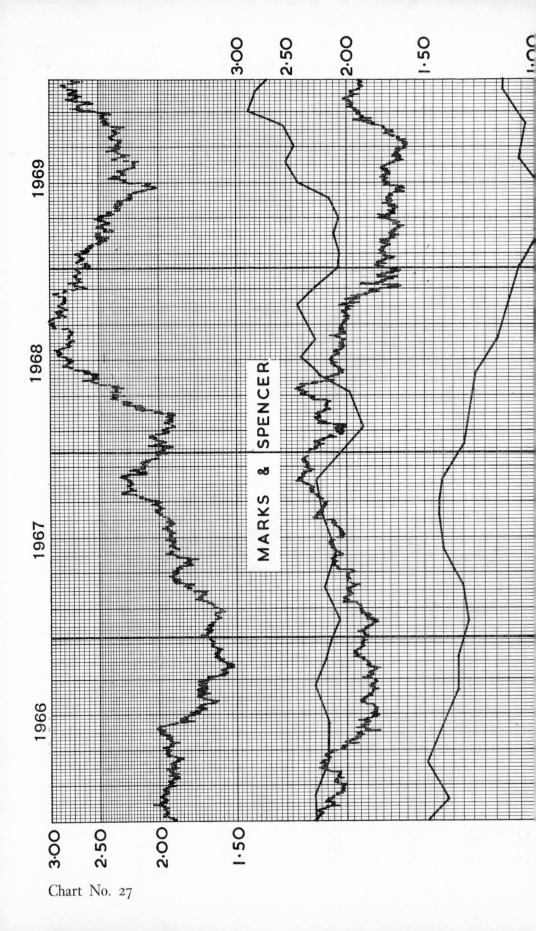

MARKS & SPENCER

Chart No. 27

average performance. In the second quarter of 1965 the ratio began to show improvement (the rest of the market was going down and Marks was not). But the improvement was not persistent; the ratio crawled up and recovered about half its fall but could work no higher. Marks were falling and recovering just about as much as the market in the second half of 1966. In front of the devaluation of 1967, the ratio crawled up again to its best 1966 level; then investors decided that devaluation was not a good thing for Marks & Spencer and it slipped back to the 1965 low point. From the first quarter of 1968 the ratio began to improve, reaching in the autumn a level above the previous year's best; but after that the share failed to keep pace with the market and the ratio dropped back to the turn of the year. For the next unhappy 15 weeks Marks matched the decline of the market very closely, and it is only at this point that a better than average performance began.

The moral of this story is simple. Throughout this period there were hundreds of thousands of investors who believed that Marks & Spencer was a good share to buy and a good share to hold, but in view of the fact that it was consistently offering a lower than average yield and putting up a poorer than average performance it was really a good share to sell.

The next share we look at has a very different character. The share is Mather & Platt and the period studied is the same, but the share requires a separate drawing for each four year period. The company has an engineering business in Manchester and has for years been considerably diversified; it had an electrical department, it made finishing machinery for the textile trade, it made canning machinery and was the leading manufacturer of sprinklers in the fire prevention field. Our chart starts off with a worse than average performance in the troubles of 1962 and the beginning of the subsequent bull market; then from November 1962 to June 1963 the performance was better than average. But at that point relative strength began to flag and there was a worse than average performance up to August 1964 which was disastrously renewed in 1966. Up to this point the ratio had generally argued that one should keep away from or get out of the share. Then came a sudden reversal. From November 1966 the ratio could do nothing but go up till it flattened out in February 1968. Relative strength remained little changed to the end of the first quarter of 1969; then, when the rest of the market began to slide, Mather & Platt held its ground and the ratio accordingly rose. When the market rallied in the third quarter of 1969, this share went on strongly ahead and the ratio went on improving into the first quarter of 1970.

Clearly this ratio is a useful tool. If someone advises you to buy or sell a share, it enables you to see at a glance whether the share has been performing better or worse than a well known standard. But how good a

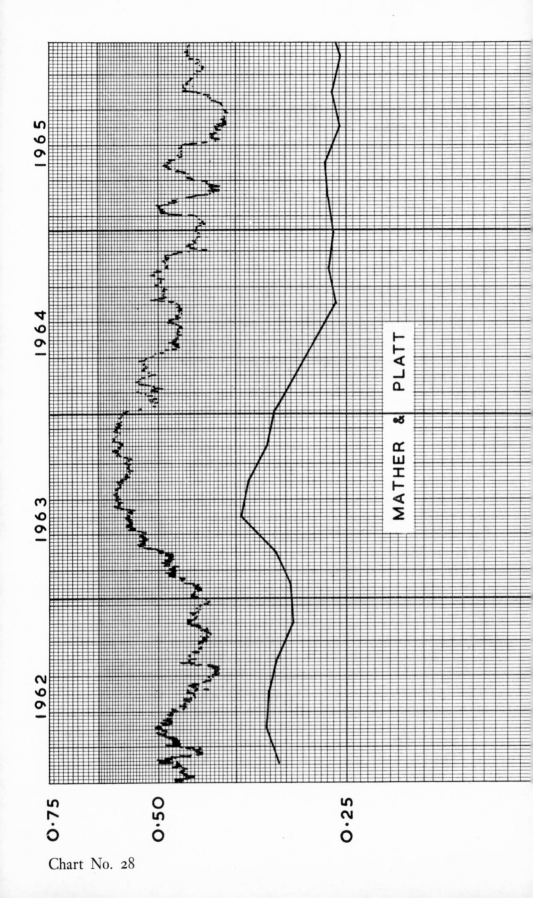

MATHER & PLATT

1962   1963   1964   1965

O·75   O·50   O·25

Chart No. 28

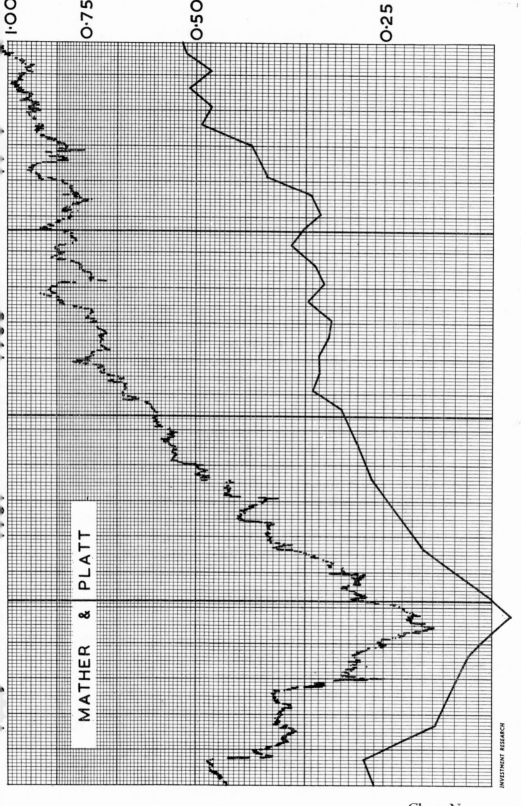

MATHER & PLATT

INVESTMENT RESEARCH

Chart No. 29

predictor is this ratio curve? The curves which we have shown have given persistent performances, better than average, worse than average, or just average. But ratio curves are often not persistent. It is a useful axiom that a price trend goes on till it stops because price trends so often go on for a very long time. But ratio trends are often like those shown for 1962–63 in the case of Mather & Platt, quite short-lived. If you want to be a successful investor, these curves are certainly something which you should watch; the successful investor is most successful if he holds shares that rise faster than average when markets are rising and shares that rise, or no shares at all, when markets are falling. It may be some comfort, in a falling market, that the ratio shows your share is falling just as fast as, or even a little slower than, everything else; but while you watch this going on, your fund is shrinking, not growing.

The uses of ratio curves are limited. If you hold a share in a rising market, you watch the relative strength to see if the share goes on being a good share to hold. If you want to buy a share in a rising market, you look at the ratio because you want to know whether the current performance is worse than average, average or better than average. Relative strength can warn you that a popular share is popular with the sort of investors who push it up or popular only with easily satisfied investors who do not worry that the bulk of the market is rising faster.

Similar in concept to ratio charts are the percentage charts which are sometimes used for plotting Activity figures. The Stock Exchange reports each day how many bargains are marked in the Official List and how many in each of the sections of which it consists. You can thus plot, from day to day or week to week, what percentage of the bargains marked fall in the gilt edged or some other section. One argues that this will show whether investors are moving into or out of any market. If investors want to buy De Beers, the number of bargains marked in the Diamond section will go up. But these investors may be raising the money to pay for the De Beers by selling Australian Mines, or Miscellaneous Mines or South African Mines, and the number of bargains marked in those sections will go up too. But clearly all the dealing with which we are concerned is funnelled into De Beers and only some of it into the other sections, and the percentages of bargains in the other sections may or may not rise but the percentage in Diamonds certainly will, and more than the percentages of the other groups we have mentioned.

These percentage curves are very volatile and it seems best to plot them on a 2-cycle log paper. However, one cannot easily accommodate a 2-cycle curve to a 1-cycle scale, and in the charts illustrating this section the scale for the percentage curve fits very awkwardly on the price graph. Chart No. 30 shows the *Financial Times* Gold Mines index for 1965–68

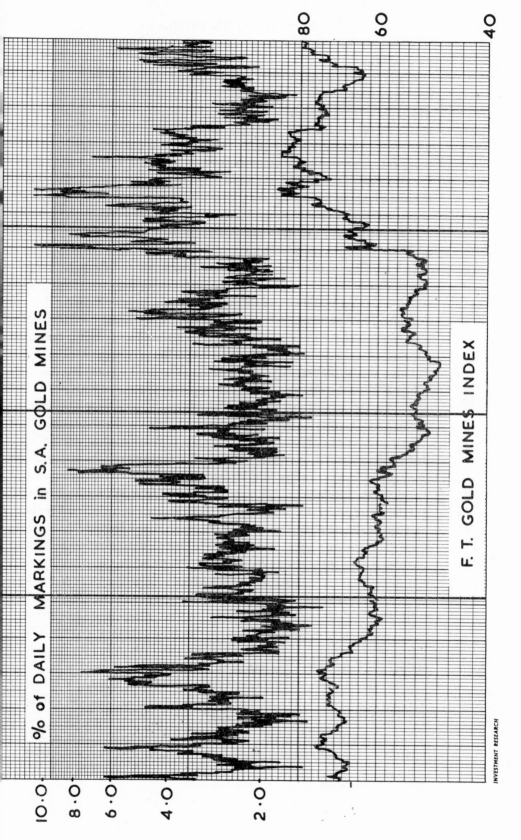

% of DAILY MARKINGS in S.A. GOLD MINES

F. T. GOLD MINES INDEX

INVESTMENT RESEARCH

Chart No. 30

accompanied by the percentage curve of Daily Markings for South African Mines.

At the beginning of the chart both curves are high; they had swung up together from a low level established before the General Election of 1964. The highest point of the %-curve just before Christmas was a little above the best level reached later in August 1965. The March peak of the price index was accompanied by a failure of the %-curve to reach its preceding peak; this suggested that the surge of buyers into the Kaffir market was not increasing and there would not be enough to push prices higher. On the other hand in the dips of the %-curve in the first and second quarters it did not drop down to the normal low levels of the previous year, and this indicated that there were still enough buyers about to keep the prices up. Then in July both curves rise strongly again; the %-curve exceeds its March high but fails to equal the top of December and the price curve almost equals its peak of March. Then both curves drop away together, and the %-curve establishes in the autumn a low range in which it had not fluctuated for any length of time during the earlier months of the year. This range is above the low range of 1964 but continues to be the normal low range for the %-curve for the next four years.

There is a big upsurge of the %-curve in the third quarter of 1966. It is bigger than the upsurge on the Activity curve at the same time. The reason for this is that this was a period of great adversity for the equity markets and Activity in them shrank so much that the %-curve for other sectors rose. The third quarter of 1966 was a time in which almost all British securities fell, and what you see in these charts is a heroic but unsuccessful effort by Kaffirs to move against the trend. When the crunch was over, the %-curve fell as buyers withdrew from the Kaffir market, and the price index followed into the bottom area of 1966–67. On the occasion of the next rise the %-curve was much more helpful. It is challenging its summer peak of 1967 almost before the price index starts moving. It runs up to a high level, the highest so far on our chart, in the first phase of the price rise and in the eight week pause that follows it never drops back to its old low levels. Curiously it reaches its lowest levels in the last third of January 1968 when prices are poised near their recent high level and then both curves go soaring up to twin peaks in March. The curves both drop back and rally towards the end of March, with the rally in the %-curve feeble. Price struggles back to its old top in May but the %-curve shows a thin, spiky rally that falls very far short of the March tops. The crowd of investors moving into Kaffirs has now thinned down, and the message of the %-curve is that the party is over and it is time to go.

The %-curve for gilt edged over the same period, Chart No. 31, also presents some interesting features. The %-curve starts at what soon seems

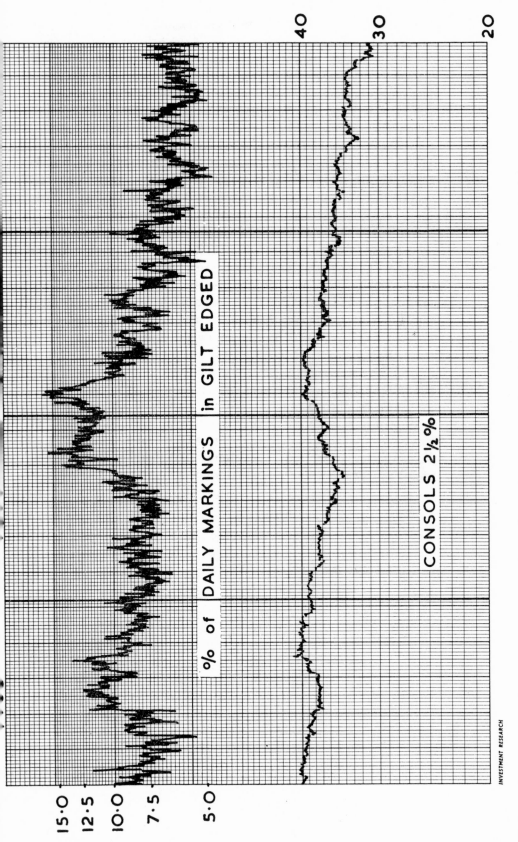

% of DAILY MARKINGS in GILT EDGED

CONSOLS 2½%

INVESTMENT RESEARCH

Chart No. 31

a high level, and there can be no doubt, if one looks at the price curve, that this represents pressure to get out of the market. By summer the %-curve is even higher, but the price curve is in a line at a lower level, and the next development is a rise of the price curve out of the line together with a rise of the %-curve to a new high level. This plainly means 'buyers about'. There was a rally—quite a good little rally—but the %-curve has drifted down as if the buyers were no longer in force, and sure enough the price curve follows the %-curve down. The next turn comes in September 1966 preceded by a rise of the %-curve through July and August; this rise will be largely the counterpart of diminishing Activity in the Industrial sections of the market. But in September the %-curve asserts itself more strongly with a good surge upwards, and the price follows. The %-curve reaches a high level in October, falls gently back while price goes on rising, and achieves a slightly higher level in February. Price is high in February. Then the %-curve turns determinedly downward eight weeks before Consols $2\frac{1}{2}\%$ reach their best level for a second time. From that peak in April the price turns down and goes on drifting for more than a year, with no cheering indication from the %-curve till late in the first quarter of 1969.

Obviously these marks ratio charts are not easy to use. Sometimes they give useful indications; sometimes they do not indicate anything. On the few occasions when rises in the %-curve accompany declines in price, either because sellers are actually pressing on the market under study or because the decline in Activity in the other falling markets is pushing up the percentage under study, the interpretation, without the benefit of hindsight, seems very difficult indeed.

CHAPTER THIRTEEN

Trend and Resistance

The theory of trend channel is simple; the practice unfortunately fails to conform to the theory and is not simple. The phenomenon is illustrated in classical form in Chart No. 2 and over a much shorter and more normal period in Chart No. 5. Why should an index of securities, in the second case of gold producers, move within parallel trendlines for a period of more than three years? More astonishing, why should Consols $2\frac{1}{2}\%$ remain in a single trend channel between parallel boundaries from 1946 at least as far as the first half of 1970? One would suggest in answer that a security, or a group of securities, if given at any time a sufficient downward impulse, tends to move to a level where the timid man with stock is no longer willing to sell and the timid man with money is no longer unwilling to buy, or, if the impulse is upward, to a level where the bold man with stock is no longer willing to hold and the bold man with money is no longer willing to buy. One would also have to assume that these levels change at a constant rate as long as the trend persists. The lower trendline is then the changing level where the optimists become buyers sufficiently willing, and the pessimists sellers sufficiently unwilling, for the secondary trend to change; the upper trendline is the changing level at which the pessimists become sellers sufficiently determined and the optimists buyers sufficiently vacillating for the secondary trend to change. In some cases the trendlines are not parallel, but while they are often not parallel in the early history of a trend it is quite frequent for new boundaries which are parallel to appear before the trend is completed. In a number of cases the trend widens as the price falls, and this can be explained by the narrowing of the market, the widening of the jobbers' turn, and the bigger proportional size of the smallest fraction (now decimal) in which it is practical to deal.

In the primary rise from 1940 there seem to have been two trends, both rooted not in the bottom of the market but the bottom of the first secondary decline. (We are discussing here the *Financial Times* index and its precursor the *Financial News* ordinary—the Moodys index illustrated in Chart No. 1 has a different trend structure). The steeper trend took prices upward past the invasion of Europe in 1944, but then there came a prolonged sideways movement from July 1944 to March 1946. The trend had changed. It was not reversed; it had just grown less steep and there was at first no evidence how much less steep. But in 1945 black disaster overwhelmed the market; the Labour Party won a triumph at the General Election and secured an overwhelming, not merely an absolute, majority. Down went the share index under a sufficient impulse. Then it rallied. The sufficient impulse had felt the trendline. After the rally the index drifted rather aimlessly. Its progress in 1946 is described in Chart No. 4, but the curious thing is that the low point at the end of March brought it down close to the trendline drawn through the election low and the bottom of the first secondary reaction in 1941. From this bottom trend the index leaped into activity. It rushed up through spring enthusiasm to a summer peak in June, tried to hold the level in August and failed, and subsided in autumn, in sympathy with New York, down as far as the bottom trendline whose course we have described. There, once again, it rallied, and the last phase of the rise began. The peak was reached in January 1947. Within a few weeks Mr. Shinwell came down from the Ministry of Fuel & Power to the Commons one Friday and told them, late in the afternoon, that on Monday there would be no power for the factories. Naturally the index hastened its decline from the peak, but the decline was checked once again on the still rising lower trendline. The rally continued to May but failed to equal the January peak. Another attempt was made in June. In July the efforts to climb were obviously less effective, and, at the end of the month, the market broke. It cut through our trendline round 128, after a peak level six months earlier of 140·7; the bear market which had been concealed since January in the old bull's clothing revealed its true nature and the dead bull's hide lay empty for all to see.

At this point we must turn to resistance, or rather to support and resistance, to use more precise terms. Resistance tends to stop a rise of price, support to stop a fall of price. What we have been considering in connection with the trendline of the *Financial News* ordinary index from 1941 onwards is obviously support. But this is inclined support; each time the support works, it operates at a higher level. We must also consider horizontal support (and whatever we say of horizontal support the same applies conversely to horizontal resistance). Let us take a hypothetical share at a price point O. From O it rises to A where it stops, perhaps because it has met resistance, perhaps because it has risen far enough. From A it retreats to P, which lies above O. From P it advances to B, above A, and then retreats to Q, which is on the same level as A. A chartist would expect it 'to find support at A' and would not be surprised to see the downtrend reversed at this juncture and a new uptrend started, which might carry the share to C, above B, from which it would retreat to R,

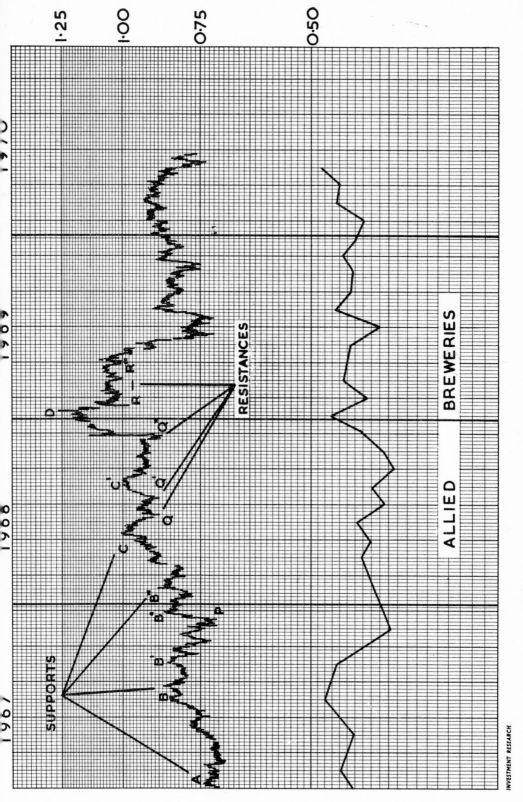

Chart No. 32

on the same level as B.

Of course, this is an ideal description and actual cases are generally nothing like as tidy. Let us look at the progress of Allied Breweries through 1967–70 in Chart No. 32. We start with a rise to A, just under 0·75; from this peak there is only a mild reaction and the price progresses, about twenty weeks later, to B round 0·85. There is a row of tops at the B level, B′ and B″ and even B‴. But between B′ and B″ there is a drop to P at 0·72, corresponding closely enough to A. The rise progresses eventually to 1·00 which is marked C; there is then a reaction to Q and Q′ at 0·87, corresponding closely enough to B. Then comes a third reaction to Q″ followed by a rise to D at 1·25. Where should the reaction take the share? Down to the level of C, and the four low points in the R series are all clustered close to 1·00, the level of C. The share declined further, pausing just above the BQ level and finishing its decline, up to the date of writing, on the AP level just under 0·75.

What is the explanation of this behaviour? John Magee, who collaborated with R. D. Edwards in *Technical Study of Stock Trends*, advances the view that sellers at A see the price slip back and think they have dealt very cleverly. Then the reaction ends, the advance is renewed, and they are bitterly disappointed; their clever deal has turned out badly. So they resolve that, if ever the stock comes back to their price, they will repurchase. In the same way at Q and R the buyers at first think their purchases have been exceptionally well timed, but by the third quarter of 1969 their clever purchases have turned out very badly and they resolve that, if ever the stock moves back to their price, they will sell. So in the summer of 1969 and again in the first quarter of 1970 there were sellers in plenty between 0·88 and 0·90. This theory differs from the popular view. It is widely, but superficially held that if a trend, up or down, has ended at a certain level, a later trend, approaching that level from the same direction, is likely to be ended at the same point. Thus Charter Consolidated in Chart No. 35 tops out at 4·50, not necessarily the highest level ever—who knows what happened to the stock in the days of Cecil Rhodes before its glamour was dimmed by the payment of its first dividend? This was a price at which the rise stopped, not a point at which the rise was stopped. When a rise stops, it comes to an end because there are not enough buyers to push the share up any higher. When a rise is stopped, the price has reached a level at which there are a large number of sellers. If the rise has not been pressed till it has eroded all the sellers waiting at that price, some of them will be left behind, ready to sell if the share reaches the price again (if it has been pressed till it has eroded all the sellers, it is most unlikely that the rise would stop at that point where there are no sellers left). So an old bottom is not likely to afford support unless it is resting on some old top,

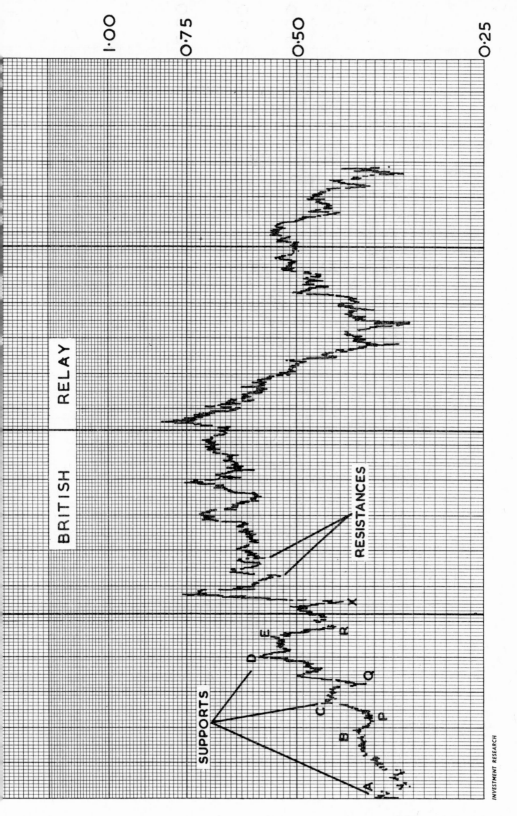

BRITISH RELAY

SUPPORTS

RESISTANCES

1·00
0·75
0·50
0·25

INVESTMENT RESEARCH

Chart No. 33

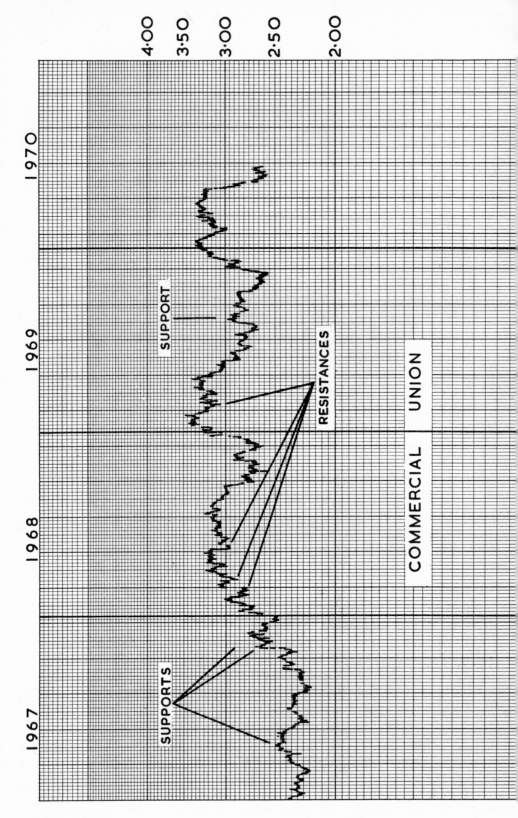

Chart No. 34

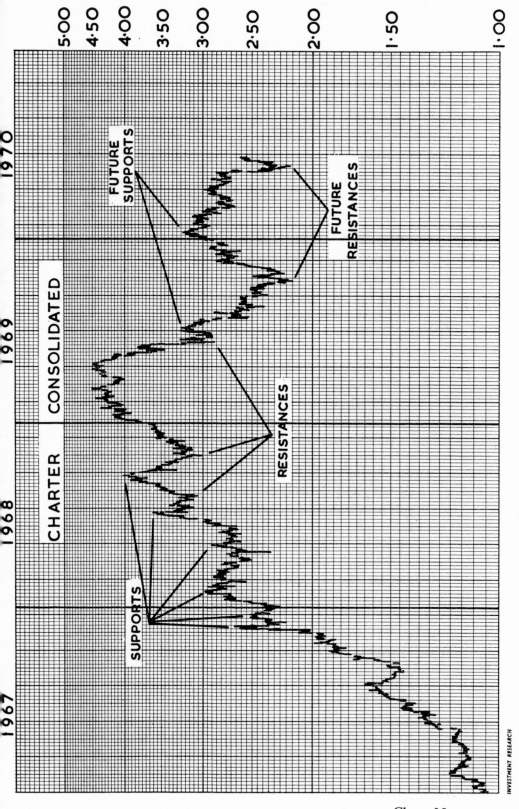

Chart No. 35

and an old top is not likely to offer resistance unless it lies under some old bottom. Inexperienced chartists, when they first grasp this theory, are often disappointed because they find supports and resistances penetrated.

The theory does not lay down that a support or resistance must reverse a trend that meets it; it lays down that there will almost certainly be sellers at a resistance, buyers at a support, but whether they will be numerous and strong enough to reverse a trend is another matter. Look at Chart No. 33 for British Relay. There you have your succession of rising tops A, B, C and D, all potential supports in a subsequent decline; below D there is another minor peak E which does turn out to provide support. Support was found during the rise on P, Q and R, corresponding roughly with A, B, and C. Then, by some misconception the price drops to X, at 0·42, from where it soars on good news, without acknowledging any resistance, to 0·75. You will notice that two subsequent peaks, associated fairly closely with general market tops, reach approximately the same level. This share did turn back three times from the same high level, but there is nothing in the charts of the previous eight years to provide a reason for the reversal.

We have talked so far of support and resistance, but we must also consider support-and-resistance. A share comes down to an old top and finds support and rallies. It then reacts, falls through the support level at the second attempt and rallies to it and turns back. Support has become resistance. If a new rally takes the share through the level, next time it comes down to it, there will be some support there. So a support-and-resistance level can persist for months or even years. On Chart No. 34, Commercial Union, look at the number of reversals round 2·95. This corresponds to the low points under the 1961 top. There is obviously some important support round 2·60, and this corresponds to a long area of distribution in the decline from the 1961 peak, a fall that worked itself out only after several years.

Before we leave the subject, let us consider the very strong rise of Charter Consolidated in 1967–68, which is shown on Chart No. 35. The rise was steep, and left very little support between 1·00 and 2·50. From that point on supports proliferate; you will note how the top of February 1968 corresponds with the bottom of October, how the top of September 1968 lays down the support beneath the top area of January to May 1969. An important support-and-resistance level has developed between 3·00 and 3·25. It is not clear from the chart whether there is any significance in the reversals at 2·15; at the time of writing in June this level looks very frail with the next significant support round 1·6. It is also worth noticing the vigour of the decline from the top. Really fierce falls of this sort can penetrate supports without a tremor, but in this case rallies, however brief, were stimulated by the support of July 1968 at 3·60, that of January 1968 at 2·95 and November 1967 round 2·60.

There is a controversy about the validity of support and resistance levels for indices. It seems likely that there is a certain validity but that it is quickly eroded by time. The holder of a particular share is long lived and his memory may reach back a long way; the explanation of support and resistance that we have given depends on human memory. If an index penetrates a previous top, made a few months ago, and then returns to it, again within a few months, it is possible that the constituents of the index will not yet have been widely dispersed and will almost all individually be finding support at the same time. But when an index returns to a support or resistance after a lapse of many years it is likely that some part of the constituents will already have penetrated it and some part will not yet have approached it, leaving only a minority of the constituents to be experiencing the support or resistance test. Therefore it seems unlikely that the tops of the *Financial Times* industrial ordinary for 1961–66 were of much importance when the index reached down to them in 1969, especially as the F.T. Actuaries 500 was not testing its 1964–66 tops at the same time.

We can now get back to trends, which we have seen can to some extent be built up by support and resistance and to some extent be reversed. The trendline which we were studying was the right hand, and more important, boundary. It is the cutting through this line which announces, not always veraciously, that the trend has changed some time ago. The left hand trendline, the upper line in a rising market and the lower in a declining, may be of tactical importance, hinting when one might consider dealing, on the short view, against the primary trend, but the right hand trendline is the strategic line from which one must guess that the primary trend has changed and with it the strategy that the investor should adopt.

There are certain cases where the left hand trend is much the better defined, and it can then sometimes be very useful. Look once again at Charter Consolidated in Chart No. 35. This trendline has four good points of contact in 1967–68; then the share makes a very determined rise in 1969 which fails to reach the old top trendline. Look back to Chart No. 3 of the *Financial Times* industrial ordinary for the long period from 1946–70. Then you will see that the time when the index reaches up to a high point and falls far short of the left hand trendline is the time when the bull market has lost its upthrust.

You would expect, rightly, to find the most regular trends in the broadest markets, like the Dow Jones Industrial Average, the *Financial Times* fixed interest stock index, the *Financial Times* industrial ordinary share index. We have already studied the rather odd regularity of the 1940–47 bull market in London. In comparison the 1947–49 bear market was irregular, but it turns out in retrospect to be far more regular than most subsequent bear markets. At least it had a well defined upper trendline. The 1949–51 rise was regular enough, and so was the unusually short 1951–52 decline. The two big rises from 1952 and 1958 were somewhat concave, especially the earlier of the two; the rise tended to accelerate as it went on. But the main characteristic of the modern bear market is its irregularity, and it will be most interesting to see in the end what shape has been taken by the formidable bear market that began in the winter of 1968–69.

The Group averages with their much narrower markets may show less even trends. The irregularities of one group compensate those of another so that the irregularities of the groups add up to the regularity of the broad markets. But you find plenty of cases where the narrow group shows a clear trend through the cycle.

In shares the trends are still less regular and more difficult to determine. But trends do emerge in the patterns which shares trace out, sometimes a fairly long trend, as in Mather & Platt in Chart No. 29, sometimes shorter trends as in Marks & Spencer in Chart No. 27. Sometimes prices run out of the trend channels, upwards for lucky holders as in Allied Breweries in Chart No. 32 and British Relay in Chart No. 33; if you want to see the same thing happen downwards, look at Mather & Platt in Chart No. 28 and the first months of Chart No. 29.

These share trends may be very valuable; however much one studies broad and narrow markets, investment decisions have to be translated into actions which concern individual shares. If the decision is a decision to buy, it may be agreed that such-and-such seems a good share to buy and then the angle of the trend channel and the position of the share in the trend channel help to the decision that it is, or is not, the right time to buy it. Or it may be agreed that so-and-so is the group in which to buy at this time and the angles of the various trend channels and the positions of the shares in their trend channels suggest which of them is the most profitable to purchase.

The most important use of trends is the strategic. At comparatively long intervals the index of a broad market will show signs that it is moving, or has moved, out of a long-established channel; this is generally though not always (1944 is an example in London), a symptom of reversal of trend. At this signal, the trader in securities, who has been buying eagerly on declines and selling reluctantly on rises, begins to sell eagerly on rises and buy reluctantly on declines. The investor who really believes that there is an investment cycle, on this signal of change from uptrend to downtrend, sells his securities and looks for safe places for his resources. Conversely if the change is from downtrend to uptrend, the trader again reverses his policy, and the investor withdraws his resources from their place of safety and begins to venture them once more in the security market.

The tactical use of trends is less certain than the strategic. It is easy to say, "Sell near the upper trendline and buy near the lower". Approach to the upper trendline (or to the upper parallel if no upper trendline has yet been established) may be a signal that the angle of trend has changed and become more favourable to holders; the share's next move may be not a retreat but a brilliant further advance. In the same way, approach to the lower trendline (or possibly lower parallel) may be a symptom of exhaustion; the rise may be ending and the share may be moving to stagnation or decline. If it is doing one of these, it will cut through the lower trendline or parallel and should be sold, not bought. But we can consider this matter, in a rising market, more fruitfully if we take account of the angle of the trend. If the upward trend is steep, which means that the share's rise has so far been vigorous, the temptation to sell near the upper trendline is strong. The position of the share enforces, if it has been well bought, that the profit is already large. Do the steepness and extent of the rise argue that it has already gone far enough? Or do they argue that a share which rises so steeply should be considered on strategic rather than tactical grounds? It is the shares that rise like this which contribute the small quota of grand appreciators, the shares that outpace the bull market and double, triple, quadruple its performance. You cannot be sure that your particular share which has started so well will turn out one of these great successes, but the prudent course is probably to wait and see rather than to rush and take the profit. If the early purchase was made on reasons which seem sound and still argue for a higher price, then the buyer will go on holding the share, but it is more usual in such cases for no reasons yet to have appeared to explain the performance. The top trendline does seem a good place for taking a profit, but before you take it think once and twice whether the buyers who have taken it there may not know something that you do not know and which will in due course justify their boldness. Such arguments are sound when a bull market is young and this sort of decision is not easy to take. They are much less sound when the bull market is older and such decisions are easy, in the confident atmosphere, to take.

Now let us consider another case where the upward trend is shallow and the share moves up to the top trendline. What is the holder to do? We must ask him the question why he is holding the share. If the answer is patently inadequate, such as "Aunt Matilda left them to me in her will" or "I bought them much higher up" or "Bill told me to buy them", he should sell (though in the third case it might, or it might not, be prudent to consult Bill). If the answer is "I thought this was a good company whose quality and potentialities the market underestimated and I am glad to see that they are now coming to their senses and I think these shares can still go on and up" then he must hold and hope that the trend has changed. If his expectations are fulfilled, let him hold till the new trend fails him, but if the share soon flags again and there is not a steep uptrend, then it is time to abandon his hopes and look for a better share in some steeper trend.

Or you may find two companies with somewhat similar interests, like Courtaulds with Nylon, Calico Printers with Terylene (Chart No. 36 covers the period 1951–54 and shows these two shares; the price of Courtaulds has been adjusted for a one for one scrip issue). Courtaulds get away first from the bear market bottom in June 1952 and Calico are held back by resistance at 1·75. But at the end of February 1953 Calico break out from the resistance and go into a steep uptrend; by mid-March Calico are still showing great strength and Courtaulds relative weakness. A switch from Courtaulds to Calico would have been justified, but in December Courtaulds made an enormous leap which showed great buying pressure. It was now prudent to watch for any flagging in Calico; by this time Courtaulds were looking the stronger shares. In April 1954 Calico ran out of steam; the price began to drop while Courtaulds were still rising strongly and steadily. At this juncture it was right to switch back to Courtaulds. The Calico trend was strong from February 1953 to October; then a secondary reaction took the share back to its lower trendline and it crawled up the trendline for weeks. Eventually it reached a peak which of course could not be recognised at the time as the top of its bull market. But when it dropped away from that peak it went through its rising lower trendline, and the technical analyst would at this juncture join the October and March tops with a pencil line and note that its flat angle seemed about the best he could expect from the share in the early future while the penetration of the trendline gave him plenty to fear. But Courtaulds had steepened its trend in October, and this trend was running strongly when the Calico trend was weakening. Courtaulds went on rising to the end of 1954 and finished with a glorious but unpredictable spearhead top at 2·8 in the summer of 1955. (This, incidentally, is a very different story from that told in the first edition, and a comparison of the two passages will suggest, first that the author has learnt a lot between 1953 and 1970, second that steepness of trend and strength of pattern are more important points to watch than position within the trend channel).

When a share is moving up in a steep trend-channel with well marked trendlines, it should not be sold. While it keeps on the left hand side of that rising lower trendline, there is always hope that it will go on. If it

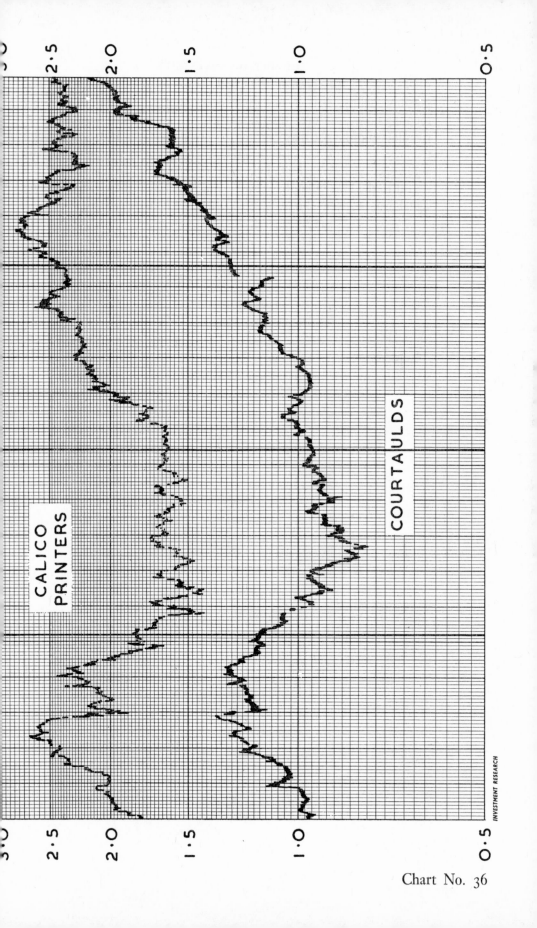

CALICO PRINTERS

COURTAULDS

INVESTMENT RESEARCH

Chart No. 36

runs away to a spearhead at or beyond the upper trendline, one may feel, possibly rightly, that it has done everything it can and must come toppling down; but even then it may gather new strength near the lower trendline and the rise may continue to new high levels. If it cuts through the lower trendline, the case for a sale is strong, but in all other cases, the arguments for leaving well alone seem the strongest. In few cases will a retreat to the lower trendline involve much sacrifice; there a clear selling signal may be given. But as long as it runs, let it go on running.

CHAPTER FOURTEEN

Prophetic Pattern

Most of the price curves that we study, whether they be share prices, group averages or broad markets, conform more or less closely to the style of movement that we described in Chapter Three and illustrated in Charts Nos. 4, 5 and 6. Single commodities traded for spot or forward positions have slightly different characteristics, particularly that the primary trend is not dominant in the same way. Further, while the curve of dividends is very stable and Activity curves are very unstable, both seem to progress towards their primary reversals with tertiary and secondary movements. In the price curves little tertiary zig-zags, whose duration is only a matter of days or at the most a very few weeks, build up larger secondary phases and counter-movements. These secondary movements too zig-zag to and fro and build up the primary movement. If the patterns were perfect, all secondary phases would proceed as far as the left hand trendline, all secondary countermovements would recoil to the right hand trendline. If this were to happen prediction would be easier. However, another anomaly is often helpful to prediction. At times the trend is interrupted. Every trend which has an angle inclined to the horizontal shows a domination either of buyers over sellers, if the inclination is upward, or of sellers over buyers if the inclination is downward. But sometimes an argument develops in which buyers and sellers appear to be in balance. It is no longer possible to determine the trend, either because the movement is for the time purely horizontal, or because the upper trend and the lower trend appear to be inclined in opposite directions. We think of these patterns as areas of argument, but the technical name for them is 'trading areas'.

There is a widespread notion that the chartists are always finding specimens of the classical formations, which we shall soon be studying, and taking advantage of the indications which these give in order to bring off profitable deals. But in the British market at any rate, and in all other markets which have come to the author's attention in recent years, classical formations are rare. 'Pattern' consists mainly of variations on the two themes of trend and support-and-resistance, and it is these variations which the British technical analyst is studying most of his time. Formations are rare; many of them are more often than not reversal patterns, and shares spend most of their lives in uptrends and downtrends and comparatively little in areas of argument. Primary reversals do not happen so very often, recently once every two or three years, and most secondary reversals are insufficiently important and well worked out to justify a classical formation. What you get most often is a simple cutting of a rising or falling trendline. From time to time, but most often round the primary reversal, one does detect the building up of a classical formation, and throughout an uptrend one may find continuation patterns being built up. In a bear market the destructive violence of a major phase of liquidation runs over all argument and it is difficult for sufficiently strongly opposed opinion to develop and work out a classical formation.

The classical trading area is the line. There is a good example, selected from America, in Chart No. 37, which shows the Dow Jones Industrial Average for 1946–49. It occurs in the first quarter of 1948 round about the lowest level which the average reached in the long period of low prices between 1946 and 1949. It lasted six weeks in which the average fluctuated, as far as daily closing levels were concerned, less than 2%. Eventually the average rose out of its line—'emerged' is the technical term—and rose steeply; when the steep rise was finished the rise continued for twelve weeks. This is model behaviour for a line, emergence signalling a new trend sustained over a profitable distance. The pattern is not very common, particularly in the *Financial Times* industrial ordinary, although a short line will be found in Chart No. 6, where that index worked in a line for a few weeks after the drop from the high point at the beginning of 1948. Here again the emergence from the line was a large and violent movement, on this occasion downwards. One is supposed not to guess, as one watches a line develop, whether the matching of buyers and sellers will end in a domination by the one or by the other. When the period of equilibrium ends, it is likely that, as in these two cases, a vigorous domination will be exercised by the buyers or the sellers, whichever has exhausted the forces of the other party and found itself victor on the field. The downward movement from the London line was valuable in two ways. For the alert operator it was a signal to sell at once, and 'at once' is important because the speed of the decline left no time for procrastination. For the student of the market, engaged on investment policy, it was strong evidence that the decline which began in 1947 had not exhausted itself in the plunge down to that year's September low. The message of this downward movement was that London was still in a primary decline. The upward movement in New York was a signal to buy, just as the downward movement in London was a signal to sell.

How useful are lines? The first trouble is that in substantial London

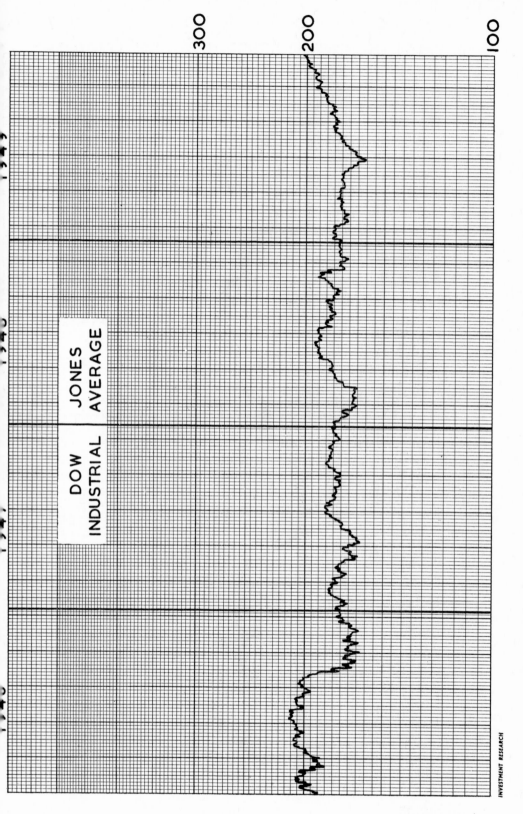

DOW JONES INDUSTRIAL AVERAGE

300

200

100

INVESTMENT RESEARCH

Chart No. 37

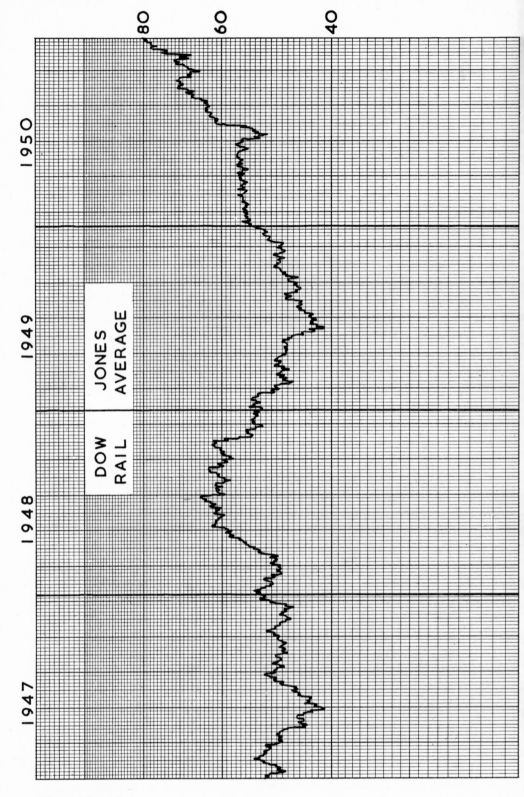

DOW JONES
RAIL AVERAGE

Chart No. 38

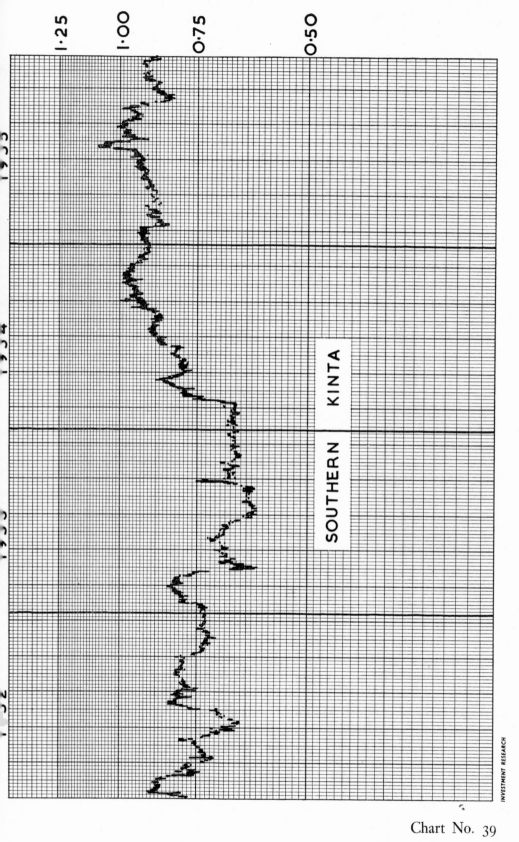

SOUTHERN KINTA

INVESTMENT RESEARCH

Chart No. 39

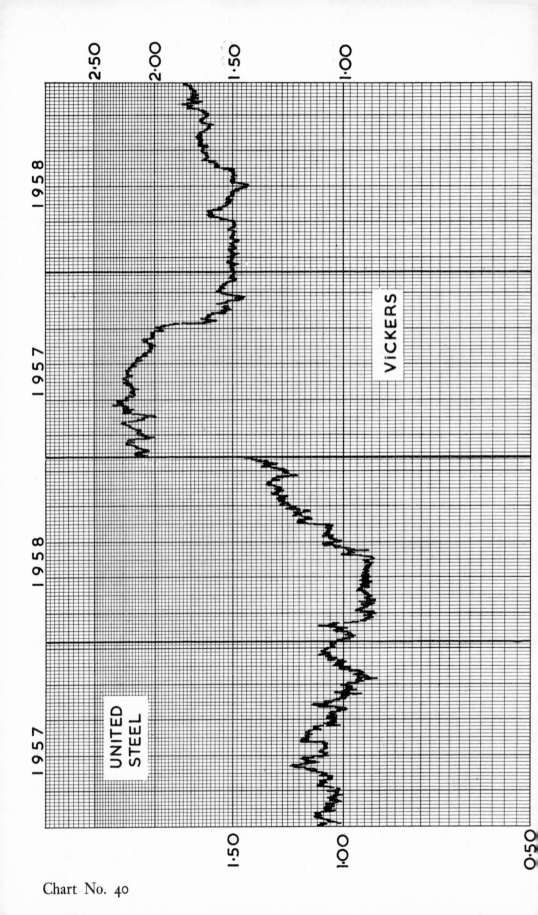

VICKERS

UNITED STEEL

Chart No. 40

issues they are very rare. When the Investment Research daily chart books were examined only five were found which seemed worth recording, and four of these will be discussed. The sample is too small for statistically valid conclusions. But the philosophy of the line seems sound, that a close balance between buyers and sellers comes to exist in a share, that it persists for several weeks and in due course is broken; then whichever party is dominant is able to push the price a significant distance in its direction.

There is however one classic case of a line's giving a completely wrong indication. In Chart No. 38 we show Dow Jones Rails (again an American example) for the years 1947–50. A primary upward movement had started in June 1949 but it ran out of steam in January 1950 and a line was formed which lasted 20 weeks. This pattern was resolved downwards (to use technical terminology) on the outbreak of the Korean War. This was quite wrong. The effect of the war was to lift up the east coast of the USA and depress the west coast, so that munitions of war could run easily in great quantities from east to west. This was most profitable for the railroads; when only one week had elapsed the market realised the mistake; the downtrend was swiftly reversed and a strong uptrend carried the average to 90 in the first quarter of 1951. Such misleading emergences from lines are rare; but abortive emergences are quite common.

There is a good and interesting line in Chart No. 39, covering Southern Kinta, a Malaysian tin mining group, in the years 1952–55. Between April and July 1953 the share bottomed twice at 0·6 and then shot up suddenly to 0·75 (the rise was probably sapped by the resistance laid down previously above 0·7). The share dropped quickly back, oscillated for five weeks between 0·64 and 0·68 and then settled into a line that lasted 14 weeks. It emerged upwards from the line in March 1954 and ran quickly up to 0·87 and continued thence upwards in a gentle and uninteresting trend to 1·08.

Our next chart, No. 40, shows two shares which were then in not widely different classes of business, United Steel and Vickers. The period covered is 1957–58, and in the early months of the year both formed lines at low levels. It was the time when the bear market that began in 1955, and was interrupted by a strong calf market in 1957, was working out its final phase. United Steel formed a line that lasted 18 weeks. The level was between 0·90 and 0·95. The emergence was upwards and the price crossed 1·50 before the end of the year (and was to get close to 4·50 by 1960). The performance by Vickers was as unsatisfactory as that of United Steel was splendid. The line was formed round 1·50 and lasted 17 weeks. An upward emergence was followed by a return to 1·50 and then a decline to 1·44. The share then rallied to 1·8; but in the fourth quarter of the next year it was down to 1·3.

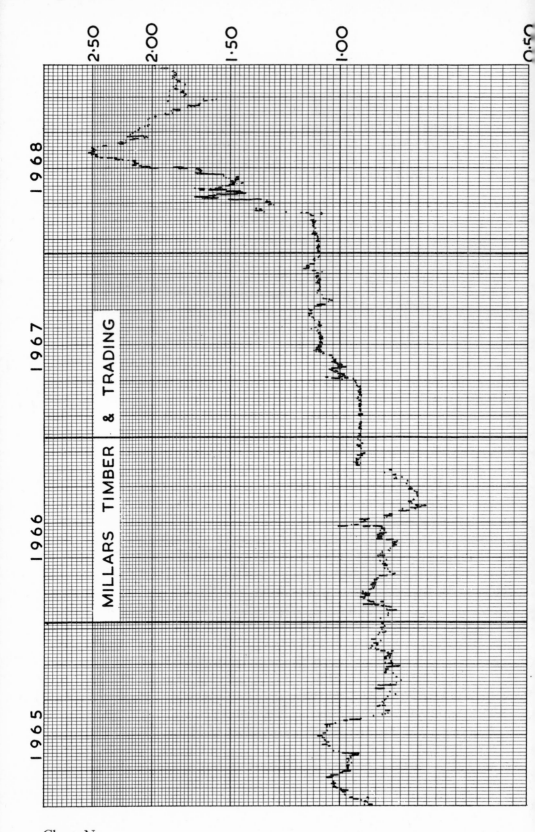

MILLARS TIMBER & TRADING

Chart No. 41

Before we leave the line we must look at one other phenomenon. Chart No. 41 shows Millars Timber & Trading for the years 1965–68. This was a comparatively small company. The share showed considerable strength at the last gasp of high prices just before the crisis of 1966, fell away quickly to a low point but then rallied at an early stage in the decline. It leapt up with a big gap in the last week of October and then ran into a line that lasted nearly six months. This looks like manipulation. The rise at the end of June 1966 looks like the entry of a big buyer and so does the early check to the decline of August. In June he bought. In July he stepped back out of the market in recognition of a harsh change of climate. Late in August he thought the share cheap enough for him to step in and pick up what stock he could, and the last week in October he boosted the price to a level at which he thought he could wear out some sellers. He held the price in a line for a long period, and in those dreary weeks of minimal change he tired out many of the holders who were hanging on for a better price. A new level was established in the early summer of 1967; but even the devaluation, which should have had most beneficial effects on a share like this with a high proportion of Australian assets, brought only a small, and ephemeral, rise of price. In the end the news leaked out and the price rose to 2·50. A line is normally caused by a balance between independent buyers and sellers, but it is not impossible for the buying and the selling that causes the price to remain steady to originate from a single source.

The line is formed by a horizontal movement with a small amplitude of fluctuation. How small is small? It seems reasonable to stipulate about 3% for an index line chart and about 5% for a share bar chart. The term is sometimes extended to cover horizontal movements with a wider amplitude of fluctuation, but we think this terminology is inexact and prefer, for this formation, the word 'band'. However, we would restrict the use of the term band to patterns where the amplitude of fluctuation lay between 5% and 10%; and we suspect that this pattern has now become very rare. It may however reappear. Working on a limited repertoire of charts in the first edition two cases were instanced, British American Tobacco (Chart No. 42) and Canadian Eagle (Chart No. 43). (We shall come back to the lettering B G and M G at a later stage). Two more are illustrated here, Ultramar in 1954–55 which is coupled in Chart No. 42 with British American Tobacco, and Canadian Eagle in 1953–54 coupled in No. 43 with the same share's four month example in 1948/49. Bands, it seems, were rare and now hardly ever happen. The characteristics of a band are that the share fluctuates for a period within a range of 5% to 10%. In three of the cases, but not in the 1948 specimen of Canadian Eagle which is a very leisurely pattern, there is frequent passage

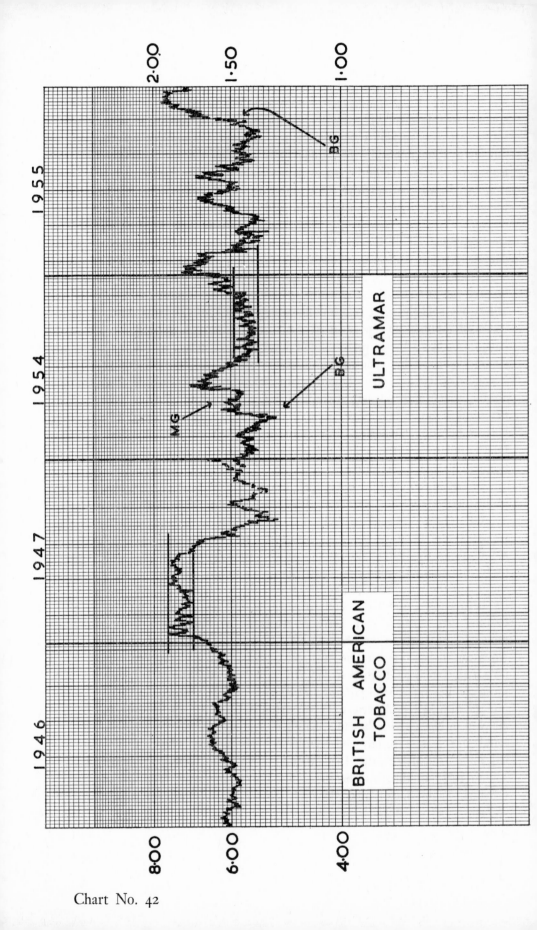

Chart No. 42

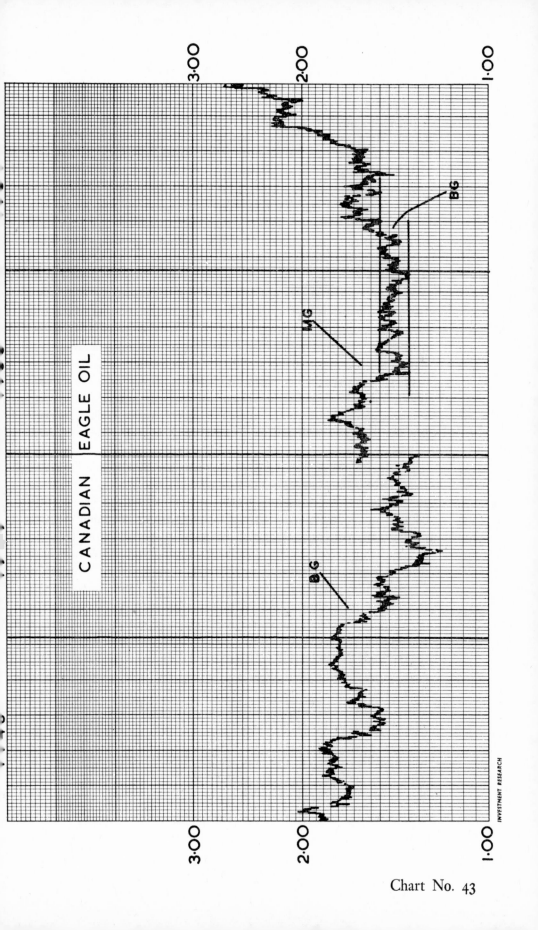

CANADIAN EAGLE OIL

Chart No. 43

between the upper and lower boundaries of the formation. Eventually the price passes out of the boundaries of the pattern and this resolution of the pattern is followed by a substantial move in the direction of the emergence. In British American Tobacco and in the second example of Canadian Eagle the pattern was formed at a most important turning point. In Canadian Eagle in 1948 the downward emergence from the pattern preceded a very important decline, but the pattern was formed not at a primary top but at the ending of a not very important secondary rally.

The very vigorous pattern formed in Ultramar in 1954 preceded a rally to the level of a previous top, but this was followed immediately by a secondary decline below the bottom of the band. This decline did not persist, but after another rally of poor dimensions (the market was at this stage very excited and industrials were rushing up to the high top of 1955) the share fell back again a fraction below the bottom of the band before embarking in a better than average upward move on the great bull market for Oils that raged in the early months of 1956. However, we should not take the evidence of Ultramar too much to heart; at times it has been an extremely bad share for chartists. British American Tobacco and Canadian Eagle were two very normal active stocks, and their patterns are extremely helpful. On the whole the slight evidence available suggests that the band is a fairly reliable pattern, but it no longer seems to occur in leading shares.

Rectangles, the name we give to such patterns with an amplitude over 10%, are not mentioned in the first edition of this book. The pattern apparently was not interesting when the first edition was being written because the good formations had fallen within our definition of bands. Further, the patterns had not shown their scope when the book was written. Two were actually illustrated as flat trend shares which the investor might well consider selling. These two were Guinness and Leyland Motor, shown in Charts Nos. 44 and 45. These lagged in their rectangular patterns from 1952 into 1954, but after the typescript and drawings were sent to the publisher they did everything, in the way of performance, that a good rectangle should. In fact, they did more. What the rectangle formation calls for is a move in the direction of the emergence equal at least to the width of the rectangle. Guinness shows more clearly than Leyland the phenomenon which technical analysts call 'pull-back'. When a share emerges from a well defined pattern the price often returns, generally within hours or days, to or possibly beyond the boundary through which it has emerged. However, there is one strong objection which technical analysts can raise against these two specimens; they lack work. The amount of fluctuation across the formation within the pattern area is small compared with that shown in Charts Nos. 42 and 43 and

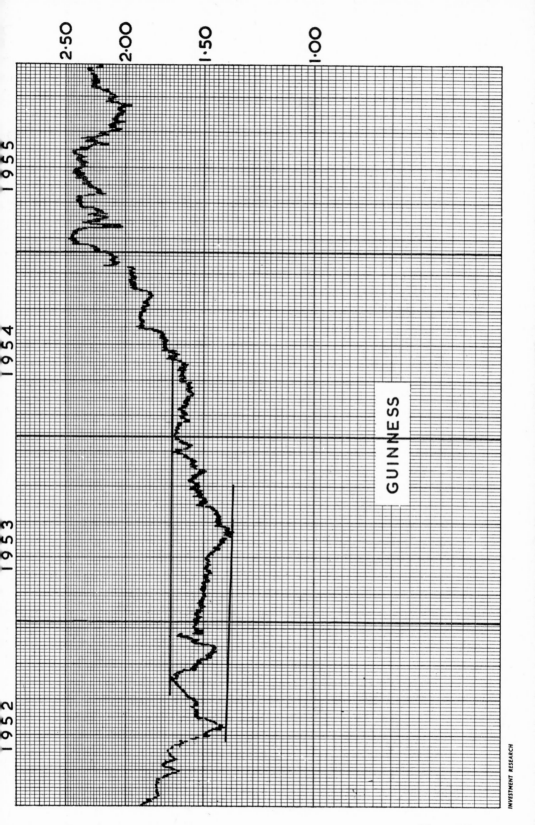

GUINNESS

Chart No. 44

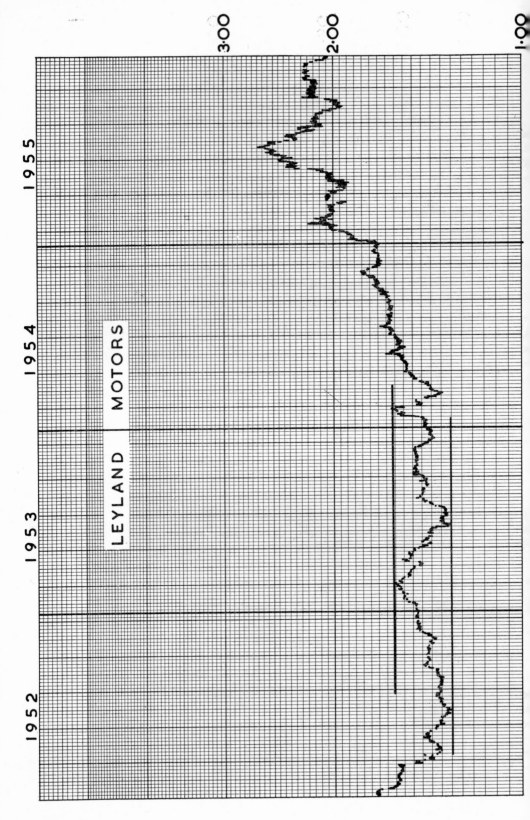

Chart No. 45

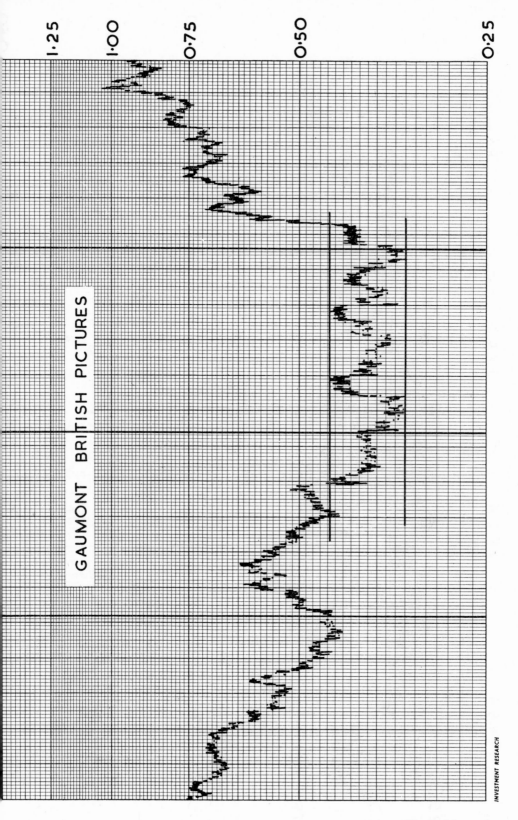

GAUMONT BRITISH PICTURES

Chart No. 46

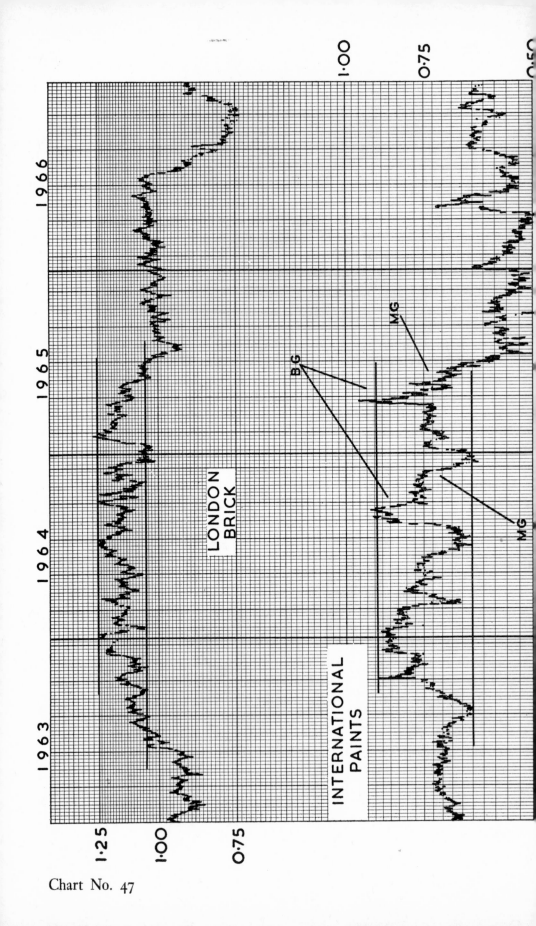

Chart No. 47

with the illustrations that follow for some more recent rectangles in Charts Nos. 46, 47 and 48.

The pattern has since become much more frequent. It was quite easy to find eight examples in the years from 1960 and a number of these are bold patterns of wide amplitude. A big rectangle was traced out by Gaumont British at the bottom in 1958 (and as the stock was very much a laggard that year the formation extended many months beyond the bottom of the market in February). This is illustrated in Chart No. 46. You will observe how the rectangle was formed underneath the resistance at 0·44 laid down by the earlier bottoms of 1956 and 1957. At a bottom a market is generally very inactive; the dealings in this rectangle are very thin except at the rallies towards the upper boundary. The pattern had a duration of 73 weeks in which the price swung up and down from 0·34 to 0·44. Then it broke out—there was no pull-back—and in three months it had reached 0·75. It crossed the pound level in October 1959 and rose still further in 1960. It is the possibility of performances like this which make the study of formations so interesting to the investor.

The pattern formed by International Paints in 1959–62 (Chart No. 47) was less helpful. There is a well-marked tendency for the price movement to be rapid between top and middle and middle and bottom; this showed up much less in Gaumont British, which was a pattern formed at the bottom. You cannot argue from this characteristic that International Paints was making a reversal pattern at the top; a continuation pattern, say halfway up, could have just the same characteristic. Lines, bands, rectangles—and triangles when we come to them—can as easily be continuation, from which the old trend is resumed, as reversal patterns, in which the direction of the trend changes. The difficulty about this pattern is that while the upward penetration of the boundary in August and September 1960 was insignificant and not well established enough to justify a speculative purchase, the strong emergence in the roaring secondary rally that was running in April 1961 was most likely to suck a chartist in. The gap that developed on re-entry into the pattern area should have warned the unfortunate buyer that this was not a pull-back but an important reversal. The share rallied briefly below the middle of the pattern area, then fell back to the bottom and plunged through to rest at 0·5.

In the upper half of the same chart we are showing London Brick for the years 1963–66. Here the rectangular area is very long, about two years. There was a false emergence at the bottom at Christmas after the first two months of Labour Government, but the share recovered to the upper boundary and then sank gradually to the bottom of the trading area and went through. But there was no immediate deep decline; the share rallied

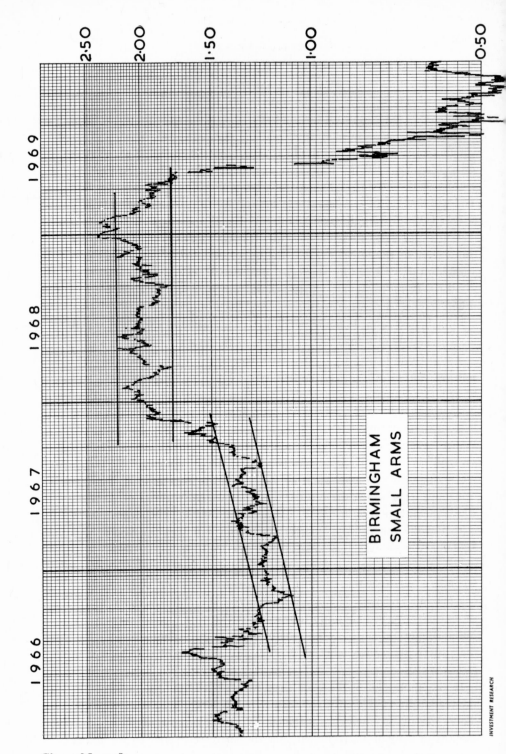

BIRMINGHAM
SMALL ARMS

Chart No. 48

mildly but always found resistance close to the bottom of the pattern. It finally fell away heavily as the July crisis of 1966 developed.

The false emergence of London Brick was not in any way a helpful development, but the false emergence of International Paints had the normal significance. When there is an emergence from a well marked pattern and it runs in the direction of the preceding trend it suggests strongly that the trading area is a continuation pattern. But if the emergence turns out to be false it indicates the contrary, that the pattern cannot generate enough strength to continue the previous trend. So the share must retreat within the pattern and either continue there till enough strength is generated or reverse the old trend. Look at Chart No. 48 which shows the movements of Birmingham Small Arms in 1966–69. The performance in 1966 was strong in the first six months; the fall in the summer took it down from 1·7 to 1·1 where it found a trend. (The trend-line drawn through the secondary bottoms of October, March and August hooks back—is it by chance?—on the bottom after the election in 1964). This eleven month trend had a fairly narrow channel, and the share soared through the upper trendline (with pull-back) in October 1967. It then ran into its rectangle which lasted about 75 weeks. At the end of 1968 the share broke strongly through the upper boundary of the formation. There was a pull-back; then the share rose strongly with a gap out of the trading area, but the rally failed just below the previous top and the share fell back within the rectangle. The failure of this upward emergence suggested very strongly that the rectangle was a reversal pattern and not a continuation. The bull market was showing its age, and one of the symptoms of a failing market is that emergences from well-formed patterns turn round back into the formation instead of fulfilling the prediction.

One of the most important things to remember about pattern is that a pattern which fails may be as significant and important and profitable to the student of charts as a pattern which succeeds. This was one of the signs that added up to form the symptoms of a bull market in decay, and a bear market in embryo.

The sequel shows that when a big pattern reverses a big rise, a share that has fallen from 2·35 to 1·7 has not fallen too low to sell.

Far the most common trading pattern is the triangle; in the years after the war a number of triangles developed in the Oil market and others appeared as reversal patterns at the tops of 1947 and 1951 and at the bottom of 1949 (British American Tobacco made one at that time and it had the same thin character as the band in that share illustrated in Chart No. 42). In the fifties and sixties the pattern seems to have become more common and it was very easy to pick out more than twenty specimens from the Investment Research chart library. The normal triangle begins

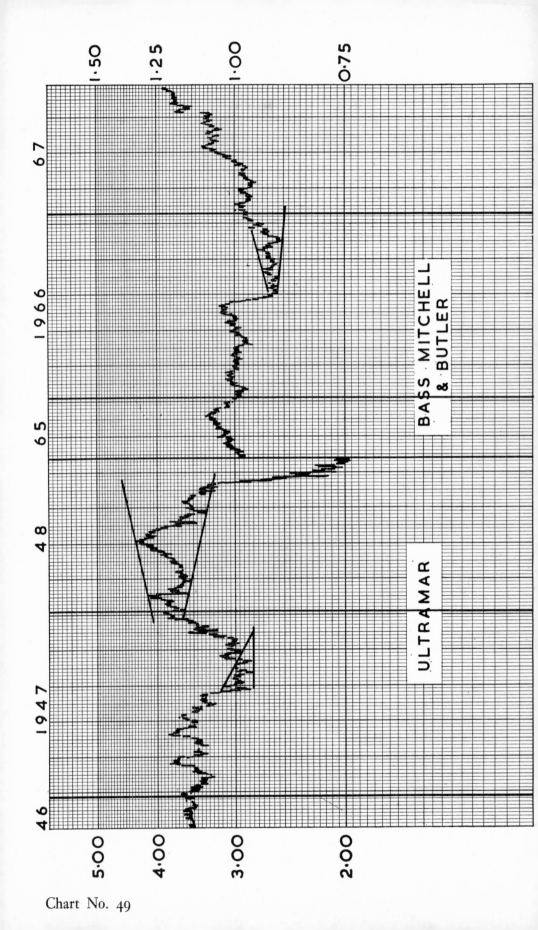

Chart No. 49

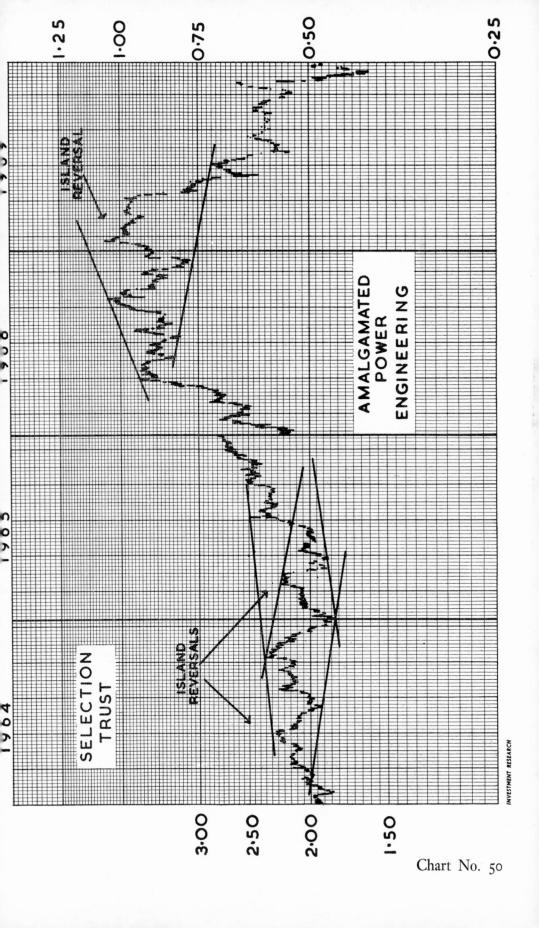

ISLAND
REVERSAL

AMALGAMATED
POWER
ENGINEERING

SELECTION
TRUST

ISLAND
REVERSALS

INVESTMENT RESEARCH

Chart No. 50

with a fairly wide amplitude and fluctuations contract as the pattern is formed; the reverse, or expanding, triangle is very rare. Let us deal with it first. The pattern, if it is a significant pattern, occurs very infrequently. Three examples were mentioned in the first edition. Of these Mawchi Mines in the latter half of 1947 may have looked like an expanding triangle in the late forties and early fifties, but it does not now. Imperial Smelting formed the pattern just before it rose steeply on the take-over by Consolidated Zinc, but this was drawn only on a weekly chart and we have no daily chart available for closer study. There remains Ultramar in 1947–48 (Chart No. 49 shows it from November 1946 to October 1948). This pattern is certainly part of a double top (a formation to which we shall come later) which was not a very helpful diagnosis; the previous top occurred in 1946. It could also be classified, much more helpfully, as a 'Head & Shoulders top with drooping neckline'. So we do not gain much from using this evidence to prove that expanding triangles are significant patterns. The Investment Research chart library was carefully scoured for specimens of this formation, and in the sixties four examples were found. Bass Mitchell & Butler appears on Chart No. 49, coupled most unsuitably with Ultramar. The chart runs from the beginning of September 1965 to the end of August 1967. The expanding triangle appears as a reversal pattern at the bottom of the market in the autumn of 1966. The share rose out of the bottom area, settled down above it under resistance at 0·75 and then resumed its rise towards the point of merger with Charrington. One could have interpreted the chart without knowing anything about expanding triangles, and the move that followed the emergence was not of large dimensions for that time. In Chart No. 50 we present Amalgamated Power Engineering in 1968–69 and Selection Trust in 1964–65. Amalgamated Power is a reversal at the top. It is, like Ultramar, a double top; but the character is different as the tops are not widely separated. Also, like Ultramar, the lower boundary droops. The pull-back in the second quarter of 1969 is a fine specimen. Selection Trust in 1964–65 shows a long trading area lasting about a year and a half. This does have the characteristics of an expanding triangle, but it could also, and much more helpfully, be treated as a diamond. A diamond is a pair of triangles, one expanding and one contracting, back to back, and the emergence in July 1965 gave a much better buying opportunity than could have been found in the expanding triangle. Finally let us mention the monstrous expanding triangle traced out by Associated Electrical Industries which started in April 1963 and was resolved upwards in October 1967! By that time the upper boundary stood 130% above the lower. This pattern was certainly striking, but it was no use at all! The expanding triangle is an infrequent and unimportant formation. It can generally be interpreted more easily by reference to the general theory of support and resistance, of trends, and the broad principles of technical analysis, and it does not seem worth any further study.

The normal or contracting triangle has in recent years been a fairly common pattern. It consists of a series of movements and countermovements, each smaller than its predecessor; so it is possible to enclose the pattern within trendlines which meet at some point in the future (in the expanding triangle the trendlines meet at a point in the past). It seems unwise to consider as triangles patterns which show only two contacts to each converging trendline; you require at least three contacts on one of the two boundaries and there cannot be less than two on the other. A triangle is usually generated by a violent movement that goes too far and is corrected by a countermovement, and the first movement in the pattern is either such a countermovement, or possibly more often the countermovement to a countermovement. Take the case of Amalgamated Roadstone in 1965–66, shown in Chart No. 51. The share rose in the early months of 1965 from 1·9 to 2·7 and then returned, in a two stage movement to 1·9. The rally to 2·3 is the first movement of the triangle (the minor rally to that level in July is not part of the pattern although the upper boundary of the triangle hooks back onto it). The share made two attempts in October to rally through 2·3 and then retreated towards 2·0. It rallied just above that figure and returned to 2·3 whence it worked down slowly to 2·1. At this stage you could draw a horizontal trendline over the top of the pattern with a double and single contact and a rising trendline under the bottoms, and these two lines intersected round 2·3 at the beginning of June 1966. The price failed to reach up again to the upper boundary, came down again to the lower limit, rallied even less effectively and dropped through the rising lower trendline. The triangle had been resolved downwards. A rally started just above 2·0 and returned to the lower boundary; this constituted the pull-back. The share then resumed its decline. You will have noted that this pattern was formed within the primary trend channel; the development of the pattern carried the price across the trend channel from a contact with the lower trendline to the upper trendline. This is not a universal feature of triangles, but the development is not uncommon.

Here we have a pattern which interrupted a downtrend; the share went down, possibly a little too far, entered an area of argument, worked out in that area whether the stronger pressures were upwards or downward, found they were downward and resumed its downtrend. The triangle is thus to be classed as a continuation pattern.

The Americans apply also a second system of classification to triangles, symmetrical (which we should call isosceles) or right-angled (which we

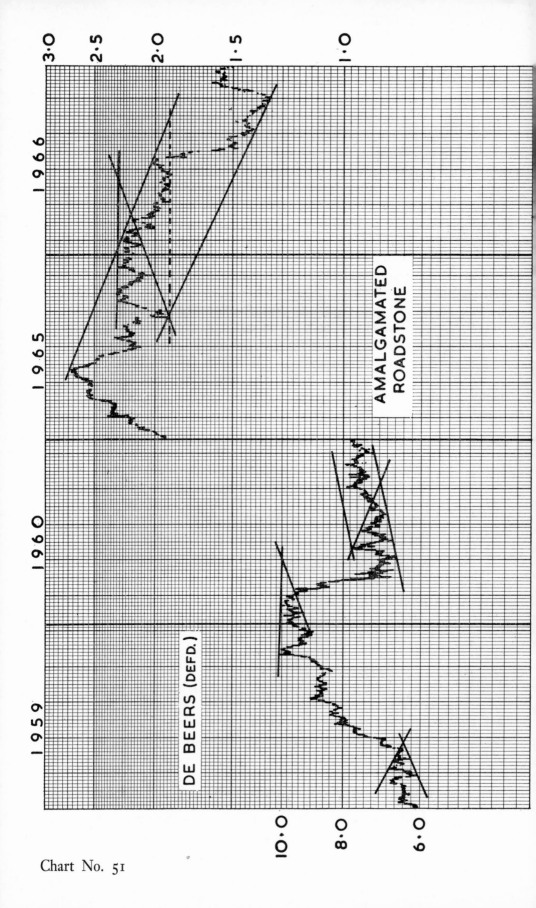

DE BEERS (DEFD.)

AMALGAMATED
ROADSTONE

Chart No. 51

might more clearly call flat-topped or flat-bottomed). As they have to fit all triangles into these two terms it is obvious that they must be applied fairly loosely. They expect flat-topped triangles to be followed by an upward movement, flat-bottomed by a downward, and you will notice at once that this pattern does not conform to their rule. In Britain it does not appear to be a good rule. But it may not be as foolish as it looks at first sight. The prediction which the triangle is supposed to give is that the emergence will be followed by a movement equal to the base. The implication, not so far noticed in any American work known to the author, is that a triangle is half a parallelogram in which you do not know, till the pattern is resolved, which boundary is the side and which the diagonal. When the pattern is resolved, the share proceeds through the diagonal until it reaches the opposite side of the parallelogram and continues in that trend. If your share breaks out through the flat side, this notion gives it quite large scope to move in the direction indicated. But if it breaks through the sloping side, the pattern is converted, as in the case of Amalgamated Roadstone, into a rectangle and little damage is done. (It was unfortunate for adherents of this theory in the case of Amalgamated Roadstone that the rectangle too turned out badly for the bulls. There are many examples of 'right-angled' triangles where the resolution is not through the flat top or bottom, and this piece of American chartist folk-lore should not be followed at all blindly in the London market).

Active mining shares are good places to look for triangles; so let us turn again to Chart No. 51 where we have coupled with Amalgamated Roadstone the picture of De Beers in 1959–60. This shows three triangles. The first, in March and April 1959, is near enough to isosceles (but it will be better in future to call them normal as isosceles is far too precise a term). It can be drawn flat-topped, but then there are only two points of contact on each boundary and that is not enough. The first is the correction of a countermovement, a rally. The price drops back and rallies, drops further, rallies to the line joining the two immediately preceding tertiary peaks, drops towards the lower boundary, and then emerges upwards. The old uptrend is resumed; this was a continuation triangle. You will note that the order of the contacts is bottom line, top line, top line, bottom line, top line and the contacts do not alternate from top to bottom as they do in a perfect triangle.

Next in the winter of 1959–60 a new triangle was traced out just under £10·0 and this was flat-topped. According to the American rule it was likely to be resolved upwards, but it turned out to be a reversal pattern and was resolved downwards. There was a sufficient pull-back after the emergence to give the stale bull a good chance of making a reasonable sale; this surely was a very helpful pattern, provided that the investor was

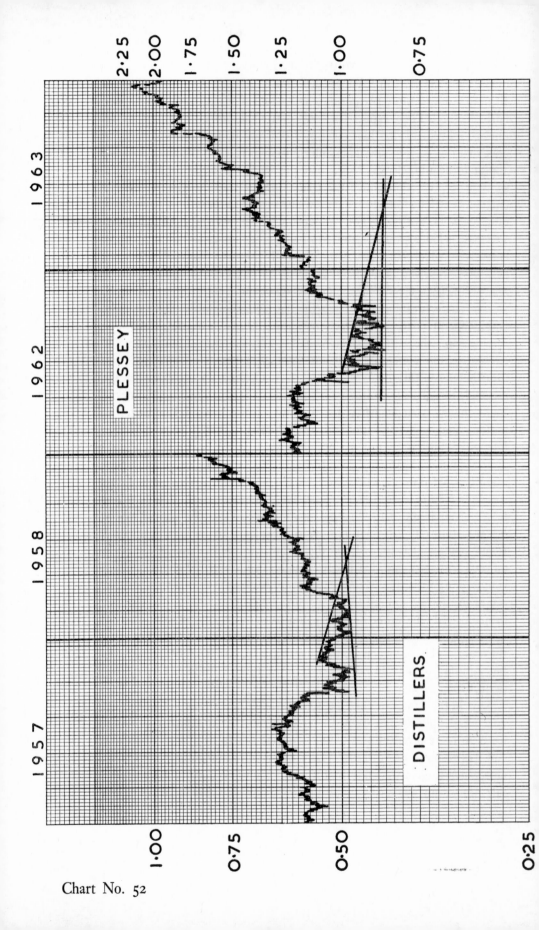

Chart No. 52

not blinded by the American expectation of an emergence through the flat side.

The fall was heavy, and when the countermovement developed it became the first leg of still another triangle. This was of the normal shape. This time the emergence was upward, but the share failed to complete the pattern by reaching the upper parallel and turned off and, early in the next year, cut downward through the lower trendline. The triangle failed to fulfil its prediction, and it offered no profit but luckily signalled quite clearly where the share should be sold and no serious loss was involved. In this share, triangles offered two splendid indications while the third time the failure was not damaging.

Let us look next at two reversal triangles in Chart No. 52. Both are flat-bottomed triangles with the emergence upwards through the sloping side. Both show the reversal pattern coinciding with the end of a bear market, a reversal of the primary trend for the British industrial market, Distillers in 1957–58 and Plessey, a much more active pattern, in 1962. In both cases the subsequent performance was highly satisfactory, outrunning by far the quite small prediction which the triangles made.

For our two reversals at the top, shown in Chart No. 53, we have shown Albright & Wilson and Rio Tinto Zinc in the years 1968–69. Albright shows three contacts on each boundary of the triangle and a downward emergence after the third contact with the upper boundary. This was followed immediately by a pull-back, very much of a last chance for the bulls. The support at 1·00 worked late and the rally was feeble, a further sign of weakness. This was a pattern that worked well.

Rio Tinto Zinc is a rather bigger pattern. You will notice that the rally from 3·25 in March failed to make a third contact on the upper boundary (it is doubtful whether you should count two contacts in January). But the general character of the pattern was such that it could be accepted as a triangle, and the well developed pull-back at the end of May provided a good selling opportunity. The share did recover later in 1969 and reached 3·5 at the beginning of 1970, but after that it suffered a very sub-stantial fall.

For good specimens of the continuation triangle in a bull market, we show J. Laing A in 1963–64 and British Oxygen in 1957–58 paired to-gether in Chart No. 54. Laing shows up as a fairly thin market and the triangle develops from a spearhead rise whose correction drops right to the support. This gives a wide base to the triangle, with the promise of a big move out of the pattern. The pattern took 30 weeks to work out and was followed by an upward emergence and a very satisfactory rise.

British Oxygen made a promising looking double bottom in 1957–58 at the bottom of the bear market. The share then rose above the intermediate

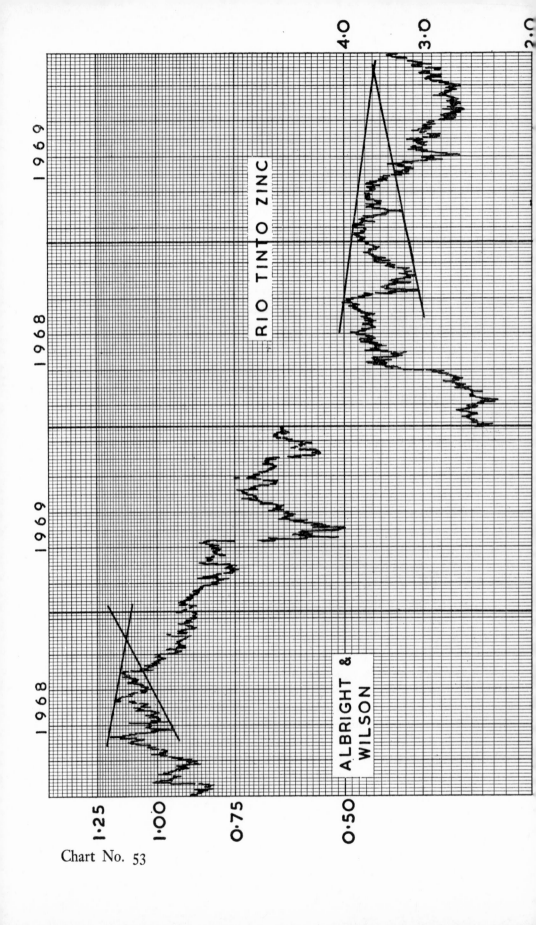

Chart No. 53

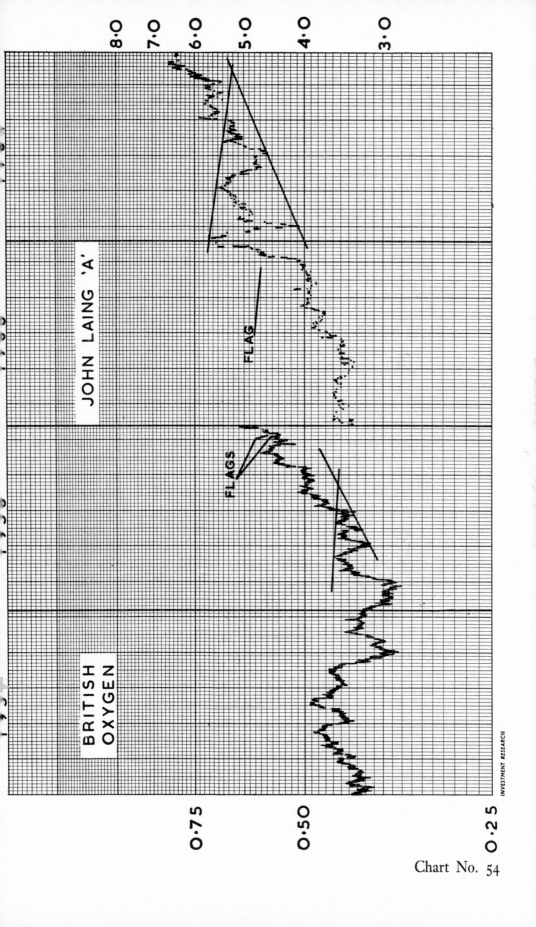

JOHN LAING 'A'

BRITISH OXYGEN

FLAG

FLAGS

8·0 7·0 6·0 5·0 4·0 3·0

0·75 0·50 0·25

INVESTMENT RESEARCH

Chart No. 54

top (the key to the double bottom pattern is a rise above the top between the two bottoms) and then ran into a trading area which took a triangular shape. The triangle was nearly flat-topped and the resolution was upward. It is this type of flat-topped triangle which usually breaks upwards, a trading area established in a strong stage of an upward primary trend. This combination of double bottom and continuation triangle was the precursor of a very large rise which gave splendid profits to the bulls who took note of these patterns.

Finally we must look at an outstanding failure in Chart 55 which shows New Broken Hill in 1967–70. Here a very big triangle developed with the first contact in August 1968 and the upward emergence in November 1969. The share made great efforts to rise when the triangle was resolved upwards, but it was too late in the day. The price dropped back astride the upper boundary of the triangle, then slipped inside the pattern again and finally went through the lower boundary in a steep decline. Perhaps the more common failure of a triangle is that illustrated for De Beers in Chart No. 51, where the price emerges through one side of the pattern, makes some progress, then falters and turns back and runs round the apex of the triangle. This is what the Americans call an 'end-run'.

Remember that the successful completion of a pattern is a potential source of profit to be exploited to the full. A failure is a warning against serious potential loss, and many failures occur at primary reversal points. The New Broken Hill failure was a helpful comment on the prospect of many other Australian shares.

The main 'consolidations' listed by Magee, the patterns which may signal a reversal of the trend or lead to a continuation of it, are triangles, rectangles and lines. He also mentions the 'flat-topped broadening pattern' which is an expanding triangle with a flat top and 'any sideways pattern with declining volume'. Of course, any pattern with a well-defined boundary that is horizontal or nearly horizontal is of interest to the chartist. The principles of technical analysis suggest that there is some substantial obstacle to progress through the horizontal boundary, that if the pressure within the pattern builds up sufficiently to overcome that obstacle then the share is likely to make substantial progress in the direction indicated. The reversal of Calico Printers at the bottom in Chart No. 36 illustrates this clearly.

The inverted Head & Shoulders, if you ever happen to meet one, is another pattern with a horizontal boundary and the same principles apply to it. He also mentions 'saucers' which are formed when a secondary rally or reaction, followed by a renewal of the primary trend, takes a rounded instead of an angular shape. Scallops, which he rightly describes as a very beautiful pattern, consist of a long series of saucers in succession. These

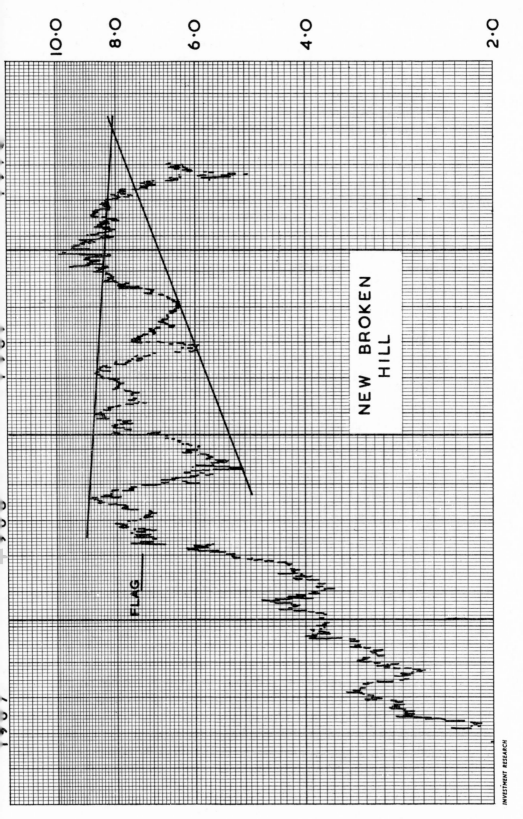

NEW BROKEN HILL

FLAG

INVESTMENT RESEARCH

Chart No. 55

last three patterns may occur sufficiently often in America to be worth mention in Magee's book; in Britain, like hurricanes in Hampshire, they hardly ever happen.

There remain two extremely important patterns, which belong to the category of sideways patterns with declining volume; these are the flag and the pennant. They are however essentially tertiary while those which we have been describing belong generally to the primary or secondary trends. Further, flags and pennants must be considered in conjunction with gaps; so we shall leave all these to a later stage.

The patterns which we have discussed so far have one point in common, namely that the observer cannot soundly guess the direction of the emergence. Further the existence of the pattern does not depend on an emergence either in the direction of the preceding trend or in the opposite direction. The patterns which we are now going to discuss depend for their existence on the emergence's being in the right direction. If there is no downward emergence from a Head & Shoulders top, a double top or a triple top, the pattern has not been completed; if the pattern is completed there ensues a prediction which may or may not be fulfilled. When one is working on patterns with two possible solutions, especially the triangle, it is possible for the curve of price to go through the apex of the triangle without any emergence, and in that case a subsequent emergence from the area of argument is not likely to be of particular interest, unless some other pattern is subsequently formed. When you see a triangle, rectangle or line, it is easy to recognise, and you expect to be told the direction of the new trend, after the interruption—for a triangle is essentially the interruption of a trend and you should not expect anything from a triangular shape if it is not the interruption of a trend. When you see a pure reversal pattern like a double top or a Head & Shoulders forming, you do not state confidently, 'That is a double top' (or a Head & Shoulders, as the case may be), but you ask humbly, 'Is that a double top?' Until the pattern is completed by an undoubted penetration of the vital boundary, the humble question cannot be answered, although you may have come earlier to the decision that the circumstances make it sufficiently likely that the pattern will be completed for a sale or a purchase to be made in advance.

The king of reversal patterns is the Head & Shoulders (reversed Head & Shoulders at the bottom). In order to study it one has to learn the anatomy and the prediction. The pattern consists of a strong rise (there can be no validity in a reversal pattern that has nothing to reverse), followed by a reaction. This is followed by a new rise to a higher level, followed by a reaction to about the same level as the bottom of the preceding reaction. The next development is a new rise which falls substan-

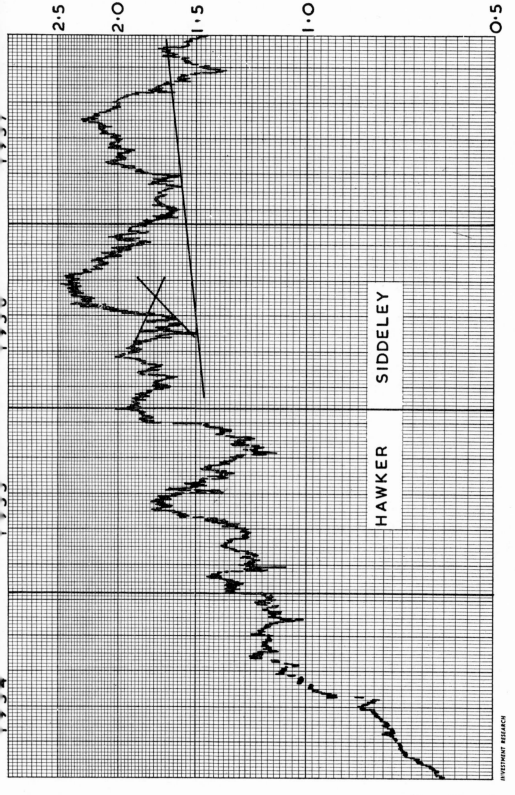

HAWKER   SIDDELEY

INVESTMENT RESEARCH

Chart No. 56

tially short of its predecessor. You now have a first rise and reaction, the left shoulder, a bigger rise and reaction, the head, a third rise, not up to the top of the head, and reaction, the right shoulder. As the reaction develops you draw a line through the bottoms of the first two reactions—you might call them the collar-bones—and that is your neckline. The neckline is vital; if the reaction from the right shoulder penetrates the neckline, the pattern is completed. What is the prediction? Expect the curve to decline further, in due course, from the penetration of the neckline by a distance equal to the vertical distance from the top of the head to the neckline.

At this stage you want an example, preferably of a fairly classical shape. We have chosen Hawker Siddeley in the years 1954–57. There was a strong rise in 1954; this provided the pattern with the essential condition that there was something to reverse. The share reached a high level in the summer of 1955, fell back in the autumn to its worst level of the first quarter, and then soared to a new high level at the end of the year. After a reaction in the spring, the share ran up again to 2·0 where it had turned back in the winter and then fell through the low point between the tops to 1·5. (This completed a double top formation but the prediction was not fulfilled, as you will see later when we deal with double tops). The share ran into a triangle that lasted only six weeks, emerged through the top side, and ran up to its final peak at 2·45. From this level a long reaction developed. This terminated at 1·63; the previous reaction had ended at 1·48. These might be collar-bones, but there was no more certainty or likelihood that they were than there was in the case of the two reactions either side of the highest price in 1955. The share rallied but crossed 2·0 with some difficulty and then struggled on to 2·28. There had been no difficulty in the rise at the end of 1955, nothing like the reversal that soon took the price back to 2·0. The chartists sharpened their pencils and drew in the neckline, joining the two collar-bones at 1·48 and 1·63 and extending the line to left and right. In the third week of September there was a negligible penetration followed by a rally. A fortnight later the price was down to the neckline again; this time the rally was more feeble. Then there is a gap in the price curve (we come to gaps later) and vigorous trading for a fortnight in a narrow range (this is the flag pattern to which we shall also come later on). The Head & Shoulders pattern was completed; the neckline was broken and any stale bull who had studied the chartist lore would have felt it wise to sell. There was another gap as the price moved down out of the flag till it reversed sharply at 1·35. The stale bulls who had not sold in the flag had not had a quick pull-back to give them a chance of getting out, but now we have a delayed pull-back, up to the neckline but not significantly through it round 1·7. Then the share slipped down and

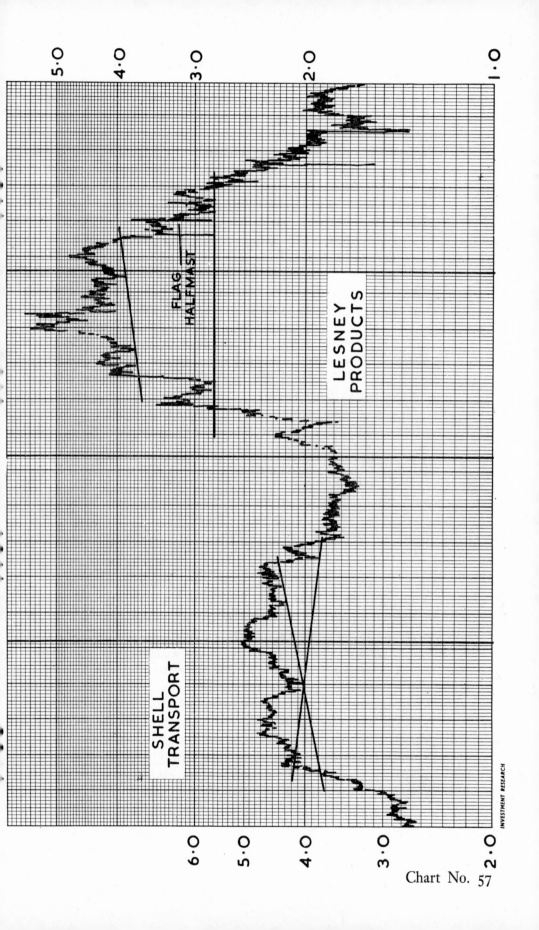

LESNEY PRODUCTS

FLAG HALFMAST

SHELL TRANSPORT

INVESTMENT RESEARCH

Chart No. 57

idled round 1·5 for the next three years or more. What was the prediction? This is the distance—for a pattern of these dimensions on the logarithmic scale, although the arithmetic scale may be relevant for patterns that are completed in a small number of weeks—taken vertically from the head to the neckline, and measured again vertically from the point of emergence on the neckline. The prediction is thus 1·0—and the share eventually grounded, after a final perverse decline in which every measure likely to improve the company's position was greeted by a further fall of price, at 0·97 in May 1962.

The working out of this pattern took a long time. A large rise is not easily nor quickly reversed, and this rise did not conform to the pattern of the share index which turned down in the summer of 1955. Instead this share rose against the general trend to a top in the third quarter of 1956 and traced out its pattern over 93 weeks. There is an even longer pattern in United Glass Bottle between May 1960 and June, or possibly, October 1962 (the June penetration is barely visible). This Head & Shoulders pattern had a duration of 98 or possibly 113 weeks; the head was formed at 1·13, the neckline was horizontal at 0·69 and the share bottomed out 0·28 in November 1966.

So when a Head & Shoulders pattern is completed, the share has often already fallen a long way, but the indication of the pattern is that it is still likely to fall a long way further.

Let us look next at a comparatively short pattern, that traced out by Lesney Products in 1968 and 1969 and illustrated in Chart No. 57. The share was rising steeply in the first half of 1968, but at midsummer it traced out, over a few weeks, the beginnings of a Head & Shoulders pattern. In this case the right shoulder was never formed, but Head & Shoulder patterns of short duration do exist and their predictions, which are usually not very large, are often swiftly fulfilled, after which the price jerks quickly back into its old trend. If a narrow Head & Shoulders appeared at a time when many other reversal patterns were appearing, it should be treated with great respect, but at this particular time in 1968 it did not appear threatening. But in due course it forms the left shoulder of our pattern. The share next ran up, twice, well over 5·0 and then retreated to 4·05. There was a triangular pattern between 4·0 and 4·5 with a downward emergence, but the prediction was not fulfilled and the share rallied to 4·75. The swift reaction from this level suggested a right shoulder was being formed and in less than five weeks the neckline was pierced. The share fell below 0·5 in the first half of 1970. You will see a second neckline at the 2·8 level; and this in its turn was penetrated with a prediction of 1·4. This prediction also was overfulfilled. Note that the prediction is for a decline of *at least* the distance from head to neckline;

Head & Shoulder patterns are thought to have failed only if the decline falls significantly short of the prediction. The duration of this pattern was 38 weeks.

Necklines need not be close to the horizontal. They can be uptilted, which foreshortens the prediction, or downtilted, which extends the prediction. This can be seen in the second share on Chart No. 57, Shell Transport over the same two years. The first pattern to emerge was a Head & Shoulders with an uptilted neckline and a rather stunted right shoulder. The pattern was completed in early June 1969 with a fall down to 3·8. The prediction was 3·65. The share rallied from 3·8 in a deferred pull-back and then continued its fall beyond the prediction. But the secondary bottom at 3·8 marked out the downtilted neckline of a second Head & Shoulders pattern. This time the prediction was 3·0 and the price fell lower than that in May 1970. The duration of the pattern was 58 weeks. How much can your neckline tilt? It must be possible to extend it into the price curve of the share on the left side, that is before the pattern begins to form; if there is no such contact the verdict must be 'No left sleeve' and the pattern is not a Head & Shoulders. You must not have one collar-bone above the other shoulder. That apparently is beyond the limit of deformity; but two heads between two shoulders, two or more shoulders on one side and a greater or lesser number on the other are acceptable. In fact, where you can see a neckline which is drawn across two or more extremes and which impinges on the price curve on its way into the pattern, watch for a large potential move on penetration of the neckline.

Do Head & Shoulders patterns ever fail? Of course they do; no chart pattern is infallible. But they are deceitful; do not trust them. You can say that they have failed if a rally from a little distance below the neckline outruns the head, but a strong rally through the neckline is not sufficient evidence. Look at the pattern of Mercantile Credit in Chart No. 58. There is a beautiful Head & Shoulders pattern with an almost horizontal neckline; the right shoulder is a bit too tall but otherwise it looks a perfect specimen. (If we had had volume data we might have been able to fault the pattern on that score). But the prediction was a fall to 0·88, and the share rallied instead at 1·05 and ran up above the neckline. But your Head & Shoulders fan would point out that the price has since retreated to a second neckline, extending the pattern to cover the period from the second quarter of 1967; at the moment of writing this, late in June 1970, the share has retreated again to this neckline and rallied sharply from it. The prediction of this larger Head & Shoulders pattern is not clear (it depends on the point of penetration of the neckline, if the pattern is actually completed), but at the moment 0·65 seems a fair guess. You need strong nerves to want to be a bull in such circumstances!

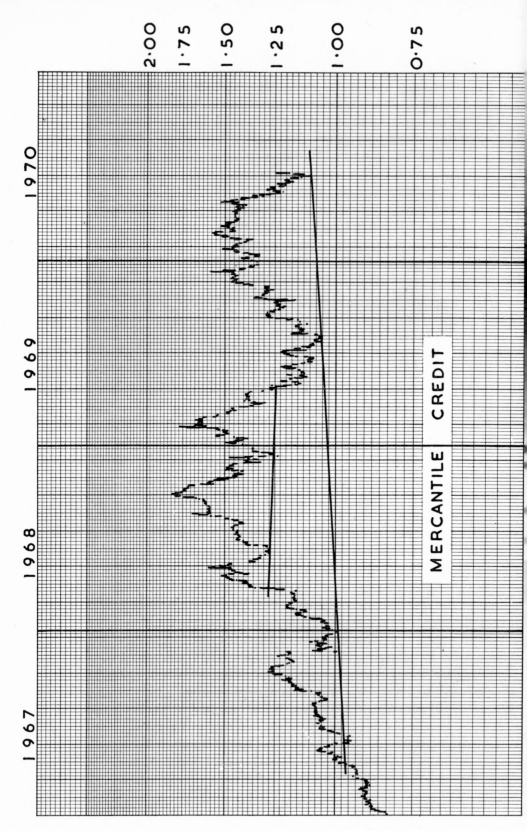

MERCANTILE CREDIT

Chart No. 58

Perhaps you should not be frightened of one Head & Shoulders, perhaps not even of two. But when you see this pattern developing on a dozen or more charts in your library, you are seeing one of the visible warnings of an impending change of the primary trend. The reason why this pattern is so frightening is that it occurs most at a time of a reversal of a primary rise; it is likely to appear in shares whose bull market has been strongly developed, where enthusiasm is strong and where a reversal of the primary trend is likely to mean the undermining of the case for holding the share. It is probably better to lose a few shares which rise further than to be involved in one fall like that of Lesney Products.

The reversed Head & Shoulders pattern is a much more cheerful affair. The chartist generally uses the Head & Shoulders pattern to avoid or minimise loss; he uses the reverse Head & Shoulders to make a profit. There is no difficulty about the pattern; it is like the Head & Shoulders only it appears upside down. It appears to be a less common pattern; when the author was looking for charts to illustrate this chapter, he easily found twice as many Head & Shoulders patterns as reverse Head & Shoulders. It is a pattern which requires vigour for its development, and a market is vigorous at the top and anaemic at the bottom. Thus the reverse Head & Shoulders patterns show smaller dimensions both laterally and vertically. Some of them are very lazy patterns, working themselves out in a rather lackadaisical fashion; these occur also in ordinary Head & Shoulders patterns at the top (there was one in Free State Geduld in 1959) but not so often.

The patterns illustrated are presented in reverse chronological order, starting with C. T. Bowring in 1969–70, which occupies half of Chart No. 59. This chart is exceptional in showing this pattern at a point which was not the bottom of the market; for it is at the bottom of the market that the reverse Head & Shoulders ordinarily appears. The pattern is duplex; there is a small reverse Head & Shoulders with a duration of 14 weeks inside a larger pattern with a duration of 33 weeks. At the time of writing the smaller pattern had already fulfilled its prediction, but the larger pattern looked for 3·4 and the highest level touched was only 3·25. Purchases might have been made on the emergences at 2·35 and 2·6, and it would have been prudent to sell on the triple signal at 2·8. The three adverse signs at this point were the decline on the gap, plainly visible on the normal charting scale, decline through the support at 2·85, and penetration of the rising trendline. The profits would have incurred the short term Capital Gains Tax and, on the second purchase at least, would have been small, but in a bear market a small taxed profit is better than no profit at all.

The second share illustrated in Chart No. 59 is Associated Electrical

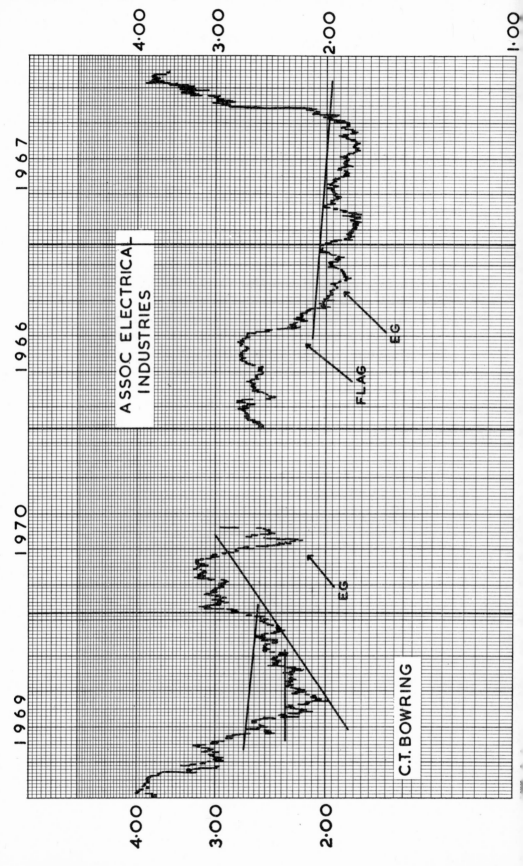

Chart No. 59

Industries in 1966–67. This is the last act of the expanding triangle referred to earlier. The share came down in the summer crisis of 1966 from 2·75 below 2·00 and there traced out a lazy reversed Head & Shoulders which lasted 53 weeks. Most other shares had started to rally as early as November 1966, but all that A.E.I. could make in that period was an insignificant left shoulder. It went on reclining in the pattern as this slowly worked out to the end of August 1967, and then came a vigorous late rise. The share rose from 2·00 to 3·75 in ten weeks, and the technical analysts who followed this pattern were no doubt duly grateful to it.

There is a much bolder pattern to be seen in Chart No. 60 where we have shown English Electric for 1960–63. The course of the ratio is interesting. This shows how the share went down at a faster than average pace in the bear market and rose at a faster than average pace in the subsequent bull market. The left shoulder is well formed, but the right shoulder is ill-developed (it is the last few weeks of a small expanding pattern). You should note the big gap that occurred at the beginning of the formation of the left shoulder, the way the trading area, after the bottom, lay under the resistance produced by the trading round the end of 1961 and in April 1962, while the expanding pattern of the right shoulder was supported on the tops of the January and April trading. The pattern needed 49 weeks for its working out.

Chart No. 61 shows Peninsular & Oriental over the four year period, 1957–60; the reverse Head & Shoulders occupies only a small part of the chart, but we need the details of 1959–60 to see how the prediction was belatedly fulfilled by the development of a spearhead top after the General Election. The chart starts off with a Head & Shoulders top in 1957; the share had come up from 1·35 in 1956 and so had little to reverse. The Head & Shoulders top was not a striking pattern, and its downward prediction was comparatively small, about 1·38 which was easily overrun. The reverse Head & Shoulders was a bold pattern; it followed the normal course for this pattern at that time, conforming to the general timing of the end of the bear market. The prediction was for a rise to 2·00 or above, and this was not achieved till October 1959. The pattern took 37 weeks to work out.

Chart No. 62 deals with Rootes Motors A for the years 1957–60; our immediate concern is with the reversed Head & Shoulders pattern worked out over 46 weeks from the winter of 1957–58. It was a lazy pattern with slow fluctuation, and the dealing after November 1957 was remarkably thin. But the emergence was bold and determined and offered good profits to those who dealt on the chart (but these profits were not as good as those won over the period from November 1956 to October 1960 from British Motor Corporation and Ford). The reverse Head & Shoulders

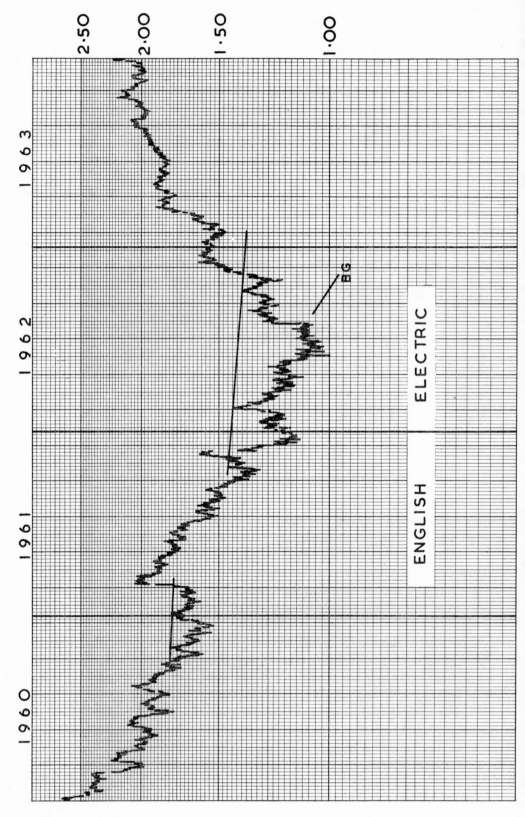

Chart No. 60

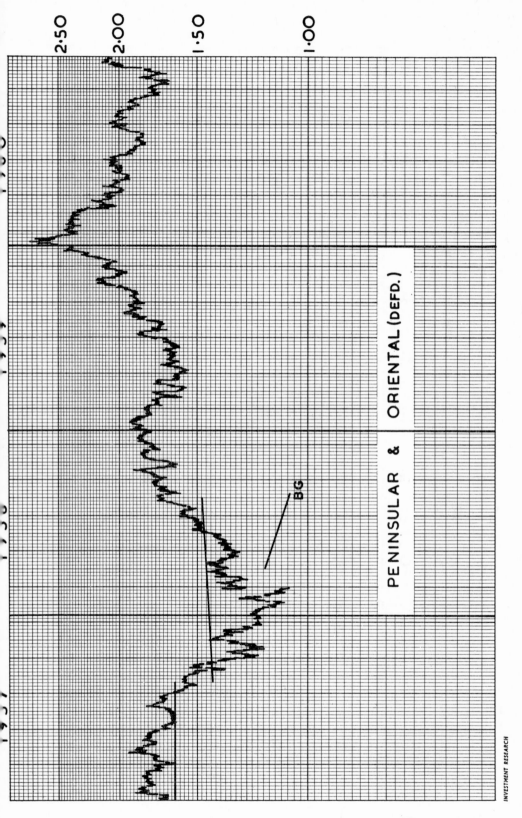

PENINSULAR & ORIENTAL (DEFD.)

BG

Chart No. 61

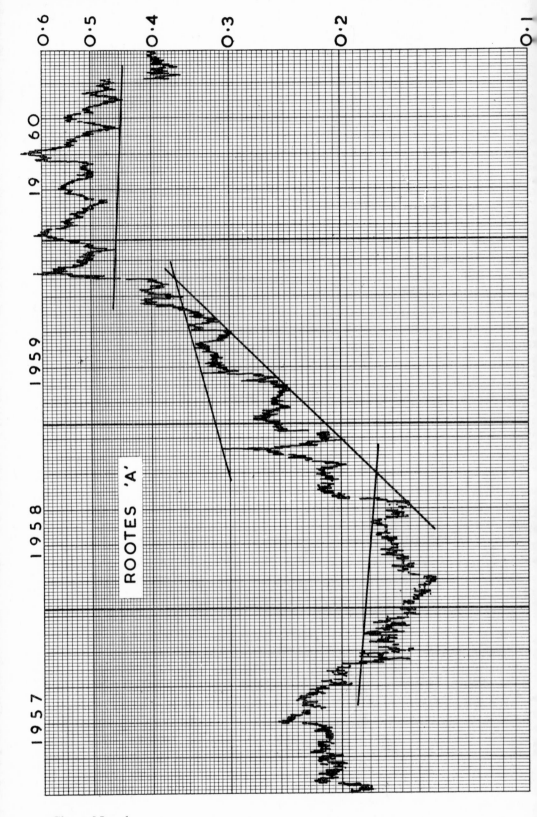

ROOTES 'A'

Chart No. 62

pattern tells you that it is right to buy the stock that makes the pattern, not that it is the right stock to buy. The chart is extended over a four year period partly because we shall want to discuss later the remarkable rising wedge pattern in 1958–59, partly for the sake of the pattern in 1960. What is the name to give to this pattern? It is hardly a triple top, especially as it is quite as well defined along the bottom side as along the top. You can, if you like, call it a broadening formation—there is too much breadth at its start to call it an expanding triangle. But why give it a name at all; what is important in reading charts of this type is the penetration of a well established trendline or neckline. In this case the neckline is clear enough as is the vigour in the anatomy above the neckline. You do not need a name; you see the neckline penetrated and will not be surprised to hear that after this incident Rootes Motors A was never the same stock again!

After the Head & Shoulders the next reversal pattern listed by Magee is the rounding turn. This is the bowl or saucer at the bottom, or the inverted bowl at the top, but it is a pattern which we do not see in the London market. Perhaps it does not come out well on the scale used for the Investment Research daily charts; perhaps we are not trained to look for it, which may be a good thing as it seems to depend for its validity on accurate volume charts which cannot be drawn for London markets. There is just one rounding turn of which we have clear and bitter memories, that of Canadian Eagle in 1958–59. If anything is a rounding turn, surely the inverted bowl of Chart No. 63 is? But just when it was coming to the stage when it ought to have gone plunging to destruction, the secondary trend changed, the trend reversed in a minor reversed Head & Shoulders, and Shell made a take-over bid. Little Head & Shoulders patterns, at top or bottom, can be very important for the secondary trend. The incident strengthens our argument that what the chartist wants to watch, much more than formal pattern, is the interplay of trend channel and support and resistance. Here the head is a second test of the support laid down by the last rally before the Suez bottom late in 1956, the neckline lies along the resistance laid down several times at 2·75, the second rally to the neckline penetrates the declining trendline. These are the indications we value, not rather imprecise patterns like inverted bowls, however useful those may be in New York with its superior volume statistics.

The next of Magee's formations is the 'dormant bottom'. This we cannot illustrate. It is a pattern that occurs in inactive stocks, mostly companies of comparatively small capitalisation. The downward trend flattens out and markings tend to disappear, even disappear entirely. Then bargains reappear on the chart, there may be a steep minor rally and reaction, volume builds up and the price begins to rise out of the bottom

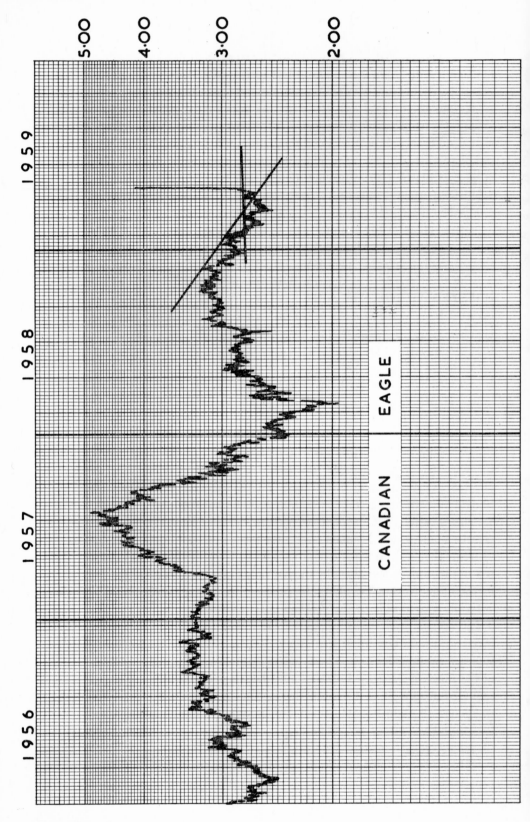

Chart No. 63

area. Unfortunately for devotees of this pattern, daily charts are required and the plotting of daily charts for the enormous number of narrow market companies whose shares are quoted in London is a profitless pursuit. We have relied on the Investment Research chart library which restricts its daily plotting, with very few exceptions, to the shares of large companies with active markets.

The triangle and rectangle, very important reversal patterns, have been dealt with already as they can also be continuation patterns, and this brings us to the controversial field of the double and triple tops and bottoms. For the broad share indices—and to a lesser extent in narrower, but well-balanced, indices—the importance is immense. The bear market bottoms in London since the war have all been reversed Head & Shoulders, except 1949 which was a double bottom. The only Head & Shoulders at the top has been 1955. The 1959 top had no formal pattern, but all the rest, 1947, 1951, 1964–66 and 1968–69 were all double tops. But the share index does not make a double top because a lot of its constituents are doing the same thing (though it may make a double bottom for this reason). Generally a number of sectors make the running in the first peak and exhaust their strength; there is a reaction, and the market gains enough vigour for a second assault which is led to a large extent by different sectors, though some which performed well at the first top may perform even better at the second.

Let us deal first with the principles of the double and triple top; they apply equally in reverse to the double and triple bottom. The pattern begins with the share's forming a top or bottom. Then a corrective reaction or rally of secondary dimensions takes the price away from the extreme. After a substantial interval the share returns to within 3% of the extreme (and for a triple top or bottom the process is repeated). The pattern is completed when the final move away from the top or bottom penetrates by a significant margin the support or resistance level shown by the secondary correction between the tops or bottoms. In some cases there is no evidence for the existence of this key support or resistance level except that it is the point at which the secondary correction was reversed. In other cases the secondary correction terminates at a level where you can see that support or resistance had been previously laid down. Obviously the validity of the formation for prediction will depend in many cases on this key level. Is it found at a price where there is real support or resistance? Or has the level been fixed because the secondary correction had simply exhausted its impetus? In the second case there seems no reason why a subsequent penetration of the level should be significant. The completion of a double top or double bottom is not achieved in the way in which a Head & Shoulders or other neckline pattern is completed. When a neck-

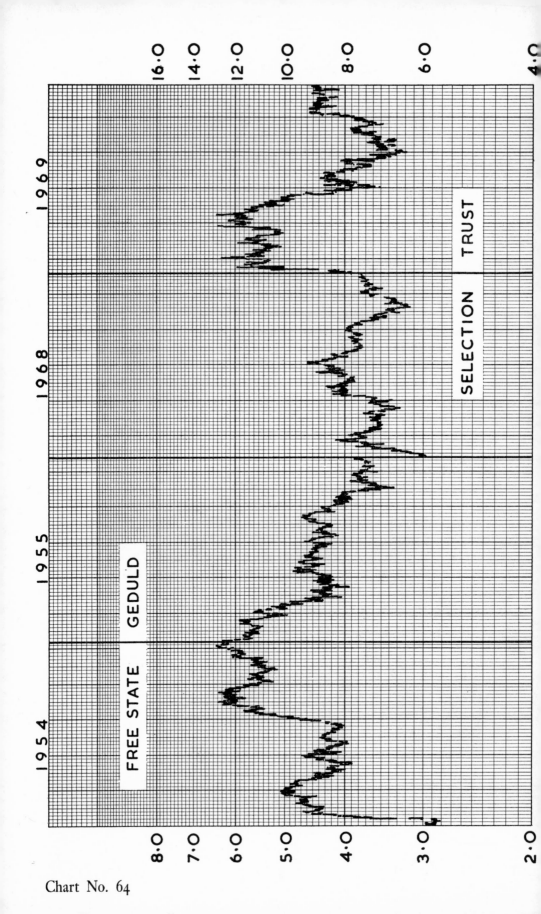

Chart No. 64

line is penetrated, you see the violation of a level which has afforded support or resistance twice and has to a large extent demonstrated its validity; but in a double top or bottom pattern, unless the support or resistance is visible, you are taking it on trust. The point is illustrated by two mining shares in Chart No. 64. Selection Trust in 1968–69 was tracing out a big Head & Shoulders top (pattern completed at the time of writing in June 1970 but prediction not, as yet at any rate, fulfilled). The head consists of a double top that worked itself out in 20 weeks. The right hand top is composite but the correction inside it is insufficient to justify the classification of triple top. The tops were established round 12·5 and the correction ran down to 10·00. This was completely clear of all previous levels of the share, except the run up to the top, and no support had been very obviously laid down. But its validity was demonstrated, previously by the reversal so close above the level three or four weeks before the correction was finally reversed, and subsequently by the minor rally staged a week before the level was penetrated after the second top. The support here was manifestly valid even though you could not see how it was laid down, and the prediction of the pattern was swiftly fulfilled. In the case of Free State Geduld in 1954–55 the pattern is much the same, a double top inside the head of a Head & Shoulders (the prediction was underfulfilled as the final decline in 1957 went only to 2·8). But the support which checked the intermediate correction of the double top was clearly laid down by the top of the left shoulder in March 1954.

Chart No. 65 shows Doornfontein for the years 1952–55. The pattern at the bottom is neither triple top nor triple bottom; it is a rectangle (and you will very often find in the context of these double and triple top and bottom formations that other indications of the charts are more informative). From this rectangle you have a false emergence downwards in the autumn of 1953 and then a penetration of the upper resistance level, which is followed by the somewhat inadequate rise to the twin tops at 1·75. The intermediate correction terminated on the support level laid down by the tops of the rectangle. The prediction was somewhat lazily fulfilled.

Chart No. 66 shows on the right a double top pattern in Renold in 1968–69. The pattern worked well enough, but it can be read as a triangle with a downward emergence. Again, the downturn from the amorphous trading area in the winter of 1968–69 was another adverse development, and the gap that appeared immediately after it at 2·55 showed how much strength there was on the selling side. Here it is the confirmations of the downward indication given by the double top pattern rather than the double top itself that are important.

The other share illustrated in Chart No. 66 is Consolidated Zinc in

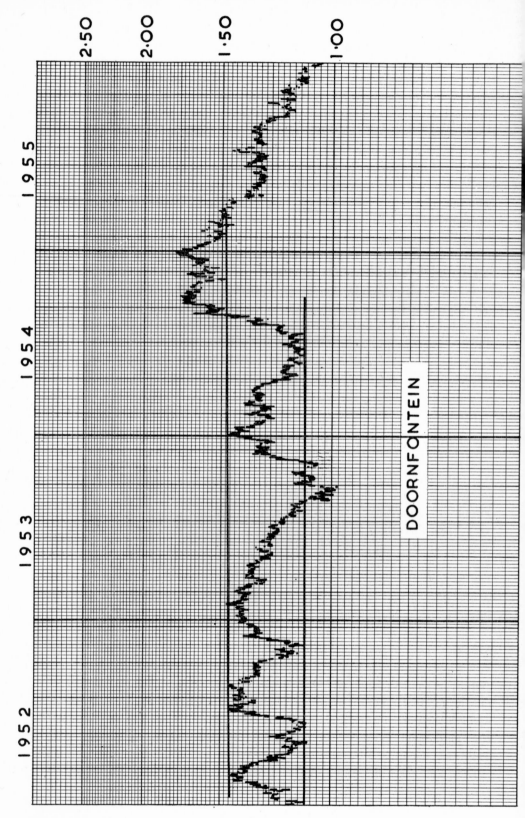

DOORNFONTEIN

Chart No. 65

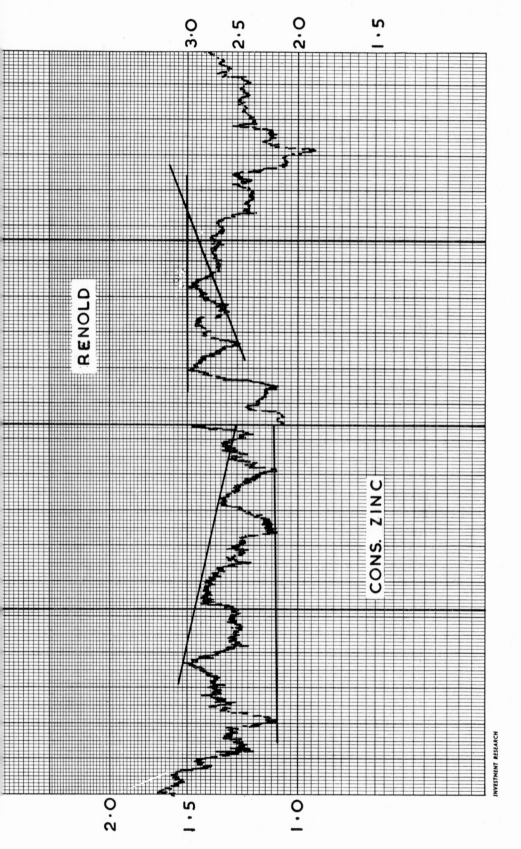

RENOLD

CONS. ZINC

INVESTMENT RESEARCH

Chart No. 66

1952–53. Here you have, if you want, a triple bottom—but what a way to read a chart that is so potentially attractive! This chart too can be read as a triangle. And remember the background; a strong bull market had emerged in London after the Coronation in 1953 and this share was a laggard in the autumn when the gaps that appeared in October and December revealed that there were large and eager buyers about. This was no case for waiting for the completion of the triple bottom at 1·56; there were better indications available at lower levels.

Our final chart in illustration of this group of patterns is No. 67, Guest, Keen & Nettlefold for the years 1952–55. Here you have a long double bottom at 1·15 (give or take the usual 3%) and an intermediate top at 1·4. The bottom area lasted more than two years, and the eventual penetration was followed by a good rise which ran up in due course to 2·7. But here again your triangular argument between March 1953 and February 1954 and the steepening trend climbing out of the trading area are better indications, and more profitable, because they put the chartist in at a lower level, than the double bottom pattern. You will have noted the minor double bottoms that were formed at each of the bottoms that mark the pattern. This type of secondary reversal is not uncommon and is watched for by operators on shorter trends. The share gave a rather splendid performance in the second quarter of 1955, dropped back and ran up at the end of the year to the previous top. Here is another double top. In March 1956 it went through the intermediate bottom, but, instead of a fulfilment of the prediction, there was a run up into new high ground at 2·75. The share then reacted to a level not significantly lower than its predecessor— does this establish another double bottom? The share rallied and cleared the previous tops in the second quarter of 1957, a level it did not regain till September 1958. This was a case where the double top and double bottom concepts were far from helpful.

These patterns can work but do not seem very reliable. Other facets of technical analysis seem able to deal more helpfully with the development of the price curve. It seems that little reliance should be given to these patterns, despite their fame and reputation. But if you see other well-known patterns, with a sprinkling of well-tried reversal patterns, developing in many shares, the appearance of a number of potential double tops or triple tops should be counted in the calculation that a change of the primary trend is likely to be in the offing. These double and triple top and bottom patterns have achieved great fame and reputation; we think this fame is deserved when the pattern appears in a major index, though even then care must be taken to ensure that you are not mistaking for a double top or bottom a pattern that is better read as a triangle or a rectangle. But when you see a double top or bottom in a share,

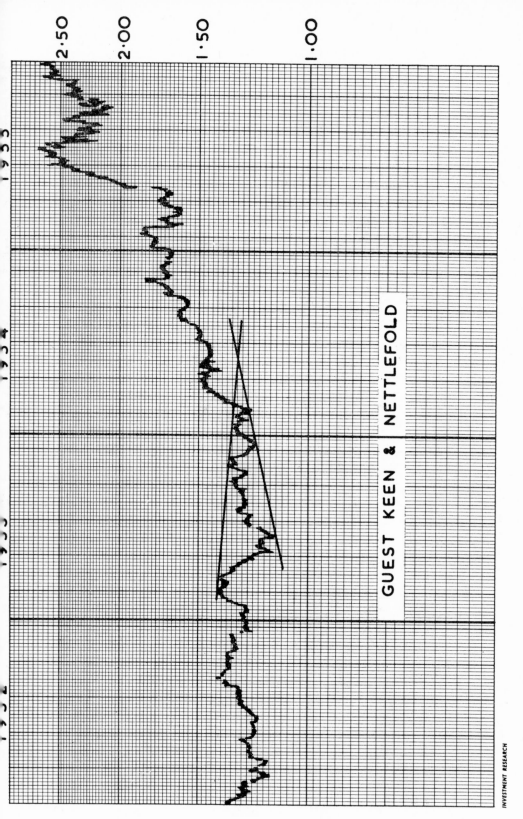

GUEST KEEN & NETTLEFOLD

INVESTMENT RESEARCH

Chart No. 67

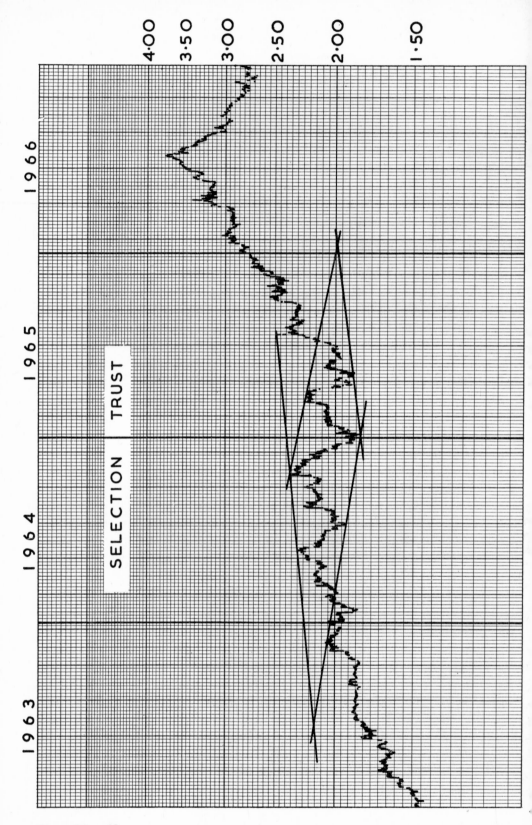

Chart No. 68

approach it with the greatest caution; it is so often not a reliable invitation to enter on a transaction that will turn out well.

Magee lists two other reversal patterns, the diamond which he says is not a common pattern and the wedge. We suspect that diamonds are an unimportant pattern. The formation is essentially a pair of triangles back to back (in the English, not the American, sense of that phrase); where the pattern develops in a fairly short time and does not work out successfully it tends to vanish into the adjacent plotting like a successfully camouflaged vehicle. If we cannot see the patterns that do not work out well, we cannot form an opinion on the value of the pattern.

Chart No. 68 shows Selection Trust for the years 1963–66. The pattern is not a reversal in this case; it is one of the quite common halfway hesitations which do not take any particular shape or last any particular time but interrupt a trend somewhere in mid course. (In fact, the Selection Trust uptrend may be treated as having run on through the 1966 decline). The down-tilted support· resistance line that starts on tops in November 1963 and ultimately forms the lower boundary of the left half of the diamond is a phenomenon familiar to chartists, but to begin the pattern where our chart shows the beginning seems quite arbitrary, and we wonder whether a diamond can have anything except an arbitrary beginning. The pattern then works out as an expanding triangle into the autumn of 1964 when it begins, this time quite naturally, to turn into a contracting triangle. A chartist who treated this as a contracting triangle and did not bother about diamonds would have had good reason to be satisfied.

Chart No. 69 shows a diamond and a wedge. The diamond is in Courtaulds at the top in 1968–69. This is a reversal pattern. It was recognised as a diamond by Investment Research and used as a selling signal. But in this case too the beginning seems arbitrary, as the striking down-thrust to 1·375 in May 1968 does not form a part of the pattern. Equally good results could have been obtained by reading the pattern as a quadruple top which degenerates into a contracting triangle and points the new trend when the lower limit of the triangle is penetrated. You do not need the diamond concept in order to interpret this chart correctly. Diamonds, in short, are unnecessary to the technical analyst; he gains nothing by bothering about them.

Wedges are a different matter. Magee treats them as reversal patterns, but we do not count them as at all reliable. The pattern needs to be watched closely up to the last moment to determine whether it is a reversal pattern or not. A wedge is a triangle set out of the horizontal; its converging sides are both tilted in the same direction, one of course more steeply than the others. In our experience the best way to treat these patterns is as uncompleted parallelograms, just like ordinary triangles; sooner or later one

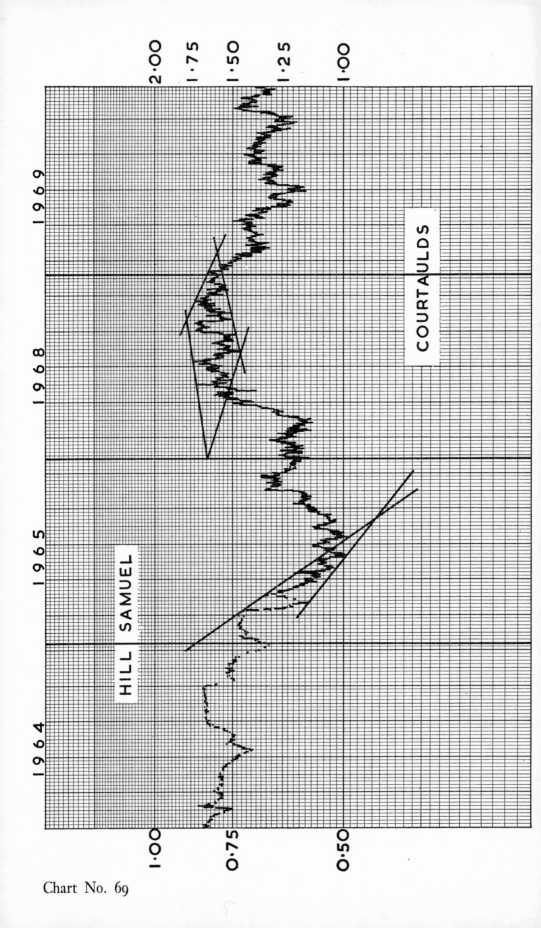

Chart No. 69

trend will turn out to be dominant and be a side of the parallelogram, while the other side is proved, by its ultimate penetration, to be only a diagonal. There was a very striking pattern of this sort in the chart of Beechams in the late forties; a steeply down-pointing triangle appeared in the chart and the share eventually broke through the left hand trendline and duly completed the parallelogram. The theory of the wedge is quite important. It assumes that the pattern shows a series of thrusts away from the right hand trendline, each of them weaker than its predecessor. As a weakening pattern it is bound, sooner or later, to end in reversal. If you turn again to Chart No. 69, you will see this happening in the case of Hill Samuel in 1964–65. The share had topped out before our chart begins, but it is interesting to note the nice example of a line in the summer of 1964. In March 1965 the share entered a steep downtrend and four successive downthrusts all failed to penetrate the lower trendline which converges sharply to the upper. This pattern illustrates clearly enough the basic theory of the wedge; it also shows how difficult a pattern it is to use. The correct and illuminating lower trendline cannot be drawn till June 1965, and within a week or two of drawing it the share rose through the well-attested upper trendline. From this development a technical analyst would have assumed a change of trend, and he would not have run the risks of being deceived by false penetrations of the two other lower trendlines which he could have drawn earlier. Chart No. 70 illustrates these weakening upthrusts in the case of Provident Clothing from 1967 onwards. Two alternative lower trendlines can be drawn; on the less steep of the two the wedge begins with the rise in the second half of 1967, but if you use the steeper lower trendline you must not count, as part of the pattern, the peak of November 1967. It is true that the trendline of your pattern hooks back onto this peak, but for an extreme to be counted as part of a wedge it must follow a movement based on the right hand trendline (otherwise the next thrust terminating on the left hand trendline may not be weaker). In due course this pattern worked out as a wedge should, with a sharp drop, pull-back to the penetrated trendline and steep descent. But does the wedge pattern really help? The concept of weakness shown by shortening upthrusts does help; the failure at the second top in January 1969 to go on to the old top trendline is an indication of weakness that occurs quite often in the working out of a top. Next the share fell through two supports and both alternative trendlines, quite enough evidence to justify a sale without any reference to the wedge pattern. Again and again we find that trendlines and support and resistance give the technical analyst all the clues that he needs and seem much more reliable than the more recherché patterns.

Two more examples are given in Chart No. 71, British Motor Corpor-

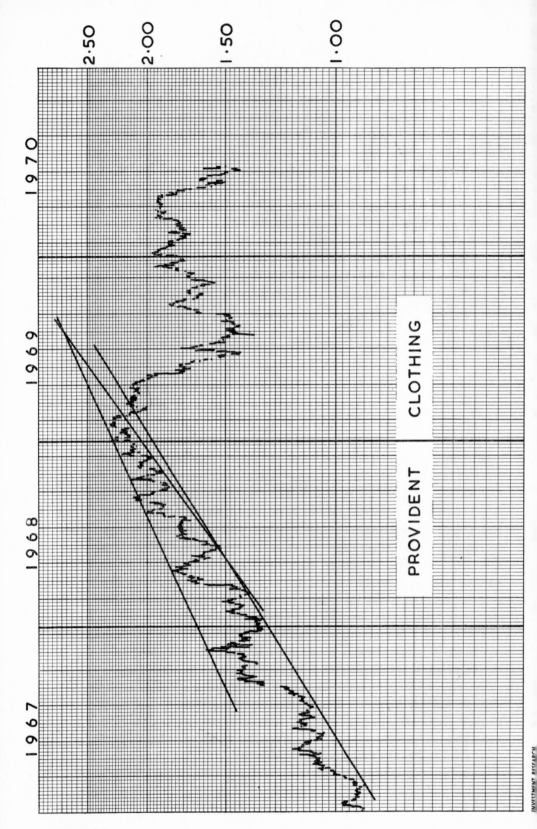

PROVIDENT   CLOTHING

Chart No. 70

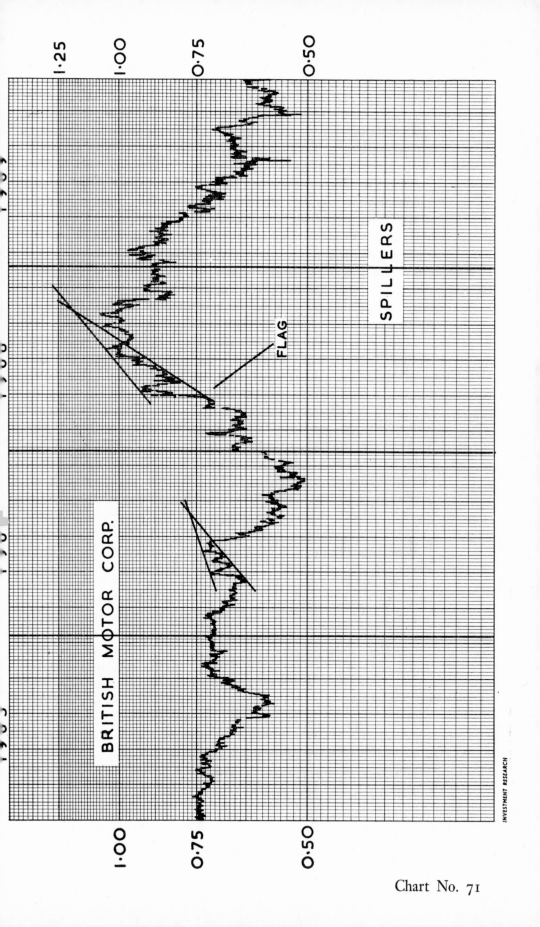

Chart No. 71

ation in the early summer of 1966 shows the correct pattern, a rising wedge followed immediately by a sharp break downwards on penetration of the trendline. But the Spillers wedge is a counterpart of that shown for Hill Samuel in Chart No. 69; it leads into a conventional reversal pattern, and the sharp break downwards does not come till the conventional reversal pattern has worked itself out.

The remarkable rising wedge in Rootes Motor, to which we referred earlier, was a symptom of strength, not of weakness. After the splitting of the shares, when holders received for each £1 Ordinary share (with a vote) one 5/- Ordinary share plus three 5/- non-voting A shares, the controlling group was in a position to sell three-quarters of its interest and retain control of the company. Very large sales of the A shares appear to have been made between 36p and 43p (see Chart No. 78, p. 272). These sales left behind resistance which the new buyers of 1958 found much too tough for them, but their successors in 1959 gradually fought their way through. What the wedge pattern here shows is not weakness but the strength of the buying in the steeply rising lower trendline and the obstacle which was facing it in the flatter upper trendline. Part of the laying down of this resistance appears in Chart No. 78.

There is one other development to be discussed here; it is a symptom rather than a pattern. If you turn back to Chart No. 61 you will see how Peninsular & Oriental, at the end of 1959, ran into a high-pointed top. This is called a spearhead top. It is symptomatic of a fairly late stage in the development of a market top (except that if the market is working out a Head & Shoulders, the spearhead tops of individual shares are more likely to coincide with the head than with the right shoulder). Specimens are easily found in 1955, 1959–60 right at the turn of the year, in 1966 but not 1964 and in 1969 but not 1968. When one sees these patterns afterwards, one gets the impression that a last desperate effort is being made to push the share in question up while there is still time. While a share may make a spearhead top, a possibility of which the investor must remain fully aware, it is most unlikely that a broad representative index like the Dow Jones Industrial or the *Financial Times* industrial will do anything of the sort. These indices do make Head & Shoulders tops as the *Financial Times* did in 1955 and the Dow in 1961, but generally the market takes a second look at the highest point before the primary downward trend gets under way. The second look may take the index to a new high level as in 1959, and in that difficult case the second bear market rally in 1961 was so big that it established a new high. The spearhead is a symptom of the individual share, not of the broad market average, but if you see a number of them developing it is time to examine the market very carefully as it is likely to have passed its second look at the top.

CHAPTER FIFTEEN

Gaps and Flags

You find a gap in a share chart when the prices at which it is traded on Tuesday do not anywhere overlap the prices at which it was traded on Monday. For very large gaps look at Charts Nos. 44, 61, 62 and 67. Very few gaps are as large as this, and quite small gaps may be significant. Gaps may be caused simply by the thinness of the market. These should be ignored unless their size declares that they are significant. They may be caused by arbitrage, the attempt to profit from differences in price arising between different stock exchanges. For example New York goes on trading in Royal Dutch till eight o'clock at night, and Amsterdam probably disposes of most of its business for the day while London brokers are still at breakfast. Sydney and Melbourne do their business while investors in Britain are asleep. Arbitrage gaps should not be ignored; there is significance in the fact that investors elsewhere are driving the price up or down while our exchanges are not open. But the significance is not the same as for a gap in an active stock that is traded solely on British stock exchanges.

Flags are consolidations within the tertiary trend, and always a steep trend. They are always continuation patterns, which does not mean that the pattern is 100% reliable but simply that it is not a flag if there is no continuation. (If you deal on the assumption that it is a flag and it turns out not to be one, the result is very often not disastrous; quite often after a brief reversal the share moves off again in the direction for which you had hoped). The perfect flag is simply a rectangular block of trading that interrupts a steep movement up or down. The duration of the pattern is supposed to be not more than three or four weeks, but we have already drawn attention in the case of the Selection Trust diamond to the existence of halfway hesitations within primary and secondary trends, and it seems most likely that a flag is a compact tertiary development of the same kind. Flags do work after periods longer than four weeks, but if the pattern gets much older than three weeks it is prudent to look on it with some suspicion. The flag can droop instead of flying straight out as if in a strong wind; it can tilt up and it can even fly at half-mast. Or it may be a pennant, which is a flag whose shape is triangular or pointed; perhaps the pattern in Hawker Siddeley (Chart No. 56) in October 1957 is a pennant. Pennants seem difficult to find and are probably rare in our market, but the closely plotted logarithmic scale used by Investment Research may not be good for showing up flags and pennants.

Good regular flags appear in Chart No. 54 both in John Laing and in British Oxygen at 0·575; there is also a mildly drooping flag in the British Oxygen chart at 0·55. A slightly less regular flag appears in Spillers in Chart No. 71. There is a bigger specimen in New Broken Hill (Chart No. 55); a large number of the gaps in this chart are likely to be arbitrage gaps.

Flags are just as likely to appear in declines as in rises; and then instead of drooping they are likely to point up. There is a specimen in Canadian Eagle in June 1948 (Chart No. 43). There is a rather irregular pattern—but clearly of the flag breed—in Ultramar in April 1954 (Chart No. 42); this pattern lasted well over the four week limit and contains a false start upward. There is a downward drooping flag in the decline of B.S.A. at 1·75 in May 1969 (Chart No. 48); the investor who said "I think this is a flag" and sold must have felt relieved. Plessey (Chart No. 52) shows two somewhat irregular drooping flags in a steep uptrend in July 1963. And there is a very good rising flag in a decline to be seen in Shell (Chart No. 57) at midsummer in 1969. Lesney (Chart No. 57) shows a splendid selection of patterns; among them is a good half-mast in April 1969.

The flag belongs to the family of halfway patterns. Measure from the start of the movement to the top of a flag in an uptrend and the movement is likely to continue, if the pattern really is a flag, for a similar distance upwards from the bottom of the flag pattern. The same applies in declines.

So much for flags; let us now turn to gaps. Gaps can occur anywhere.

The Leyland Motor pattern (Chart No. 45), which begins in the major phase of liquidation of 1951–52, is naturally a thin pattern in the bear market. It grows thicker in the subsequent recovery, but in the subsequent declines the gaps become wider and more frequent as the market grew progressively thinner while the pattern worked itself out. This is quite a normal development within long patterns.

There are three, possibly four, regular positions for gaps. A gap is caused by an excessive weight on the buying or selling side which forces the jobber to quote in the morning a price substantially higher or lower than the levels at which he was dealing the day before. Thus it is likely to appear immediately after a reversal when a number of investors are rushing to get onto the new trend at the earliest possible moment. This is called the breakaway gap. Nearly three-quarters of the thirty stocks of the *Financial Times* index left gaps on the Friday after the 1970 election.

Turn back to Ultramar in Chart No. 42. A secondary reaction came to its end during the last week of March 1954, and the new upward movement starts off with a breakaway gap. This is marked BG on the Chart. The price goes up, and comes down just below the gap within three or four days. This is known as closing or covering the gap. It happens very often, but it does not happen always. When it happens quickly, as in this case, the phenomenon is obviously akin to the pull-back, which we have observed already on breaks through necklines, trendlines and emergences from formal patterns. It gives the investor a second chance of dealing close to the gap. The share then ran up into a horizontal movement of the flag type, but the trading area has no definite shape and lasts five or six weeks and has a gap, of no significance, inside it. In due course the advance of price is continued, and a new gap appears as the share emerges. This is marked MG because it turns out to be a midway gap, formed when a share comes out of a consolidation formed halfway up its rise. The price goes on rising until it has covered the distance predicted by the flaglike formation and the midway gap. There is a good little gap on the emergence from the band in the winter of 1954, and a second breakaway gap (also marked) when the share moves out of its secondary bottom area in the autumn of 1955.

In Canadian Eagle (Chart No. 43) there are a number of good specimens. In 1949 there is a breakaway gap when the share emerges from the band in which it had spent the previous winter. In 1953 the share produced a midway gap as it went down into the band in early summer. There is a good breakaway gap at the end of the band; this is the gap inside the pattern which the build up of buying pressure produces. There is enough strength now to push the share through the top of the band, where there is a second gap, followed by a further rise and, within three weeks, by a pull-back. This rise ran out of steam below 1·75, and the share had to come back to the top of the band, and then right inside the band, before sufficient steam was developed to send the share off on the next leg of its upward movement. (It topped out at 3·6 in the summer of 1955). There are also good specimens of breakaway and midway gaps in International Paints in Chart No. 47. The very large gap which appears at the beginning of May 1962 will be dealt with later.

We must now turn back to Gaumont British in Chart No. 46. Here we find an important, but much rarer, gap, the exhaustion gap. Sometimes, when a movement has run a long way in a steep trend—and here we have a share which more than triples its value in 48 weeks and ends with a spearhead run of 40% in five weeks—the movement ends with very strong buying pressure and sellers very scarce. In these conditions a gap is natural; Gaumont British shows two. But then it sometimes happens that these were the last buyers, and a market which was all buyers on Monday opens on Tuesday without a buyer in sight. The sellers look for takers of their stock and have to find them lower down. So the trend has changed downwards, although the last gap was pointing upwards. That is the exhaustion gap (it occurs also, with the conditions reversed, through extreme pressure of sellers, at bottoms). It is not generally, according to Magee, a primary reversal symptom. In the case of Gaumont British it was the top of the share for 1959, but the market's top came eight to ten weeks later. Nor was it the end of the rise for Gaumont British, which reached substantially higher levels in the next year.

If you turn on now to Chart No. 47 you will see that the big gap of May 1962 must be treated as a case where the midway gap and the exhaustion gap were merged.

For an exhaustion gap at the bottom, look at Chart No. 59 where the decline of C. T. Bowring in 1970 was arrested after a series of downward gaps. This almost qualifies as an island reversal, but this is better illustrated in Chart No. 50 where Selection Trust shows islands at secondary tops in May 1964 and March/April 1965. (The isolated bargains at the secondary bottom in 1965 appear to be due more to the thinness of the market than to any significant buying or selling pressures). Clearly an island reversal is formed when an exhaustion gap is quickly succeeded by a breakaway gap in the opposite direction.

You may see references to running gaps. These occur in fast moving shares in places other than the standard breakaway, midway and exhaustion positions. A running gap soon after a breakaway is encouraging; it seems most likely that there will be a flag and a second half of the movement to come. A running gap after a midway is less cheerful; it implies that the pressures are still high, but the speed of the movement may be bringing it quickly to the exhaustion point.

There are probably thousands of gaps to be found in the London market every year. The proportion of them which is important is small. But the importance is large, and it is this which justifies the study. Gaps occur at important reversals, and you must remember that the importance of a reversal cannot be seen at the time. A drop of 10% is reversed, and that does not seem important. A breakaway gap says, 'Look at me; I may be starting a new move that will run 100%'.

CHAPTER SIXTEEN

The Change of Trend

We have discussed already the things that happen when the market as a whole is making a primary reversal, and we have described the various patterns made by shares. But we have not talked about the very common case of the share which goes up, stops going up and starts going down or vice-versa. In this chapter we shall first look at this behaviour in shares and then go on to analyse the general market reversal in terms of trendlines rather than of individual patterns.

Let us start with the declining trend. Chart No. 72 shows the case of Ashanti Goldfields for the years 1960–63. In the first quarter of 1960 it dropped into the trend channel which it subsequently defined. The broadening channel was not unusual; before the commission scale was changed, the expenses of dealing (expressed as a percentage) tended to rise as a price fell into the low ranges, and even after the change in the commission scale the jobbers turn may have widened as prices fell. The chart reproduced here was taken from the weekly section in the Investment Research catalogue; these charts show Friday's close and none of the intervening bargains are shown. The decline went through three phases. The first ended at 0·70 in December 1960, the second at 0·44 a year later and the third at 0·37 in May 1962. Each phase was followed by a secondary rally which carried the price back to the top trendline. But in the summer of 1962 this rally was succeeded by quite a small decline, after which the price rose through the upper trendline, pulled back to it and soon surpassed the preceding secondary top. The share seemed a very tempting purchase, provided one had some faith in Ashanti Goldfields, as soon as recovery from the pull-back made it most likely that the trend had changed. The investment did not turn out very well; the share ran into a somewhat unconventional top area in April 1963 and by November had shown that this was an altitude that it did not relish. The transaction should then have been closed at a profit. What distinguishes this reversal from the others which we have discussed previously is that there is very little work done in the reversal area. The share has made a habit of hitting the top trendline again and again, and there was nothing to show there was anything different here till it drove through the line and recovered from its confirmatory pull-back.

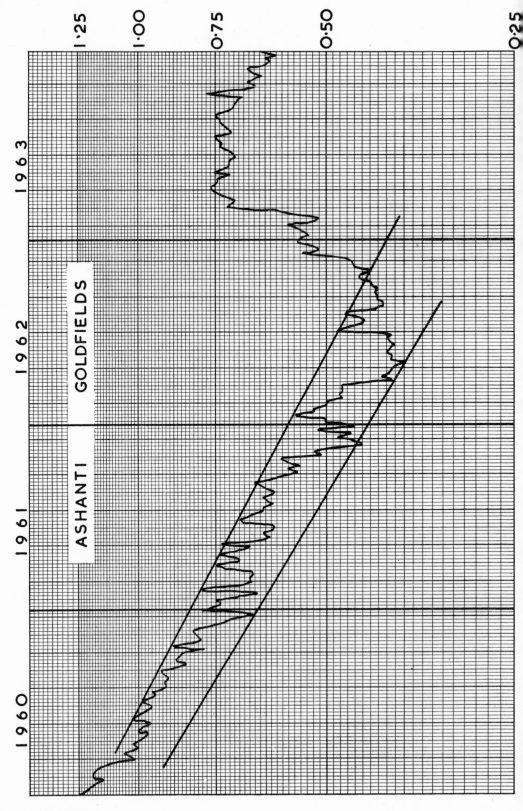

Chart No. 72

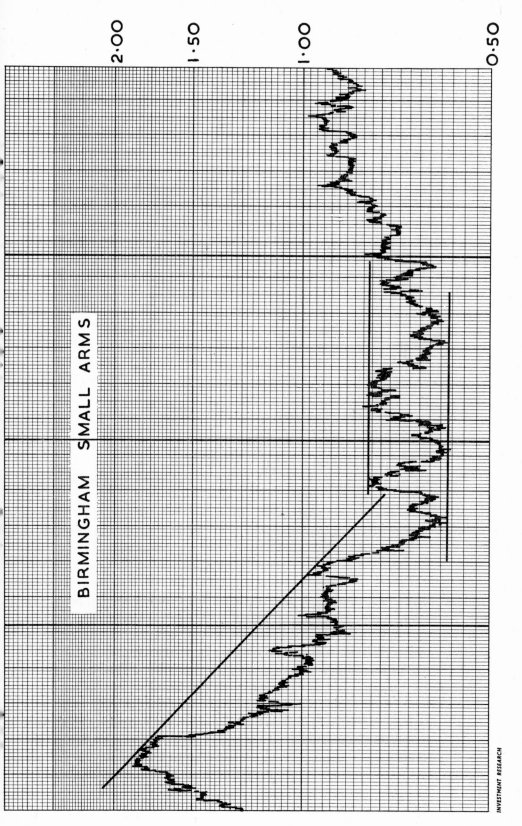

BIRMINGHAM SMALL ARMS

2·00
1·50
1·00
0·50

Chart No. 73

Birmingham Small Arms in Chart No. 73 shows much more work in its reversal, but the work is done after, not before, the emergence through the downtrend. The share dropped from a fantastic peak in 1961, when many other shares reached fantastic peaks, and in the next fifteen months lost five-sixths of its value. It then rose through its descending trendline but turned back under 0·80 and returned within the trendline. But it did not move significantly into new low ground and worked out a long rectangle from which it did not emerge till the last week of April 1964. The lesson to be learned here is that one should not be in too much of a hurry when a trendline is broken. In this case the rally ran up to 0·8; there was a resistance area at 0·83 and another at 0·85; if the share went straight through both of those, which it almost certainly would not, it would have shown its strength and would be worth backing. If it turned back from the resistance, its subsequent conduct would probably reveal whether a new uptrend had been established or not. By the beginning of the new year one knew two things, that the market was in a primary uptrend, and that B.S.A. had turned up again at its previous low. If one knew the cyclical character of the share, which had been a true friend of the chartists right through the post-war period, it was tempting to read the rectangle as an accumulation area, and that is what it turned out to be. The share went into a nice uptrend, which ran to June 1966; then the July measures brought it down, deceptively, alas! through the rising lower trendline, after which it promptly recovered and went on to its 1968 top. The cutting of a trendline is not an infallible signal.

Chart No. 74 shows British Enkalon for the years 1965–68. This shows a much less steep trend. The less steep trend means that the signal is given at a much higher level. Further, other shares with similar trends have proved most disappointing; let us instance Tanganyika Concessions which reached its low point in June 1964, cut the descending trendline in January 1966, and then equalled its previous low in December. It is true that after this double bottom at 0·50 it enjoyed a glorious rise to a double top at 3·00, after which it cut the ascending trendline and fell below 2·20 before it recovered and ran up over 3·50. After this digression, to prove once again that trendlines are not entirely trustworthy, we return to British Enkalon. There is a deep drop below the trendline in July 1966, and the share did not return to it till November 1967. Then it ran up into the resistances laid down earlier under 0·4, found support on the upper side of the declining trendline and later on the rising trendline which went back quite clearly to September 1967. This was a good trendline as it turned the share up again at the end of its horizontal movement in the winter of 1968–69, after which the share ran up a second time to the 1968 top. In this pattern the key lies not so much in the descending trendline

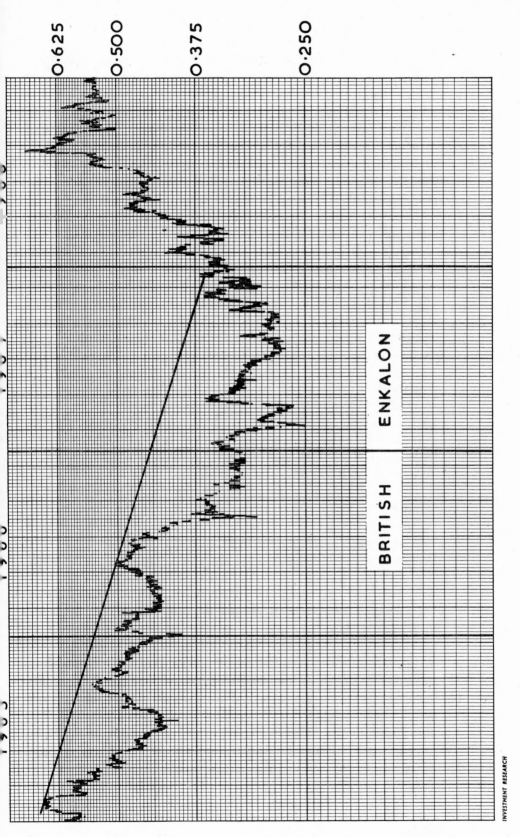

BRITISH ENKALON

0·625
0·500
0·375
0·250

INVESTMENT RESEARCH

Chart No. 74

from 1965 as in the development of the rising trendline in 1967.

The principle of the rising trendline is more simple. There is one golden rule; if your trendline is steep and your share is on the left hand side of it, hold fast to it and let it run to your profit. You do not want to take profits when your share is on the left hand side of a steeply rising trendline; you want to cling to the darling that is doing you so much good. It may be prudent, if the share runs far away from the trendline in a fantastic rise, to let it go, but in good bull markets fantastic rises have a way of going even further!

There was nothing fantastic about Laporte in 1957–60 which is illustrated in Chart No. 75. One difficulty here is that the trend emerged very slowly. It is true that you can join the top of the secondary rally in November 1957 to the top of the rising secondary phase at the beginning of June 1959, and you have got an upper headline. It is only after this is broken that you get the bottom trendline delineated. But there might well have been a lower trendline which was cut, at a midway gap, by the reaction from 1·125; it took some nerve to hold through the test of the support in the line at 1·15. Once that danger had been survived the share stayed on the left hand side of the new and convincing trendline. In this case the share dropped back from its peak and rallied on the first support, dropped through the first and second support, cut the trendline and pulled back to it, aided, no doubt, by support from the small line of the previous July. After the pull-back the decline continued, and this was surely enough evidence to let the share go at last. It did not recover adequately in 1961 and dropped as low as 0·8.

The case of Rhokana is interesting; the course of the share is shown in Chart No. 76. You will see here that while it is important, when you buy on emergence through a downtrend, to have confidence in the share you buy, when you sell on downward penetration of an uptrend you must have confidence not in the demerits of the share but in the validity of the trend. The share had put up a very undistinguished performance after its 1951 peak and after a five month rally from the summer of 1952 had fallen substantially lower in 1953. It emerged in a somewhat lazy manner in the spring of 1953 from the downward secondary phase and by January 1954 had lost much of the ground gained. But in the fourth week of January 1954 a reversal with a good breakaway gap suggested that there had been an important change, and the share ran up steeply in a slightly expanding trend channel to the top of 1955. Then the share dropped slightly and rallied almost to its old top, dropped again to the trendline and rallied, then drove down through the trendline leaving a gap. What should be done in a case like this? The outlook for the share seemed good. Copper was strong; it had come up from £300 in the first quarter of 1955 and was

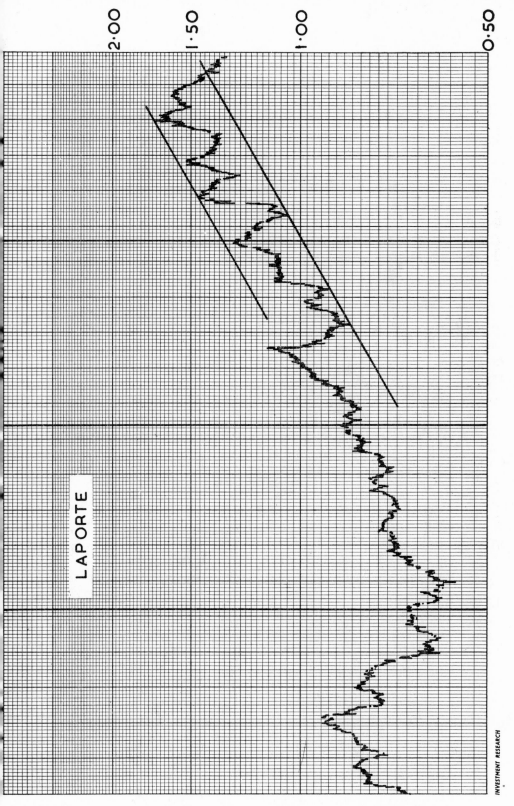

LAPORTE

Chart No. 75

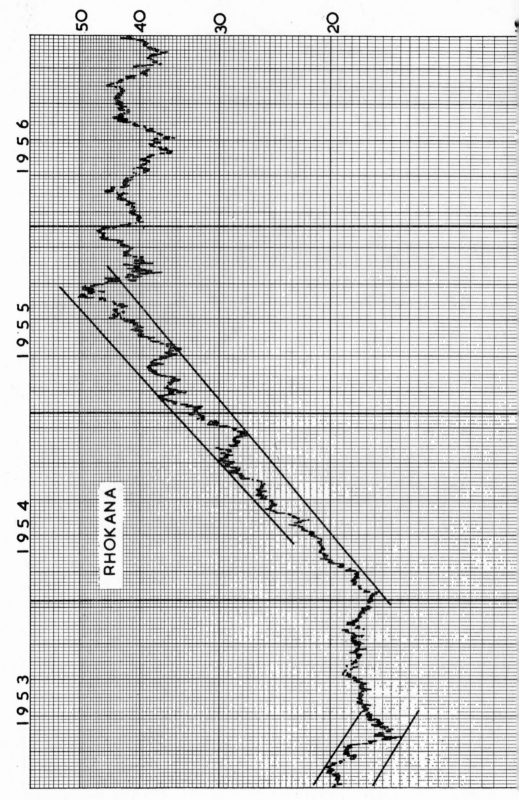

RHOKANA

Chart No. 76

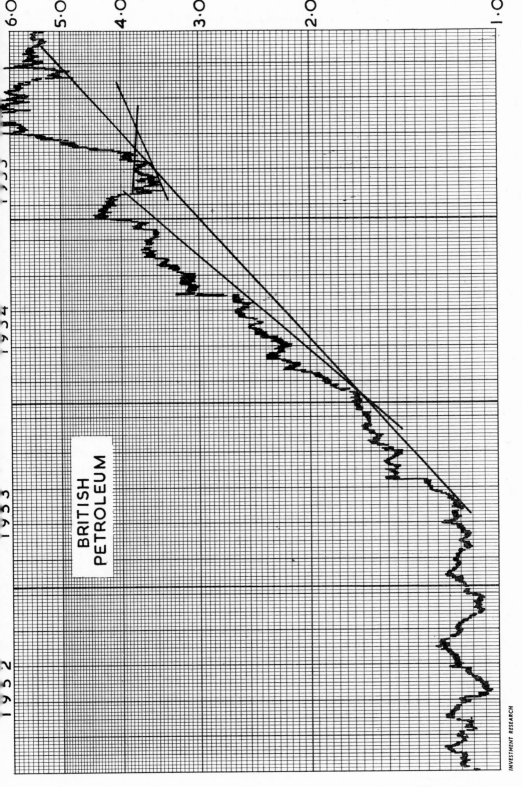

BRITISH
PETROLEUM

Chart No. 77

still in a rising trend; in fact it went on rising, and thus arguing the case in favour of Rhokana, till it reached £438 in March 1956. The man who believed in the trendline sold, probably rather badly, on the downward emergence from the flag at 40 at the beginning of October 1955. The man who believed in the share and copper saw the metal up to £438 in March 1956. When would he have changed his mind? At a better price than 40? Let us hope so; for copper went all the way down to £160 and the share bottomed at 20.

For a less favourable outcome of this chart technique we would like to have looked at British Petroleum over the same period. Unfortunately the share's fluctuations were too wide for the chart scale which we are using[1]. It multiplied its price by five between June 1953 and July 1955, dropped to an uptrend, rallied, and came down and cut the trendline at 3·9. You will note that on this chart one can draw two trendlines, one passing through low points in the summer of 1953 and beginning of 1954, the brave man's trendline, and a steeper line from the beginning of 1954. It is this second and steeper line which was cut at 3·9. Instead of going on down, the share formed a triangle which in due course rested on the brave man's trendline. It came out of the triangle upwards and rose almost vertically over £3 in nine weeks. The reversal came near the turn of the Industrial market in the summer of 1955; but British Petroleum started building up a new triangle in the autumn and emerged from this upwards once again at Easter in 1956. The end of this great rise had not come yet; it ran up a couple of pounds above its previous top. It then dropped, at the time of the Suez crisis from over 9 to under 6, passing through our second trendline at 5·3, and rallied in the next year to 8·5. Those who had sold on the penetration at 3·9 (and not rebought on the emergence from the triangle) saw the share down, by February 1958, below 4. The investor who bought early into the rising trend and held as long as the share stayed on the left hand side of his trendline (whichever it was) would have taken a very good profit. The man who held on might have achieved a better price; or he might have found himself holding the share through the brilliant bull market of 1958–59 in which the share had no performance at all.

Clearly the technique is not certain of successful results, but it does provide a method by which you can run your profits with a considerable feeling of security that you will not be left in some share that is plunging towards annihilation and conversely also a means by which you can keep out of a declining share until it has given you some visible reason for believing that its major liquidation has been completed.

[1] However, see Chart No. 77 on page 261 for year 1952-55.

While single shares can turn round in a comparatively few weeks, the reversal of a market generally requires a substantial period of time. Bull and bear markets do not develop uniformly. The great rise from the 1940 bottom to the top reached in January 1947 was interrupted by a horizontal movement that lasted from soon after D-day to the eve of Dr Dalton's first Budget. The subsequent bear market shows a clean pattern with a strongly marked declining top trendline, and it lasted more than two and a half years. The bear market of 1951–52 shows a clear enough down-trend, but it was deceptively short. After 1955 there was a clear down-trend to the winter of 1956–57; then came a strong rise followed by a new decline to much lower levels. The strong rise gives that bear market a main downtrend with a very flat angle, but what are we to make of the next bear market of 1960–62, where the rally of 1961 out-topped the bull market of 1958–59? Certainly the shapes of the markets in the early sixties were most unsatisfactory. There is a clear uptrend for 1962–64, but as in 1960–62 there is no upper trendline for the bear market. Prices were as high in 1966 as in 1964; the bearishness of the market lay on the underside of the pattern, lower in 1965 than the worst of 1964, lower in 1966 than the worst of 1965. This was very much the pattern of 1960–62, when we saw the *Financial Times* index lower in 1961 than in 1960 and lower in 1962 than in 1961. Then in 1966 the old pattern was reborn; there was a classical bull market pattern from November 1966 to the top of 1968–69, and the subsequent bear market has developed (up to the summer of 1970) in two main stages of decline with a classical declining trend channel.

Investment Research published its analysis of the bear market bottoms in its Note No. 1514 which we reprint here.

By our reckoning there have been five major bottoms since the war and the sixth may arrive in 1970 or later (our present working hypothesis remains that the bottom will come in the summer next year, but one function of a working hypothesis is that it is there to be changed). We do not count the low points reached in bear markets in their initial stages of liquidation, September 1947, November 1956, July 1965 or July and November 1969.

All the major bottoms conformed to recognised chartist patterns, being either reversed Head & Shoulders patterns or double bottoms. Thus we can determine an upper limit for these bottoms, but not necessarily for some future bottom which does not conform to chartist pattern, by using the neckline of the Head & Shoulders pattern or drawing a horizontal through the intermediate secondary top between the double bottoms. When we mark the intersections of these lines with the preceding falls and subsequent rises, we can determine the duration of the bottom areas. Thus we can work out for these bottoms their vital statistics.

Period	Duration	Height of Bottom Area	Pattern
1949–50	50 weeks	10%	Double Bottom
1952	46 weeks	13%	Reversed H. & S.
1957–58	35 weeks	10%	Reversed H. & S.
1962	11 weeks	$3\frac{1}{2}$%	Reversed H. & S.
	23 weeks	12%	Reversed H. & S.
1966	17/18 weeks	11%	Reversed H. & S.

Thus if you exclude the smaller of the two figures traced out in 1962, you can expect a bottom to take from four months to a year to work itself out, the upper limit to be placed 10% to 13% above the low extreme, and these two to be combined with a recognisable chartist pattern. All these qualifications were fulfilled by the summer and autumn of 1969, but that pattern developed at much too early a stage in the primary decline.

The Note, which was published on 29th June 1970, went on to examine the possibilities then present, a matter which does not concern us here.

It is possible to carry out a similar analysis for the tops of 1946–47, of 1951 and of 1955. It is not possible for the next two bull markets, those at the end of the fifties and the middle of the sixties, but the top of 1968–69 fits well into this type of analysis.

Period	Duration	Depth of Top Area	Pattern
1946–47	40 weeks	$11\frac{1}{2}$%	Double Top
1951	31 weeks	$8\frac{1}{2}$%	Double Top
1954–55	72 weeks	$20\frac{1}{2}$%	Head & Shoulders
1968–69	30 weeks	$8\frac{1}{2}$%	Double Top

The duration given for the 1955 top is obviously too long; it includes weeks that plainly belong to the major phase of accumulation. But the period between the collar-bones, the duration of the actual head pattern, was 30 weeks.

In 1945–47 it is reasonable to use the rising trendline from the Election low point; this line touches the pre-budget tertiary low of April 1946, the important secondary low of September, and passes through the descending curve of the index at 128 at the end of July 1947. As the top was only a few decimals over 140, the trendline in this case gave a helpful signal. In 1951 the rising lower trendline was clearly defined, and after a top at 140 it was cut by the declining index at 128. The bull market from 1952 assumed a concave trend. The trend channel must be defined by selecting two points on the underside of the index curve which are aligned with the low point of March 1955. This looks satisfactory; when you draw the upper parallel the line lies along the last secondary top of 1954, the first of 1955 and the final top of the market. The index went over 220, and the rising trendline cut it on its way down from the head to the right hand collar-bone at 198. Once again this indication was sound. It was, however, a somewhat difficult trendline to draw. For the bull market that began in 1958, there is no difficulty in drawing the trendline; it starts at the bottom in February 1958, touches a minor bottom in July 1959 and after several indecisive intersections goes through the index curve in October 1960. This does not look convincing nor successful; the intersection occurred at 326 and would not have been obvious till the index was down to 320. It subsequently reached a level 14% higher. On the other hand, this was a very difficult period; the index was eventually to fall close to 250, and the investor who sold on the trendline indication and stuck to it through the tribulations of 1961 would probably have done better than most. There is no great difficulty in drawing a trendline for the bull market of 1962–64; it does not start at the bottom of the market at midsummer but at the low point of November 1962. It then achieves frequent contacts with the curve of the index till it passes through at 345 in January 1964. This indication could well have been rejected, because there had been insufficient time for the working out of a top. (It was, however, as it turned out, close to the highest point for activity and the lowest point for yield, two strong indications that this was the point where the enthusiasm of the market had exhausted itself). A more plausible trendline could be drawn later on when a line passing through the 1962 bottom and the subsequent November low touched the secondary bottom of June 1964 and passed through the descending curve of the index at 350 in October 1964. The index fell below 285 in the autumn of 1966. Clearly the man who sells on a significant intersection of the rising lower trendline needs to be very patient, but his sales turn out well in the end.

The declining upper trendline of a bear market is a very different matter. Its intersection of the rising bull market in the early part of 1950 was timely; and so was its indication of the ending of the brief bear market of 1951–52. In 1957 the trendline of the initial phase of the 1955–58 bear market gave a good indication of the coming calf market of 1957 (and the rising trendline a few months later timed the exit from the calf market well enough). But the intersection in 1958 came too late to be helpful, and the first two bear markets of the sixties had no long trendlines at all.

The lesson must be that one must look for rather rudimentary patterns in the bear market bottoms and hope for a helpful pattern but have more faith in the trendline in the bull market tops.

CHAPTER SEVENTEEN

Investment Decisions

Theoretical conceptions like that of the market, or the smaller group, are undoubtedly helpful to the investor in the making of decisions, but a decision, when it is made, involves doing something, and the investor cannot do something about the market or about some narrower group. If he is going to do anything, to buy or to sell, what he buys or sells must be one or more individual stocks. So in this chapter we must consider the actual decision of the investor, to buy this or to sell that. The investor who uses charts differs from the investor who does not mainly in his respect for the opinion of other investors (it would, of course, be possible to use charts in order to deal in disagreement with other investors). But the user of charts cannot rely solely on others, and he must make his own use of the data available in the forming of his ideas. If an investor is contemplating a transaction in a certain share, he should take account of certain matters for which he can refer to a chart and of certain others for which he cannot. The first and overriding factor is a chart factor. Is the market right for whatever it is he proposes to do? If he is thinking of buying, he should think of buying only when the market is rising or when it appears likely to be turning from fall to rise. The second factor is also a chart factor. This is the question whether the time is right. Nobody can hope to buy at a primary or even a secondary bottom, but the investor does want to assure himself that he is not dealing for a movement which is almost completed. In this matter of timing he must be content to be always wrong, but he must assure himself before he deals that he is not too badly wrong. The third factor is the question whether the share is right. This question may depend on the figures already published, which are data available to all. It may depend on the facts which may have been published, and are thus available to all, or which may be known only to some and be making their influence felt on the chart through the transactions of the informed.

In a discussion of this sort we must concern ourselves first with transactions initiated in the course of a primary upward trend. Transactions on a reversal are wholesale and are governed mainly by decisions about the change of trend; transactions entered into during the course of the upward trend are later amendments made with the purpose of improving the original selection of stocks.

The first figure usually considered used to be the dividend. You must remember that before the 1948 Companies Act we did not have consolidated balance sheets and consolidated profit and loss accounts. Directors disclosed not the earnings which their accountants told them the company had made but what they thought it was good for the company for the shareholders to be told. Fundamental analysis was very much further from being an exact science than it is to-day. Since the 1948 Act, and much more since the introduction of Corporation Tax in 1965, we pay a high degree of attention to earnings, and we shall be coming to them in the next paragraph. The dividend provides the income which may be the investor's inducement to buy and which must be the inducement of the ultimate permanent holder into whose hands every temporary holder is hoping that the share will pass at a higher price. Divide the dividend by the price and multiply by 100 and you have the yield, the income to be received from an investment of £100, provided that there is no change of dividend. Much investment is based on a comparison of yields. Every investor wants the highest ultimate yield (if not for himself for that ultimate buyer who is to pay the enhanced price that gives the profit), but, as dividends change from year to year, the share which yields £2·2% on the latest dividend may be a better investment for long-term income than the share which yields £12·2%. As the whole range of yields is always changing and as the general curve of yields mirrors, by no means exactly, the curve of price, a single yield in isolation is of very little use. Of more value is the conception of rating (at present quite out of date but what had become unfashionable by the end of the sixties may be restored to favour by the return of a bird-in-hand philosophy in the early seventies). It was assumed, for the use of rating, that the market ranks shares by their yields. A rating figure can be obtained by dividing a representative yield, say the F.T. Actuaries 500, by the yield of the share in question and multiplying by 100. This gives you a figure over 100 for shares with yields below the average (and one presumes that they are below the average because the shares are better than average) and a figure under 100 for shares with yields above the average. (Moodys used their own indices, which are not calculated daily, and reversed the process; the principle was exactly the same, but the better shares had the lower ratings figures). Two uses can be made of the rating figure. You can compare it with previous ratings of the same share to see what is happening to the market's opinion of it and deal with the change or against the change. You can compare it with another share's rating (but this is the same thing as comparing one share's yield with another's). However, if you compare ratings and not yields, you can look not only at the relation between the current yields on the two shares, but you can also see how opinion about each of them has been changing.

Behind the dividends lie the earnings. Investment analysis used to pay considerable attention to the 'earnings yield' but, when the Corporation Tax came in, their attention was turned to its reciprocal, the Price: Earnings Ratio. The modern way of rating shares is by their P/E Ratio ratio, that is the ratio of the share's P/E to the P/E calculated for the F.T. Actuaries 500 share index. The earnings spring from the management's use of the company's assets. So the student of figures must look at the earnings per share and the assets per share—and it is important to look at these figures for a series of years and not for one year only. The trend of earnings is more important than the earnings of any single year. In the case of assets the trend has become difficult to determine because the revaluation of assets has become fashionable. As the basis of revaluation is disclosed, it is possible to calculate what the assets per share would have been on the former basis and thus link the figures after the revaluation to those before it.

There are other figures worth watching. The net current assets are computed by adding together the current assets, mainly stock in trade and work in progress, debtors and cash and subtracting the current liabilities, the creditors, loans from banks and other sources which are repayable on demand, the tax due at the end of the financial year and the dividend. If the net liquid assets are growing faster than the cash (or if their growth is causing the bank loans to grow too fast), the company may be ill able to spare the money required for an increase of dividend. Or the company may need to make an issue to replenish its cash resources. Equally, you must watch the depreciation and the profits retained after payment of the dividend; these are the main sources of the company's flow of cash which can be used to finance either capital investment or an expansion of the liquid assets. In the notes printed after every company's accounts you will now find details of the outstanding commitments for capital expenditure, where the contracts have been signed, and the outstanding amounts authorised by the board for which no contracts have yet been signed. You can compare what the company intends to spend on plant, machinery and buildings with the resources available to it. If the fixed assets are growing, the earning power which the new facilities should bring may not be realised at once. (In an inflation an increase of fixed assets may represent nothing more than the replacement of an old machine by a new, 40% more efficient than the old and 400% more expensive. Growth of fixed assets after the middle fifties often brought with it little growth of earning power). You can also relate the turnover, which must now be revealed, with the trading profit and calculate the margin of profit. Some companies reveal these figures half yearly or even quarterly, and one can then form an idea of how their profitability is changing.

The figures are published once a year and they are published by the company. It is reasonable to assume that the shares are seldom bought except on an opinion formed with a knowledge of the latest published accounts. The actual buyer may never have seen the figures, but the friend of a friend who originated the chain of buying probably had seen them and had taken them into his calculations. In addition to the figures one must consider the facts. As we move from one Companies Act to another, the companies have to publish more and more facts, but it is by no means necessary that the facts should be published by the company. The company will normally publish the facts that the law requires, but there may well be other facts highly relevant to the question whether the share should be bought or not and the company may be under no obligation to publish them, or at any rate not at the time when some investor is considering a purchase of the shares. Facts may be published by some person or body other than the company, for example by a stockbroker or a financial journalist who investigates the company, or they may appear in a government publication originating from the Central Statistical Office or the Board of Trade. Even more often they remain for long periods unpublished. Unlike the figures, which are available to all, the facts are often available to some or perhaps to none. During the fifties, for example, investors bought thousands of shares in the Calico Printers Association because that company owned the patents for terylene and was drawing a royalty from Imperial Chemical Industries on its production in Britain and later from other producing companies overseas. No figures were published at that time; the company became more enlightened in the sixties and full details were then given. Somebody must have known what the royalty amounted to; it is possible that none of the people who knew bought any of the shares. Effectively those facts may have been available to nobody. There was a somewhat similar case in South African gold mines which turned to the production of uranium; there was in those days no publication of the price to be paid to the mines nor of the value of the metal in a ton of their ore. These facts must have been known to some of the officials in the mining finance houses and their dealings will have been informed by the facts. Other investors had to rely on rumour or on the curves of the charts. The facts are as important in changing the price of a share as are the figures. But the facts are generally unpublished and uncertain, at least until the annual report for the year in which the chairman learnt them is published. The facts relate to figures that are to be published in the future, perhaps quite a long way in the future, while the only figures available to the investor are those published in the past. When the investor is considering a transaction in ignorance of the facts, the question he must ask himself is, "Are these facts more important than my figures?"

The predicament which we are considering is that of an investor who believes that the market is rising but thinks that his resources might be better invested, either because he has not so far devoted a sufficient proportion of his resources to ordinary shares or because the shares which he is holding no longer seem to him to be those which are likely to serve him best. What he needs are shares which will enjoy a large appreciation in a short time. On a chart such a share has a steep trend. We may divide shares into three classes, steep trend shares which are rising much faster than the average, normal trend shares whose appreciation enjoys a pace that is about the same as the average, and worse than average shares whose trends may be flat or actually declining. If a share is declining in any trend longer than a normal corrective reaction, it should have no place in your portfolio while other shares are making good progress. The purpose of investment is to hold shares that are rising, not shares which are falling. But one cannot deal quite so curtly with the flat-trend share. Turn back to Chart No. 45 and look at Leyland Motors in the early fifties. Let us suppose that an investor is considering a new purchase; is there any reason why he should devote any attention to a share whose trend is flat like this? There are two possible reasons for such a purchase. The first is a belief that the figures, or the facts, which relate to the company are such that a steepening of the trend is likely which will turn up the angle of the share's ascent and make it steeper than average. This is a reason based on a view about the primary trend of the share; such an investor contemplating buying the share believes that the sideways movement is either an interruption of a much steeper trend which will be resumed or a base from which such a steep trend is shortly due to spring. There can be another reason for buying, based on the secondary trend. If the trend channel is exceptionally wide, as it was in the case of Leyland Motor, it is possible that the appreciation of the share over a secondary phase may be more generous than that obtainable from some other share whose primary trend is much steeper. Leyland provided more appreciation in the secondary phase from June 1953 to February 1954 than was shown by many other shares whose primary trend was much steeper. The same sort of arguments may be used for continuing to hold a flat-trend share. If the facts and figures seem likely to justify a much higher price in the not too distant future, then it may be argued that in due course the flat trend will turn much steeper and the share is worth holding for this change of trend. The argument about the secondary phase is valid only if the share is placed close to the lower boundary of a wide trend channel. But, if the scope of the secondary phase is an insufficient attraction (can it ever be sufficient in competition with a steep primary trend?) or if the facts and figures do not seem to justify a future steepening of the trend, the flatness of the trend is a sufficient argument for a sale of the share. Indeed, the first question which a flat trend like Guinness in Chart No. 44 should prompt in the mind of a holder is, 'Is there any reason why I should continue to hold this share?' The nearer the share approaches to the upper trendline or parallel, the more urgent this question becomes. If the figures are unprepossessing, if the facts appear to be unattractive, approach to the upper trendline should be a signal to sell. On the other hand, especially in the case of a share with a narrow trend channel, piercing the upper trendline may be an excellent signal to buy a share whose figures or facts appeared attractive like Rootes Motors early in 1954. This is shown in Chart No. 78. It may be very useful for an investor to know in advance that a certain share has qualities that should in due course justify a higher price. But, if those qualities do not draw attention to the share for eleven months, the investor may waste in a flat trend eleven months that could have been more profitably spent in a steeper. It is useful for the investor to know in advance, but he should act on his knowledge when the facts of which he has long been aware are at last going to impart to the trend that upward twist which brings swift appreciation. The penetration of an upper trendline is often a sign that this is happening. So we see that action near the upper trendline must depend not only on the behaviour of the share but on the investor's knowledge of the company as well.

We have also to consider the action of the investor when a share nears its lower trendline. If the trend is flat, is there any need to buy? The trend may turn steeper on the next rise, or, less profitably, on the next but one, or it may never steepen at all in the remaining life of the bull market. The case for buying into a trend which is not steep seems poor; the secondary swing may have some interest if the channel is wide, but if it is narrow there seems to be no attraction at all. For the gain from the secondary swing will be negligible, unless the primary trend is twisted upwards; if the primary trend seems likely to be twisted upwards, waiting in a narrow trend for an approach to the lower trendline shows an excessive greed which is likely to frustrate the investor's object.

We may now turn to the steep-trend share. The steepness of the trend can be justified only by figures or by facts which are very different from those of shares whose trends are normal. (Of course, the facts may not yet have been published and the steepness of the trend may be due to the activities of investors with special, not necessarily illegitimate, information). Look at Aveling Barford in Chart No. 79. Here the chairman had succeeded somehow in writing a speech which read in London as if he intended

271

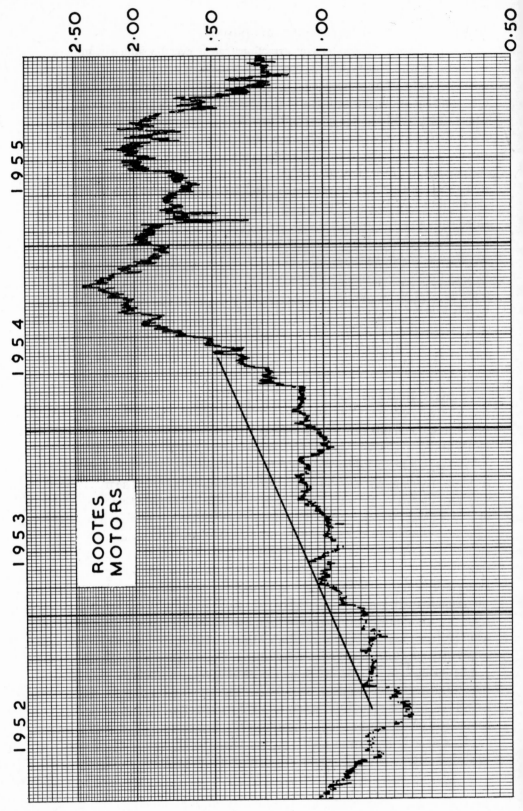

ROOTES
MOTORS

Chart No. 78

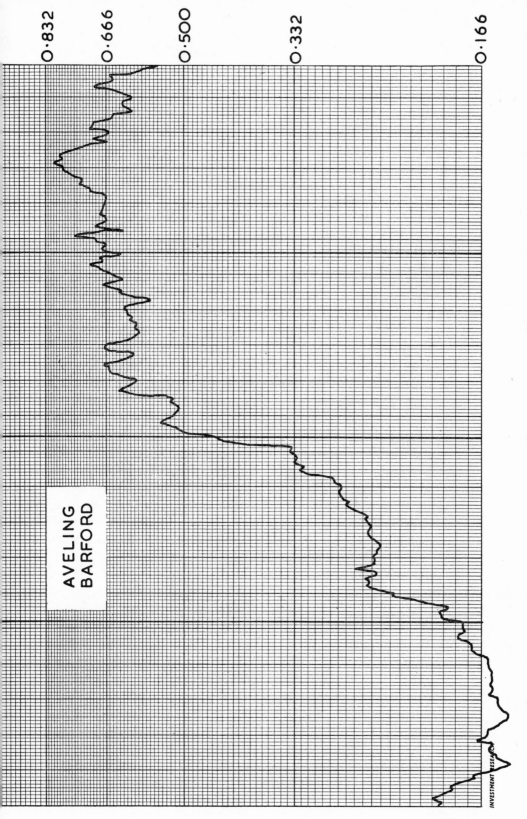

AVELING
BARFORD

INVESTMENT RESEARCH

0·832
0·666
0·500
0·332
0·166

Chart No. 79

not to increase the dividend but which sounded, when he delivered it in Grantham, as if he had high hopes of an increase. (The author, to assure his possession of a quite certain fact, persuaded Mr Barford to read the relevant passage in the speech a second time). But the question 'Do exceptional figures or facts justify this trend?' is not one which a holder should ask except when the share approaches the upper trendline. As long as it can run along between its steep trendlines, the holder can hold quite contented. If an investor is watching such a share and sees the trend develop, as it had developed by the second quarter of 1953, and sees it react from the upper trendline and then turn up again without going down to the lower, he can reasonably be tempted to buy. If it turns down and penetrates its lower trendline, he must then ask questions or accept the penetration as an instruction to sell. If it turns up towards its upper trendline, then he must ask the question and do his best to find a satisfactory answer. If it goes through the upper trendline, he must give it a chance to show if it can achieve a steeper trend; only when it has shown that it cannot should he begin once again to question its merits. The winter of 1953 was no time for selling Aveling Barford. If the share fails to penetrate the upper trendline, a sale near it is often a satisfactory termination to an investment, unless the share seems still to be full of steam and likely to prolong its steep rise.

When one considers a steep-trend share which one does not hold, the position is very different. Then the question 'Do exceptional figures or facts justify this trend?' is one that needs answering. If the share stands near its lower trendline, like Ford Motor in Chart No. 80 round the beginning of January 1954, a purchase is tempting, but if the facts and figures do not justify the steep trend, a penetration of the lower trendline, supposing it occurs, will present a difficult problem. Such a penetration will argue that the facts assumed by the purchaser are not deemed as favourable by the market as he had expected, and the whole basis of his purchase is thus destroyed. After such a penetration of the lower trendline great care must be exercised; the share may proceed upwards in a trend less steep, the trend may become flat, or a reversal pattern may be formed. The buyer must not allow any loss that may be incurred to influence his dealing. If he still finds good arguments for expecting better than average appreciation, he holds; if his hopes of better than average appreciation look like being disappointed, he sells. If, however, one is considering a purchase when the share stands near the middle of a trend channel, it is plain that the investor is facing the problems already described as those of a holder. Near the upper trendline a purchase may still be sound, if the channel is narrow, as was the case when Ford was approaching the inner top trendline in the first quarter of 1954. With the narrow trend channel

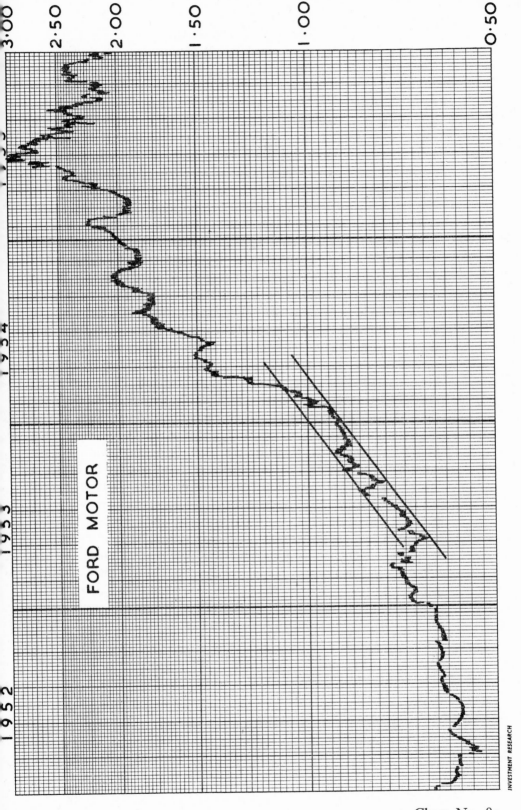

FORD MOTOR

Chart No. 80

a position close to the upper trendline cannot be dangerously far from the lower. But what is the holder to do when he sees, as Ford crosses 1·25, that a second upper trendline can be drawn whose presence the share is, for the moment at any rate, acknowledging by a pause? The answer is that one should at first hold to see if the share can run on; if it can, you let it rise, sliding up the point at which you are determined to sell close behind it. It is especially important not to be too eager a seller near the upper trendline when the whole primary uptrend develops a concave character, as happened in 1952–55.

When we turn to Chart No. 81, which shows Randfontein over the same years, the trend channel is much wider. In 1952 we don't know where the trend channel is to be drawn. Early in October, when the share turned down from 1·25, the trend appeared to be almost flat—all the chartist could do was to join the March top to the October top. But the reaction did not persist, and by the end of November the share had risen above 1·25. One could now draw a lower trendline AB at a steep angle, and the share was in a strong rise and pulling gently away from the steep trendline. This share was now looking very promising, and some optimistic chartists will have drawn the upper parallel from P, probably with a very faint pencil, as an upper parallel should properly be drawn from a point later, not earlier, than the beginning of the lower trendline. The faint pencil worked; the share hit it at 2·25, and the chartist now has two parallel trendlines, AB and PQ. Now this is a wide trend channel, and purchases have been growing progressively more dangerous as the share rises away from its lower trendline. The investor who buys above 1·75 in this chart is running a fairly high degree of risk and will need most exceptional facts and figures to justify his action. After the contact with the upper trendline there was a period of great excitement with much fluctuation which produced a further rise with two more peaks, each of which, however, lay further from the trendline than its predecessor. In the middle of April an exhaustion gap appeared, and the share soon dropped below 2·0. The rally was ineffective, and the share soon dropped through the rising trendline but achieved a sharp reversal in the last week of September. It suddenly went leaping ahead, equalled its previous top, dropped back and then went ahead with a gap. At this stage the share was once again looking an inviting purchase. It was possible to draw the lower trendlines BG and an upper parallel through Q, and this gave a wide trend-channel with plenty of upward scope. The share hardly paused for breath till it reached 3·5; then after a fortnight's hesitation it went ahead and reached the upper parallel at X. Again great activity developed near the top trendline, but at X the fluctuations did not continue upward as they had at Q. The share drifted to 3·1, rallied but could not penetrate the resistance at 3·4 and then went down

276

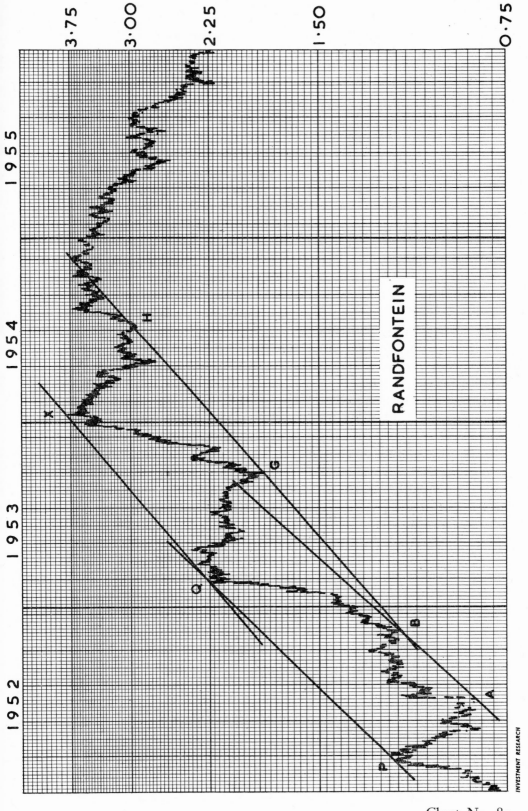

RANDFONTEIN

Chart No. 81

INVESTMENT RESEARCH

with a gap. That was a signal to sell, reiterated months later by the succession of failures, within the trend channel and beyond, to regain the level of January. The share that crawls up close to the lower trendline and then sinks through it is a share to sell, especially if this is part of the making of a double top pattern.

For the secondary trader the ideal is to sell near the upper trendline and buy near the lower. The primary trader may be tempted to sell near the upper trendline and, if his judgement is good, he may gain some time (as in a sale of Randfontein round 2·2) even if the share eventually reaches a much higher level. It is most important to remember that any share, even a share with a steep trend, may bolt through the upper trendline if its prospects are sufficiently attractive. Equally important, an approach to the lower trendline may imply that a normal secondary reaction is nearing its end and offering a good opportunity to buy. But, if the trendline is already obvious, it is probably old and may be nearing the end of its useful life; probably the better opportunities occur in cases like Randfontein where it can be seen that a new steep trendline can reasonably be drawn. There are no hard and fast rules about steep trends; you want to catch them as young as you can and stay in them as long as you can, resisting all temptations to take your profit too soon.

We have been concerned so far in this chapter with the selling of shares on which profits have been made, and that sort of selling is comparatively easy. Why is it so difficult to sell a share which has not done well, or which has done well but has not been sold and is now standing at a disappointing price? One reason, possibly, is that a sale at the current price involves an acknowledgement of a mistake, and many people are unwilling to acknowledge that they have made a mistake. This gets complicated with a second source of error, a personal involvement with the stock. This can take several forms. Some people come to believe in their stocks and to assume that the lowness of the price is due to the errors of the market, not the weaknesses of the share. Perhaps that is an accurate diagnosis, but, if it is, the question must follow when the market is going to see the error of its ways. When you are playing in the market, you must play with the market, not against it. Many investors confuse the shares which they hold with the companies which issued them. The excellence of Marks & Spencer as retailers does not necessarily imply that their shares must be good investments, and through most of the sixties the shares gave a poorer than average performance, although the market continued to accord them a lower than average yield. The investor is investing in the market as it is, not in the market as it ought to be, and he should also be humble enough to wonder whether his judgement of how the market should behave is really better than the sum of the judgements of the investors who are shaping it.

Another weakness that is common among investors is the attributing of last year's facts to this year's problems. The facts about Lesney Products in 1969 were not the same as the facts of 1968; from the beginning of the year the market was anticipating the publication of the 1969 facts, and the investors who waited for that publication were heavily penalised. There is also another kind of involvement which is possibly even more dangerous. The investor buys a share which goes down, and this the investor takes as an insult. He determines to get the better of this insolent share which has gone the wrong way, and what follows is a battle between the investor and his investment, conducted with no real regard for the maximisation of profit. What is important for this investor, once he is thus involved, is to make a profit out of the share which he has bought, not to make himself as much profit as he can in the time at his disposal.

Many investors say that they believe that if they hold long enough they will see their price again. Some of those who bought Vickers in 1955 are still waiting in 1970. Some readers will object that Vickers is not a fair example, that one should not pick a stock with a reputation like that. They should remember that what we are concerned with is not the reputation of Vickers in 1970 (and the fact that it has not so far gone below its 1965 bottom suggests that this is improving) but with its reputation in 1955 when the damaging decision was probably taken. The share that is going to let the investor down badly probably still has a dazzling reputation at the time when he decides to hold it, and most likely other shares with similar reputations will behave in the way which their good reputations demand. In almost every bear market there are shares which go up, others which go down very little, but these are not distinguishable, till after the event, from shares which will fall the average amount or two or three times as much. All the shares which rose in the bull market were pushed to higher prices by investors who believed that the companies would do much better, and in most cases this belief would be backed by figures showing increases of profit. So at the top of a bull market all shares, or almost all shares, look good investments, and it is probably a matter more of luck than of skill if the investor who holds on is clinging to shares which subsequently behave well or badly. But for most shares a bear market is a period in which supports give way and in which resistances prove powerful.

One finds sometimes a comfortable belief that as time passes each bull market rises to a peak above its predecessor. This is unfortunately less true of individual shares, but it is not true of market indices either. If one relies on the London & Cambridge series before 1914, one finds that the two bull markets at the beginning of this century both failed to lift prices to the best levels of 1900. Then came a series of rising tops, with

1919–20 well into new high ground, 1928–29 above 1919–20 (though many well-known shares of those days had to wait longer before they equalled their peaks made just after the first European War), 1936–37 probably above 1928–29, 1947 above 1929 but 1951 no better than 1947. Then came the steep rises to the peaks of 1955 and later to 1959–60 with some shares, but by no means all, higher for a brief period in 1961. Then up to 1967 the latest decade was a period of poor performance, but the 1968–69 peak ran far above the best levels of 1964–66. These facts suggest that the man who relies on the recovery of his price above the high level at which he bought is likely to be proved right within ten years, but he is taking the risk that he will waste a lot of good investment time before he is free from the stock which he has tied round his neck and can go and look for a better one.

While there can be no guarantee that any particular bull market will outrun its predecessor, there is a strong likelihood that each new bull market will bring a quota of stocks with outstanding performance. For the man who sells his old stocks and waits with cash, the new bull market brings opportunity, and it is in order to be able to take advantage of such opportunity, if you can find it, that we urge the prudence of selling shares when they seem to have exhausted their upward potential individually or when the trend of the market changes and a primary downtrend appears to supervene.

But this is much more easily said than done. As we wrote earlier, it is easy to buy shares, difficult to sell them. We have tried to explain the timing of purchases; the timing of sales may be equally easy to explain, especially when we are using charts showing what happened afterwards, but the actual deed, the instructing of the broker to sell, is ten times as difficult as the decision to buy.

Let us look back first at Chart No. 81. The bulls of Randfontein had enjoyed some splendid opportunities; life was simpler in those days as there was no Capital Gains Tax. But by the summer of 1954 the share was looking rather tired. The rally after the decline from the beginning of the year had failed in August to equal the previous top; it had failed too to climb away from the rising lower trendline. The share then moved more or less horizontally through the rising trendline and this horizontality is not a symptom of weakness, although the cutting of the trendline is. Twice again it rallied to equal its best level of August, and the repeated reversals of these rallies suggested that the share could rise no higher. By the first week of January 1955 the support underneath these rallies was clearly marked at 3·3. This support was violated at the beginning of February, and by this time the case for selling was urgent. There was still good support reaching up to 3·2, and the investor who relied on this and then sold on the recovery over 3·4 was luckier probably, rather than more skilful, than the investor who threw the share overboard as soon as he saw the support violated. Later in August there were chances to sell the share on rallies at prices close to 3·00. However, some of the other illustrations we have already given will show how little you can rely on being given such a second chance. You may well get a second chance when a share behaves like Randfontein and falls away from a point like X and then rallies towards that level within the trend channel. The *Financial Times* industrial goes through this routine quite often, individual shares not so often. But that is the second chance that the market offers, and, if you ask it for a second chance when what you need is really a third or fourth chance, you are liable to be sorely disappointed.

If you look at Broken Hill Proprietary in Chart No. 82, the top pattern in the middle of 1968 had enough Head & Shoulders characteristics to justify a sale on the cutting of the neckline in August. If that opportunity was missed, a chance was given on the pull-back in September. If that chance was not taken, the rally from October 1968 to January 1969 gave the last good chance. Also in Chart No. 82 we are illustrating Vickers for the same period. Here you have a triangle at the end of 1968 with a false emergence upwards. The rise was quickly reversed, and in less than a month the share had gone through the lower boundary of the triangle. The false emergence was a symptom of weakness. The violation of the lower boundary of the triangle was a more serious symptom of weakness. The share was turning back where there was no obvious resistance, and it was going through what looked like strong support. The general behaviour of the market was discouraging. Good chances of selling were given at 1·75 on rallies to the lower boundary of the triangle. After them it was rash to expect more (the best price in the first half of 1970 was 1·57).

You cannot rely on a third chance like that given to holders of Hudson's Bay, illustrated in Chart No. 83. The share traced out a big reversal triangle from the summer of 1968 to the spring of 1969 with a lower boundary at 8·5. This was penetrated, perhaps not significantly, in May 1969, but the share rallied back into the triangle. It did not stay inside but broke out downwards with a gap, clear evidence that the downward thrust was powerful. In the next two or three days there was a pull-back which gave what might have been a last chance. However, about four weeks later the share made another attempt to rally to the underside of the triangle but failed. Here again was a very brief chance. Then the fall continued steeply to 6·5, and on that level the stock formed a base and rallied through the winter to give one more chance just inside the triangle.

The chartist myth lays down that when a primary uptrend is reversed

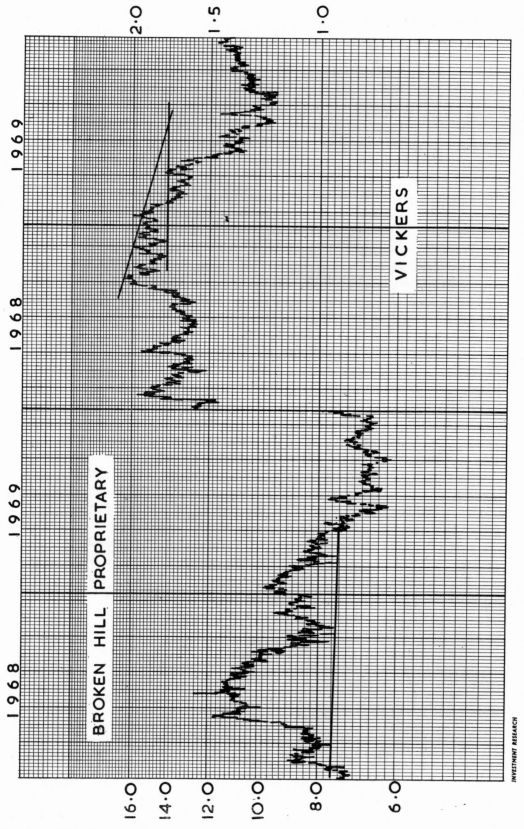

BROKEN HILL PROPRIETARY

VICKERS

INVESTMENT RESEARCH

Chart No. 82

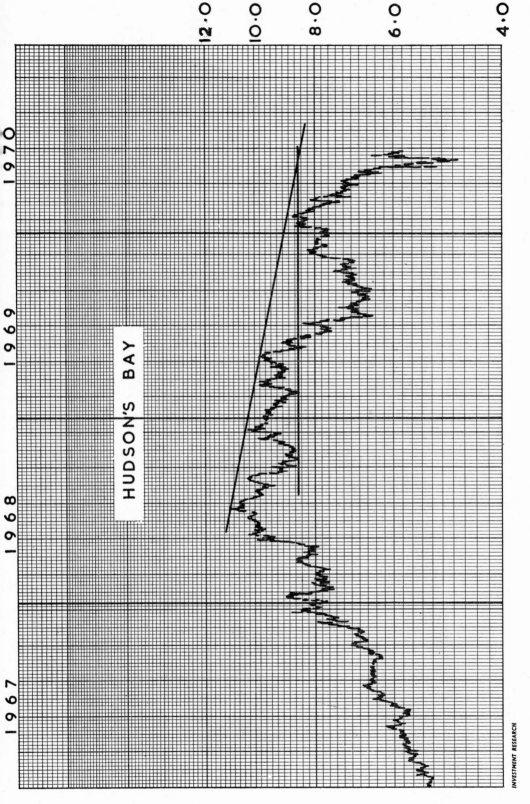

HUDSON'S BAY

INVESTMENT RESEARCH

Chart No. 83

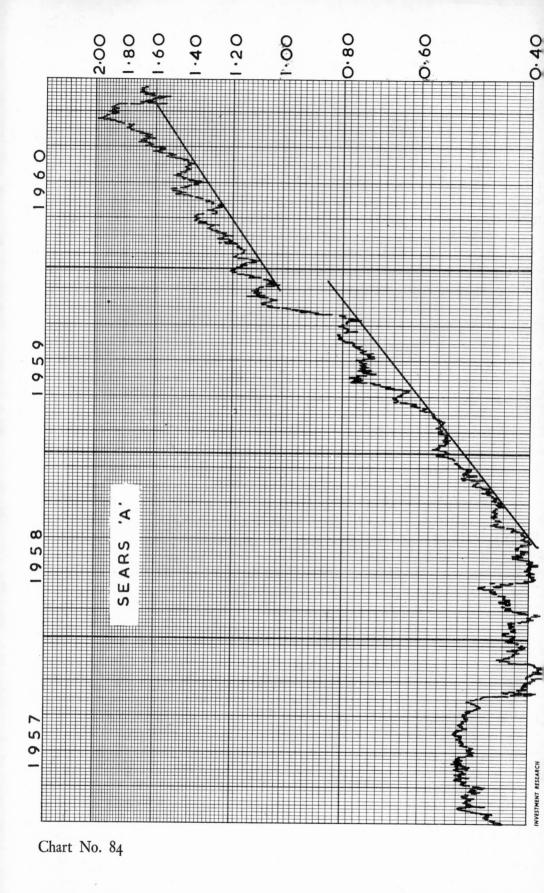

SEARS 'A'

INVESTMENT RESEARCH

Chart No. 84

you should cling only to the strong stocks. Sometimes this is possible as in Chart No. 84 where the rise of Sears A was not interrupted by the adverse developments of 1960 till the decline in the autumn of that year, and a hardy bull, riding the lower of the two possible trendlines, might have clung to his holding even through that set-back. More often the chart develops a bearish pattern which prompts a sale, and it is only after a too serious initial set-back that the true strength of the share emerges. But even then, shares which prosper in early stages of a primary down-trend may well attract selling at a later stage. This may happen simply because the share which has kept its price up generally shows a yield which finally becomes uncompetitive when much higher returns can be obtained from shares with first class names. Or it may happen because the industrial and commercial difficulties which a primary decline nor-mally brings in its train eventually overtakes the companies which have continued to prosper in the earlier stages.

The last word about selling in bear markets is quite simple. Generally the sooner it is done the better; you should strive to make your sales as near the top as possible. If the shares you have sold later advance to new high levels, do not worry; think instead of the low prices at which you will be able to buy other good shares.

CHAPTER EIGHTEEN

Basic Tools and Basic Rules

Anybody who is going to take charge of investments, whether his own or someone else's, whether as a professional or on a do-it-yourself basis, needs a set of basic tools and basic rules. Of course a large proportion of the professional analysts in London do not rely at all on the technical methods discussed in this book, although we suspect that many of them have their own ways of reaching the appropriate conclusions. On the other hand if there were many chartists in Britain in 1945, when Investment Research started business, they kept very quiet about it. Things are very different now. There is a Society of Investment Analysts, with a journal called *The Investment Analyst*, and matters of technical analysis are from time to time discussed in its pages. More recently the Association of Chartists and Technical Analysts has been formed. The demand for photoprints from the chart library maintained by Investment Research has grown, not regularly from year to year, but by substantial progression from period to period. A number of brokers and merchant bankers were going so far as to buy copies of the whole British daily chart library once a month; most of these are now satisfied with the same library on microfilm —but now they receive it once a week. From time to time the *Sunday Telegraph* calls a forum of technical analysts, and it devotes enough space to their views to argue that the public interest in our mystery (a fine professional word used by the Executioner in *The Yeoman of the Guard*) has grown to gratifying proportions. In New York the situation is different; there is hardly a broker or investment house that does not maintain a technical department or at least employ a competent technical analyst.

The simple argument for the use of charts by the ordinary investor is that he is trying to use stocks and shares as a vehicle towards greater wealth, and, if you want to board a vehicle with the idea of getting somewhere, it is just as well to know where it has come from and to see where it is going. It is not enough to rely on what you hear about a share. The share that everybody praises is the share that everybody has bought, and, when you buy it, who is left to keep the price up?

The extent of your investment apparatus must depend on the amount of time and of resources that you are prepared to devote to the subject.

The brokers with big research departments are now spending tens, maybe hundreds, of thousands a year; the man who is investing a fortune of four or five figures must operate on a vastly smaller scale. Six basic tools should be enough, backed up by daily reading of the *Financial Times* (with the special purpose of extracting the statistics of your six basic tools).

First of all you need a share index which represents fairly enough for your purpose what the market is doing. We have already given reasons why the *Financial Times* industrial ordinary is the best for this purpose; we should like the wide coverage of the F.T. Actuaries, if it were not weighted, but a weighted index shows not what investors are doing but what is being done to values by investors. This index should be plotted daily, possibly it will suffice if you plot the whole week's business from Saturday's paper (but you will need the *Financial Times* every day except Monday in order to extract from it other data which you will require).

Second you require a fixed interest indicator. This is not a simple matter. We do not favour the *Financial Times* government securities index nor the *Financial Times* fixed interest stocks index; both of these contain dated stocks for whose maturities no adjustment is made and thus these indices are liable to stand higher at a later point than at an earlier, not because the rate of interest is lower but because many of the constituent stocks are so much nearer their redemption dates. The simplest fixed interest indicator to chart is Consols $2\frac{1}{2}\%$; dividends are paid four times a year and so the distortion caused on ex-dividend dates is minimised. But the stock is no longer looked on as being truly representative of the movement of interest rates, as gilt edged with no fixed date for redemption has reasonably become especially disliked; however, times may change and, if past precedents are any guide, Consols will enjoy a much higher repute by 1980. The most scientific indicator readily available is the gilt edged index published in the F.T. Actuaries series.

The third basic tool—and here we bow to current fashion—is a chart of the P/E Ratio. This is calculated for their 500 shares by the F.T. Actuaries, and it is possibly ideal for the purpose. The use of this tool is for deciding how cheap or dear shares are. The ratio moves up and down in wide swings between bear market and bull; it became fashionable to use it in Britain after the introduction of the Corporation Tax, before which we used to talk, with somewhat less reverence, about the Earnings Yield (the Earnings Yield is a reciprocal of the P/E Ratio). The use of the P/E Ratio for deciding how cheap or dear shares are assumes that share prices are not affected by fixed interest yields. Investors have been learning in 1969 and 1970, if they did not know it before, that the yield on Government stocks and industrial bonds and debentures can exert a strong influence on share prices.

287

The fourth tool is Confidence, described in Chapter Five. This indicator should, by precedents from before the war, have been a useful leading indicator for the share market, but after 1949, when it was very successful, it has failed to lead and will probably continue to do so until changes of dividend round the primary reversals once again outweigh the changes of gilt edged prices. But it is probably a better indicator than the fashionable P/E Ratio of the dearness or cheapness of the market.

The fifth tool is the Advance/Decline Line. This was described in Chapter Eight; you need it to confirm that your narrow index of 30 leading shares is really representative of what the market is doing (the broad F.T. Actuaries index with its 500 shares is not much help here, because not many more than 30 shares will carry so much of the weight that the movements of the remainder make very little difference to the course of the index).

Confidence and the A/D Line you have to calculate yourself. If you want to prepare your own Confidence indicator and start plotting it from scratch, you can divide the F.T. Actuaries gilt edged yield by the F.T. Actuaries 500 share yield, and this should work satisfactorily. The Investment Research calculation is, for historical reasons of continuity, rather more complicated.

No calculation is needed for the sixth tool, which is the *Financial Times* industrial activity index. Here it is probably best to plot the 5-day mean, although for detailed analysis it is useful to have the record of the single daily figures as well.

These are the tools you need for the making of your strategic decisions. The daily figures for each should be plotted, if not daily, at least once a week; one plot a week may suffice for the P/E Ratio and for Confidence (if fashion does not insist it may be possible to dispense with the P/E Ratio altogether) but you need five plots a week for the share index, the fixed interest indicator, whatever it is, the A/D Line and the Activity index.

Beyond these tools you need access to a chart library. You may well want to maintain your own library of shares in addition to the main tools mentioned above, but you want to use charts with plenty of back history, at least two years and a much longer period may in some cases be useful. Photoprints of leading shares showing the daily range can be obtained from the office of Investment Research in Cambridge; many other less prominent shares are plotted weekly (showing Friday's close only) and charts can be ordered, plotted on this weekly basis, for any share quoted on the two pages of the *Financial Times*. By ordering a chart as soon as the idea of buying a share enters your head you have time to look at a little of its history, to see where the trend has taken it, and if it is forming a possibly significant pattern, before you make the decision to buy. (Investment Research receives orders by letter, telephone and telex, and, if they come at a reasonable time, the chart required is photoprinted and posted the same day. The day's delay is not normally a serious matter, and inspection of the chart can save you from falling into many a serious trap).

Your own chart library may consist, beyond the basic tools, of half a dozen or a dozen shares in which you are interested. If your interests are very large, it may cover very many shares, share groups, ratios, activity charts and activity ratios, overseas securities and averages, and commodities. Most active investors in Britain think it prudent to know something of what the Dow Jones Industrial Average is doing. It does not seem wise to plunge into a purchase of Copper shares just at a time when the price of Copper has started to plunge; on the other hand there must be many people in Singapore who would argue at the moment that a good fall in the price of rubber would be far more embarrassing to the manufacturers of synthetic than to the owners of rubber plantations. These are interesting thoughts in July 1970 when Copper and Rubber shares seem to be strong and the corresponding commodities weak.

This basic equipment, which can be as extensive or as meagre as your needs demand, should enable you to make a fair determination of the development of the investment cycle and a reasonable appreciation of the course of any individual share. Possession of these basic tools is the first step towards obedience to the basic rules.

The first rule is 'Watch the main trend; use it as your friend and never let it be your enemy'. If the main trend is upward and you buy badly, in most cases time and the current of the main trend will sweep your share up past the price that you paid for it. If the main trend is downward and you buy well, you will probably have one chance, and one chance only, of selling your purchase at a useful profit and, if you miss that chance, you may not see that price again for one investment cycle or for many.

The second rule, for those who do not run a sufficiently extensive chart library, must be 'Choose your shares on figures and on facts; time your purchases and sales by chart'. The ordinary investor can usually obtain a sufficiency of figures from the company analysis cards, which brokers obtain from Moodys or the Exchange Telegraph; specialists may require to study balance sheets over a long period. The facts may be known to you personally at first or second hand, or you may deduce from the behaviour of the share on the chart that there must be facts of an importance sufficient to swing the weight of investment from the buying side to the selling or vice-versa.

The third rule is 'Use the charts, if you keep enough, to point to the figures you should look at and the facts you should look for'. The great advantage of using charts is that the user can call to his aid the knowledge of other investors who are quite unknown to him. This advantage must not be thrown away; all study of charts should be made with this question fully cocked, 'What are they doing and why are they doing it?'

The fourth rule is 'Rules cannot help you unless you develop judgement, nor judgement unless you keep to the rules'. The chart has a simple rôle, rather like the governor of an engine. It is a controller of speed. Every investor who thinks about the market or about any individual share is likely to be ahead of the market or behind the market. A share that you chart starts to rise for no reason known to you; the chart gives you a prod forward because you are in this case behind the market. A share which you think should rise insists on falling, although you are possessed of reasons which convince you it must rise. Perhaps you are wrong, and the chart puts you right. Perhaps you are right, but right too soon; the chart puts a brake on your impetuosity and prevents you from doing something that will be right but is still wrong when you want to do it. Usually you know less than the market, and the chart is urging you on to keep pace with the events that are not yet revealed. Sometimes you know more than the market, and you want to take advantage of your knowledge before the time for that has come. Most often the market knows what you know and knows also something that you do not. But what is known to the market is not known to the whole market. The investor should strive to know as much as possible of what the market knows and as much as possible how the market behaves. The chart will tell him how the market behaves, and from its behaviour he can deduce something of what it knows.

INDEX